THE RECONSTRUCTION OF
POLITICAL ECONOMY

The Reconstruction of Political Economy

An Introduction to Post-Keynesian Economics

J. A. KREGEL

with a Foreword by Joan Robinson

A HALSTED PRESS BOOK

JOHN WILEY & SONS
New York – Toronto

First published in the United Kingdom 1973 by
THE MACMILLAN PRESS LTD

*Published in the U.S.A. and Canada
by Halsted Press, a Division of
John Wiley & Sons, Inc., New York*

Library of Congress Cataloging in Publication Data

Kregel, J   A
    The reconstruction of political economy.

    "A Halsted Press book."
    Bibliography;   p.
    1.   Keynesian economics.   2.   Neoclassical
school of economics.   I.   Title.
HB99.7.K72   330.15′6   73–14684
ISBN 0–470–50733–0

Printed in Great Britain

To my Father

Contents

List of Figures

Foreword

When I came up to Cambridge, in October 1921, and started reading economics, Marshall's *Principles* was the Bible, and we knew little beyond it. Jevons, Cournot, even Ricardo, were figures in the footnotes. We heard of 'Pareto's Law', but nothing of the Walrasian general equilibrium system. Sweden was represented by Cassel, America by Irving Fisher, Austria and Germany were scarcely known. Marshall *was* economics.

There is a deep-seated conflict in the *Principles*, of which Marshall himself was uneasily aware (especially in connection with 'increasing returns') between the analysis, which is purely static, and the conclusions drawn from it, which apply to an economy developing through time, with accumulation going on; but somehow we managed to swallow it all.

When I returned to Cambridge in 1929 and began teaching, Piero Sraffa's lectures were penetrating our insularity. He was calmly committing the sacrilege of pointing out inconsistencies in Marshall, and at the same time revealing that other schools existed (though they were no better). The elders reacted by defending Marshall as best they could, but the younger generation were not convinced by them. The profound inconsistency between the static base and the dynamic superstructure had become too obvious.

Professor Pigou, long before, had worked the static element in Marshall's theory into a neat logical scheme. He introduced the concept of the equilibrium size of firms to rescue Marshall from the dilemma between increasing returns and perfect competition. This was being taught as the orthodox interpretation of Marshall, though many points in it were under dispute.

Recently I have used Pigou's name as a convenient label for the static element in Marshall and credited Marshall himself with the dynamic element [92]. Perhaps this is too flattering to Marshall. Both elements were present in his thinking and he showed great agility in appealing, in each context, to whichever would best suit his purpose of presenting a mollifying picture of the private-enterprise economy.

I worked out a theory of imperfect competition, inspired by Sraffa's article (published in English in *Economic Journal*, December 1926) on 'The Laws of Returns under Competitive Conditions', against the background of Pigou's static analysis. My aim was to attack the internal logic of the theory of static equilibrium and to refute, by means of its own arguments, the doctrine that wages are determined by the marginal productivity of labour.

Meanwhile a much more powerful attack on equilibrium theory was being mounted by Keynes. It was obvious enough in real life that a free market does not guarantee equilibrium, for the world economy had fallen into the great slump, but it took a long time to find out where the mistake lay in the theory and to sketch out a new approach. Unbeknownst to us, Michal Kalecki, writing in Polish, evinced the same solution, in the main, as Keynes. His version of the General Theory of Employment was less rich than Keynes's but in some respects more coherent. He brought imperfect competition into line with the analysis of effective demand and laid the basis for what is nowadays called the 'Cambridge' theory of distribution.

In 1940, as a distraction from the news, I began to read Marx. Seeing *Capital* in the light of the Keynesian revolution, I found much in it that the professed Marxist seemed to have overlooked. They had replied to Keynes with the slogans of sound finance and the gold standard. Only Kalecki had seen the point of the schema of expanded reproduction in Volume II of *Capital* and he had built a 'Keynesian' theory on them. For me, the main message of Marx was the need to think in terms of history, not of equilibrium. This, of course, was the message of the Keynesian revolution too, but I had applied it only in short-period terms. I had been so much under the influence of Pigou's methodology that I had written a 'Long-period Theory of Employment' in terms of comparisons of stationary states with different rates of interest. Now I began to catch a glimpse of an approach that would emancipate us from the dominance of equilibrium analysis.

As for the labour theory of value, I could not make out what the fuss was about. It seemed obvious that the transformation problem, that is, finding a system of prices yielding a uniform rate of profit for all capitalists, was just a puzzle (though it was not solved till Sraffa showed the way). Nothing of importance could turn on it.

Marx had a way of expressing his views of history and politics in bits of algebra. I did not think that pointing out and correcting mistakes in the algebra could affect the force of Marx's view of history and the powerful political doctrine that he derived from it. The 'law of value' in the sense of the diagnosis of exploitation in the capitalist system as a whole cannot stand or fall with a theory of the prices of particular commodities. But some fundamentalist followers of Marx were offended at the mere suggestion that his algebra needs to be corrected.

There was an important point of substance, however, mixed up in the algebra. If there is a long-run tendency for the rate of profit to fall, there must be a tendency for wages to rise in terms of commodities. This, not the transformation puzzle, is the inconsistency between Volume I and Volume III, and it has never been satisfactorily sorted out.

The other difficulty in Marxian theory is the relation of money-wage rates to prices. If Marx really believed that trade unions could raise the share of wages in the value of output merely by raising money-wage rates, why did he think it necessary to have a revolution?

It seemed to me that Keynes, or rather Kalecki, was a great help to the Marxists in clearing up contradictions – whatever the fundamentalists may say. Certainly it is not so easy nowadays for the academic economists to dismiss Marxian theory as pure rubbish, which they were formerly happy to do.

After the Second World War, the economists accepted Keynes, and governments accepted responsibility for maintaining a high and stable level of employment, each for its own national economy. The centre of interest then shifted to the problem of long-run growth.

Responding to the challenge of Roy Harrod's *Towards a Dynamic Economics* I set about to try to make a generalisation of the General Theory. A long-run theory requires to deal with the rate of profit on capital. Keynes had been concerned only with the state of expectation about future profits – the 'marginal efficiency of capital'; Kalecki dealt with the share of gross profit in the value of output; Marx appeared to have two incompatible theories; Harrod seemed to confuse the rate of profit with the rate of interest on rentier wealth. Sraffa's introduction to Ricardo's *Principles* gave invaluable hints, but the treatment of the subject in his *Production of Commodities by*

Means of Commodities was still unpublished. Where was a theory of the rate of profit on capital to be found?

A *rate* of profit is a return *pro rata* to a quantity of capital. I posed the question – does a quantity of capital mean a list of specified machines, stocks of materials and means of subsistence; or does it mean a sum of money, of which the purchasing power over investible resources depends on wage rates and prices?

To my surprise, this question aroused a fury of indignation. 'Everyone except Joan Robinson knows perfectly well what capital is.' It became a standing joke in the profession – 'As Mrs Robinson is not in the room, I suppose I may speak of a quantity of capital.' But the only answer to my question that anyone offered was to say that if the capital goods were 'malleable' the question would not arise. No amount of teasing could shake this position. The description of capital goods as putty, jelly, 'steel', leets or ectoplasm was cheerfully adopted when expounding new growth models; and although, after the 'reswitching debate' in 1966, Professor Samuelson had to admit that he had lost faith in jelly, these descriptions are still being used today.

The argument was not really anything to do with the problem of valuing capital. It was concerned with reconstructing a pre-Keynesian equilibrium in which the accumulation of means of production is governed by the desire of society as a whole to save, and where full-employment is guaranteed by real wages finding the level at which the existing stock of jelly will be spread out or squeezed up to employ the available labour. To reconstruct equilibrium, it is necessary to escape from history. The purpose of 'malleable capital' is to overcome the difference between the future and the past.

The situation in the teaching of economic theory at the present time is unsatisfactory, not to say shameful. I have been trying for the last twenty years to trace the confusions and sophistries of current neo-neoclassical doctrines to their origin in the neglect of historic time in the static equilibrium theory of the neoclassics and at the same time to find a more hopeful alternative in the classical tradition, revived by Sraffa, which flows from Ricardo through Marx, diluted by Marshall and enriched by the analysis of effective demand of Keynes and Kalecki.

The economics of equilibrium is a Moloch to which generations of students are still being sacrificed. I hope that I have been able to rescue a few here and there, not in order to offer them an easy life but to appeal for their help in the serious task of developing an analysis that deals with the economic problems of the world in which we live.

JOAN ROBINSON

Preface

Political Economy, as it was understood by the Classical economists, stands today discredited by both the neoclassical theory that took its place and by the Keynesian short-period theory of effective demand. The 'neoclassical synthesis' which integrates Keynesian short-period and neoclassical long-period theory leaves the Classics in the stone-age of economic science, historical ancestors without modern application.

To historians of economic theory the triumph of the neoclassical synthesis should appear as most inappropriate, for the basis of Keynes's formal training in the economics of Ricardo and Marshall left a strong imprint on his own contributions to economic theory. It would seem more appropriate to link Keynes's own theory with the long-period theory of the classical political economists. The possibility of such a relation has become obvious with the post-Keynesian construction of a long-period theory based on Keynes's short-period theory which closely resembles, in both content and concern, the classical theory of Ricardo and Marx.

Thus I have seen fit to call the combination of Keynes's short-period theory and the post-Keynesian extention of that theory into long-period terms a Reconstruction of Political Economy in the sense of the Classics. A reconstruction in the sense that the approach shares the problems and concerns of classical Political Economy with the inclusion of the theory of effective demand in a monetary economy (or without Say's Law and the Quantity Theory of Money). In this sense a Keynesian theory has no place in a neoclassical synthesis and cannot be attached to the neoclassical concept of equilibrium. The relation of post-Keynesian theory to the Classical is quickly seen from the emphasis that this theory places on social relations, the distribution of income and the analysis of an economy that changes and grows over time.

This Keynesian reconstruction of Political Economy was not at first apparent to readers of Keynes and owes most to the 'generalisation of Keynes's General Theory' by Professor Joan Robinson. In the presentation of the post-Keynesian reconstruction of Political

Economy I have relied mainly on the works of Professor Robinson, trying to show how they evolved towards a full-fledged alternative to the currently orthodox 'neoclassical synthesis'. That this evolution was not an instantaneous or simple procedure is obvious from the fact that we are now nearly forty years away from the birth of the General Theory but the 'Keynesian revolution still remains to be made both in teaching economic theory and in forming economic policy' [94]. The broad historical evolution of Professor Robinson's ideas is traced out in the Foreword that she has kindly provided for this book.

The major portion of this book is based on lectures that I have given for a number of years to a wide variety of students in a number of different countries. The format attempts to meet three specific problems that I have most widely encountered in the teaching of post-Keynesian theory.

First of all, most students are well, if not too well, schooled in the nuances of the neoclassical synthesis. This creates a number of communications problems, for much of the nomenclature of the two approaches is the same but has very little in common in meaning. It thus is necessary to place the theories in historical context and to highlight the widely differing intentions of a common terminology. Part One of the book is used for this purpose and is probably the most important and most difficult for the student to grasp. It tries to free the reader from preconceived ideas and methods in order to take up the post-Keynesian approach afresh.

Second is the problem of time, but here meant in the sense of study time. The post-Keynesian literature is large, and not always well integrated. Part Two thus attempts to put the basic method, mechanisms and propositions in their barest and simplest form, trying to prepare the reader for the more difficult original works. Thus the presentation is in no sense complete, but tries to give the flavour of the post-Keynesian method.

The third problem is the tendency for students (as well as professional economists) to be sceptical about the generality of the theory. Just as Keynes was incorporated (wrongly) as a special case dealing with a special problem (the slump), the post-Keynesian theory is often criticised as being not fully general or positive, but only critical and negative, e.g., related only to the criticism of neoclassical capital theory. Thus interest in the theory is limited because it is only a negative critique, not a fully positive alternative approach. This is to miss the potential contribution of the approach. It is my view that it is such an alternative and should be approached as such. Part Three tries, feebly, to show applications of the alternative approach to various problems. It is not my intention to provide, *in toto*, this alternative. Much of the work has been undertaken, much is still to be done. Economic theories are not produced pre-packaged to be picked off shop shelves. To ask for an alternative to the necolassical theory comparable in precision and beauty is naïve. But the potential for a truly alternative approach exists, the problem is to expose and explain this potential so that further positive applications can be made. This cannot be done if everyone waits for someone else to do the work. If this book can create an interest in further applications of the post-Keynesian approach it will have more than served its purpose.

Although the analysis presented in Part Two of the book is based primarily on the contributions of Professor Robinson, it must be recognised that she has not been the only economist to contribute to the post-Keynesian revival of political economy. Part Four takes up differences and similarities of the major alternative approaches, all of which are based on the work of Keynes.

The discontent with the equilibrium approach of the neoclassical synthesis, and general equilibrium theory in particular, continues to grow. The reader is directed to Kornai's *Anti-Equilibrium* [40] for a critique by a practioneer of the general equilibrium theory, and a positive alternative approach that has much in common with the post-Keynesian approach. Recent works by Kaldor [32] and Harrod [20] which appeared too late to be dealt with in the text are also recommended.

As I have already mentioned, the book presents the post-Keynesian theory in a form that I have found useful in the class-room and the lecture hall. It is in this sense a very personal interpretation, and is not meant to rework or replace the original contributions, but to prepare the way for their study and further application. To the extent that this presentation is not misleading or misrepresentative I have greatly benefited by aid and criticism from Joan Robinson, P. Davidson and G. C. Harcourt. I am also extremely grateful to J. L. Eatwell for his comments on the revised draft, especially in relation to chapter 9 which I have been able to, hopefully, much improve as a result of his suggestions. For the time and effort that has been given I am greatly indebted. Their good nature, however, does not imply full or complete agreement with the manner in which I have treated and applied the material presented. I especially thank Professor Robinson for providing the Foreword. I need not add that this does not implicate her in the sense of providing a seal of approval for the present work, for which I take sole responsibility.

J. A. K.

Part One

1 Preparing the Way

The main task of the chapters that follow is to try to present in a simplified form the principles of what has come to be called 'post-Keynesian' theory. That is, the theory of growth and distribution most closely associated with the writings of Professor Joan Robinson. In addition, I want to compare and contrast her position with other Keynesian writers such as Kaldor and Pasinetti, as well as with Keynes himself. At the same time the book will try to be both positively and negatively critical, extending the possibilities of the theory by changing some of its assumptions and viewpoints. In this way, hopefully, it can be seen that the 'post-Keynesian' extension of Keynes's *General Theory* is general in the same sense, and general in the sense of rehabilitating the Classical interests in growth and distribution as the prime concern of political economy.

To help you in this task, I urge you to empty your minds of all preconceptions and prejudice. If you have been taught to think of all consumer decisions in terms of the relation of prices to final utilities to the end of maximisation of utility; and of all production decisions in terms of factor prices and marginal value products to the end of maximisation of profit, consciously try *not* to order the world in this way. Try to think, not in terms of what you already know, but afresh. Much misunderstanding in economics generally (and in growth theory in particular) could be avoided if we were willing to momentarily give up our own point of view in order to see someone else's way of looking at things.

The sort of thing I am talking about is expressed very neatly in Thomas Kuhn's *The Structure of Scientific Revolutions* [43]. It is not necessary to strictly apply Kuhn's explanation of 'progress' in the natural sciences to the social sciences in order to grasp the inherent difficulties that truly new or different points of view encounter. It is sometimes mentally impossible to conceive of both the old and the new at the same time. To see or understand one point of view may imply completely blotting out the other. This occurance Kuhn calls a 'Gestalt shift'.

Looking at an abstract figure I may be able to see the outlines of a rabbit. Someone else, looking at the very same abstract figure, may believe it to be an elephant. But for me to see the elephant implies losing the image of the rabbit; both cannot be seen at once. So it seems also with economic theory. The confusion that may be caused by failing to recognise this phenomenon can be amazing. It becomes possible for two people, each observing the same abstract drawing (or phenomenon or economic system) to talk about the same parts of it, agreeing on what they are talking about, and at the same time failing to understand one another. And is this surprising when what I see to be a rabbit's ear my friend sees as an elephant's trunk? We can talk at cross-purposes for an eternity without realising what the problem is, for I cannot conceive of his elephant nor he my rabbit. The only thing that keeps us from thinking the other barmy is that we can periodically return to square one and agree that the individual blobs of paint are the same for both of us. Then the discussion (and confusion) starts all over again, both of us convinced of the validity of our positions, but unable to convince the other or even communicate the sense of the argument.

So I ask you to do your best to try and see my rabbit, and I shall do my best to help you see it. Afterwards if you still prefer the elephant (or in turn find a duck) you are welcome to it. At the very least it will improve our communication, this to the benefit of both of us.

In keeping with this approach I will keep the emphasis primarily on the positive side of the 'post-Keynesian' approach, taking very little time to try and formally discredit the existing elephant. This has not only been better done by others, but it would take away from the presentation by switching back and forth from rabbits to elephants. One taken at a time is difficult enough. For those who are not familiar with the Critique, based on Piero Sraffa's 'Introduction' to Ricardo's Collected Works [71] and *Production of Commodities By Means of Commodities* [107] a number of good sources exist. In addition the writings of Keynes and Kalecki will be essential.[1]

---

[1] Possible suggestions include Joan Robinson and John Eatwell, *An Introduction to Modern Economics* (London: McGraw Hill, 1973), chapters 2–6; Joan Robinson, *Economic Heresies* [92]; Schwartz and Hunt, *A Critique of Economic Theory* [100]; and G. C. Harcourt's *Some Cambridge controversies in the theory of capital* [17]. A useful guide to the works of Kalecki is Feiwel [13].

THE MAKING OF A REVOLUTION

It would be a mistake to think that either the Critique or the positive theory that sprung from it was something that occurred overnight in a blinding flash of light. Joan Robinson's Foreword to this book gives testimony to the fact that it was not something sudden, but a long and sometimes difficult process which drew its beginnings in what is now somewhat mistakenly called the 'Keynesian Revolution', in concert with the growing dissatisfaction with the competitive theory of value and distribution which led to the theory of Imperfect Competition.

To understand the position of the so-called 'Keynesian Revolution' we must recall the state of English economics in the 1920s in relation to the economic conditions ruling at the time. England, quite unlike the post-First World War position of the United States, experienced slump conditions throughout the 1920s. Unemployment in this period was commonly in excess of 6 per cent. The existing orthodoxy, however, denied that such conditions could exist, at least over an extended period of time. This position, which Keynes called the 'Classical', was pillared on two principles: Say's Law and the Quantity theory of Money. Now Say's Law we all know by the maxim 'Supply creates its own Demand'. What poor old Say was trying to convey in his Law of Markets was something much more complex, yet much more simple. The Law of Markets was simply that the production of goods was necessary to provide the where-withall to buy goods. Thus the production of commodities was at the same time the creation of supply and demand in the market. Goods must be produced in order to provide the income necessary to buy them. This proposition could be used to combat the idea of overproduction or the glut of commodities, for the supply of commodities always produced purchasing power over commodities. Production would produce an amount of demand equal to the quantity of goods supplied. The proposition had little to do with the level of employment or the operation of relative prices in combatting overproduction.

In the historical context in which Say was writing it is doubtful whether unemployment as we conceive it today had much meaning. But for the neoclassicists who took up Say's proposition and told the story in terms of relative price adjustments there can be no such excuse. In the neoclassical explanation of Say's Law, if there was an excess supply of a factor the price of the factor would fall. The factor would thus be cheaper relatively to other factors and thus would be substituted for the factors that were relatively dearer. It is not always directly acknowledged, but this mechanism implies the assumption of perfect substitution of all factors and certain income elasticity assumptions. In modern parlance the theory is most easily supported by assuming income and substitution elasticities equal to unity with constant returns. It should not be surprising that the substitution assumption still remains in the corpus of neoclassical theory as applied to long-period growth.

For the neoclassicists there was always a set of relative prices which eliminated excess supply or demand and thus generated the full employment of all factors traded on the market in competitive conditions. But this left the absolute price level undetermined. There were no money prices in the model, only relative physical exchange ratios. The Quantity Theory of Money provided the equations for the excess supply and demand for money which gave money values to the relative real prices. The level of money prices was thus determined by the total quantity of money without disturbing the relative physical exchange ratios which were unaffected by changes in the total money supply.

Thus both relative prices and the absolute price level were explained. The system was neatly closed, but also neatly separated. The determination of the monetary sector and the real sector was as separate as Cambridge, England and Cambridge, Massachusetts. This is where Pigou's famous phrase about the 'veil of money' comes in. Money was just an unnecessary complication that had to be removed, seen through, to get to the analysis of the 'real' variables in the system. Since money had nothing to do with the determination of the real exchange ratios it was something that could be dispensed with as relatively unimportant to the real movement of the system.

Added to this dichotomy between the real and monetary analysis of the economic system was the dichotomy between the determination of the general nominal price level and the determination of the prices of individual products. The general nominal price level was determined through the 'equation of exchange', by the total quantity of money; while the prices of individual products were set by cost and demand conditions at the firm or microeconomic level. The theory could never adequately explain how the changes in the total quantity of money brought about the changes in the microeconomic prices that were the basis of the general price level. The strict Quantity theory was never capable of more than static comparisons of equilibrium conditions. It did not analyse the transitions between such positions. To this day Milton Friedman is still trying to find a believeable transmission mechanism that will explain the effects of changes in the rate of change of the quantity of money on individual prices and thus on the aggregate price level. At the same time he hopes to turn the long-period neutrality of the original Quantity theory into a short-period theory capable of explaining fluctuations of both prices and output.

So there are two basic dichotomies; between the determination of prices at the microeconomic and macroeconomic level on the one hand, and between the real and monetary sectors on the other. It was in *A Treatise on Money* [33] that Keynes tried to show that not only were microeconomic and macroeconomic variables linked, but more importantly that real and monetary phenomena were inextricably linked in an economy with uncertainty over the possible outcomes of future events, i.e. in what he called a monetary economy. The main thrust of his explanation was to show how the relation of savings to investment could affect the general price level. With the focus on the interrelations of money and real variables, the effect of savings and investment on aggregate demand and employment came as secondary considerations. As a theoretical demonstration it was not sufficient to provide an economic basis for the proposition to ameliorate unemployment that Keynes had been advocating since the late 1920s – namely that the government could increase employment by undertaking public investment without in any way diminishing the amount of private investment that could take place. The theoretical proof finally came in *The General Theory*, but the important point to notice for present purposes is that Keynes had expressly rejected the validity of the two dichotomies and set about to provide a theory that integrated the determination of individual prices with the overall price level by showing the interrelations between the monetary and real sectors.

FROM MONEY AND PRICE TO OUTPUT AND EMPLOYMENT

The transition of Keynes's ideas between the *Treatise* and the *General Theory* is a story that is better told in another place (see [38], vol. XIII]). Here I want to mark a sole distinction: the way in which

Keynes established the possibility of involuntary unemployment and equilibrium at less than full employment. The very complicated definition of involuntary unemployment was designed to give away everything it possibly could to the existing theory. Keynes wanted to show that the theory under its existing assumptions was capable of producing the result of unemployment if freed from its logical flaws. Thus Keynes was willing to assume that the price system functioned perfectly, that both prices and wages would move flexibly to adjust any inequality between supply and demand. It was only on these assumptions that his theory could appear convincing – by deriving a result contrary to what he called the 'Classical' model, given its own assumptions. It is thus indeed strange that Keynes's own theory is most often accused of assuming rigid prices and/or wages, or as being a special case of the 'Classical' theory in which prices and wages are rigid in the short period.

In simple terms the theory that Keynes was combatting had gone something like the following. If there was an excess supply of a factor, say labour, its price would be driven down relative to the prices of other factors. This would lead to an increase in its utilisation in production. Thus there was always a price that would clear each factor market (including price zero, identifying a free good). Unemployed factors could only exist if they were voluntarily held out of the market at the ruling price, or if they refused to lower their price (accept a lower wage in the case of labour).[2] The basic assumption of substitution of factors is clearly implicit (even if unnoticed and unobtrusive without an aggregate stock of capital) along with strict independence of microeconomic supply and demand functions for all factors traded. Unemployment could only be explained by blaming labour for demanding too high wages. This yielded the twofold benefit of absolving the capitalists from the blame for unemployment and the slump and, at the same time, giving them a stick with which to beat the trade unions.

A more sophisticated version of the same line of reasoning, but more closely aligned with Say's maxim, concerned the effect of changes in consumption and saving on the rate of interest. If demand for consumption goods declines then saving out of a given income rises. The rise in saving then drives down the rate of interest, making borrowing for investment cheaper. Investment goods become

---

[2] A full analysis of the effects of changing factor inputs on relative prices is worked out in [77].

cheaper relatively to consumption goods and therefore the capitalists demand and produce more investment goods. The increase in the utilisation of labour in the production of investment just equals the loss of employment in the consumption goods sectors and full-employment is preserved. In this case the rate of interest is the price that brings savings and investment into equality and preserves full employment. That this approach is based on the belief that saving determines the demand for capital goods (investment) is evident. In explaining the possibility of unemployment, however, the intransigence of the banking system in keeping the rate of interest higher than that required for full-employment (and thus defending their own profits) equality of savings and investment did not, however, catch on as a popular notion as easily as the story that blamed the monopoly position of the trade unions. (The notion seems, however, to have regained some currency in the United States of late.) This second version, however, resembles the first in its use of relative prices, only here the emphasis is on the rate of interest as the price of capital (savings) and the difference a change in the rate of interest brings about in the relative prices of capital and consumption goods.[3]

Keynes's main point in demolishing these explanations was quite simple, viewed with the advantage of hindsight. An economy at its macroeconomic level is by its very nature interdependent. Thus wages which appear as a cost to the firm also appear as income to households and eventually as income to the firms as the result of sales to households – the basis of profits for the firm. But what is true for one firm in isolation is disaster if it applies to the economy as a whole. For a single firm a decrease in wages reduces costs and raises profits, if it can continue to sell the same quantity at the same price. But when wages fall, overall total household incomes also fall; when incomes fall demand falls as do sales and profits. Thus a general cut in wages implies an overall fall in demand and sales for all firms and an inability to sell the same output at the same prices. Thus it could hardly be said that entrepreneurs would want to hire more labour as a result of a general fall in wages when they are having a hard time selling the output of the labour force currently employed. All students who have been taught to carefully distinguish between moves along and shifts in supply and demand curves will recognise the application of this proposition.

[3] This view has been unsuspectingly resurrected in [44].

Now the best result that could occur in the case of decreasing money wages would be no change at all in the amount of employment offered, which could conceptually occur if prices and wages adjusted instantaneously to the new conditions. In such a case there would be no change in relative prices or employment. The process that the neoclassical explanation required, a fall in wages relative to prices, could not be produced without the assumption that aggregate demand was independent of the level of wages or that full employment was guaranteed from outside the system. The net result of the proposition then must be that changes in relative prices would not (indeed could not) produce the advertised results – the full employment of all factors. The operation of the price mechanism to produce full employment failed in the crucial test on the labour market. If the theory is not applicable to the factor labour, there appears to be no reason why it will work in any other case. Full employment was something that was outside the control of relative prices.

The second 'Classical' explanation was something harder to expunge from the minds of those who were brought up to think of saving as the same thing as demand for investment. Keynes pointed out that there was a sharp distinction between decisions to save and decisions to carry out investment for they were usually carried out by different people for different motives. Again the price system could not equate savings and investment as there was no way for the price mechanism to communicate the decisions of the savers to the investors. Since saving was a decision to forego consumption for an undetermined period, unless the actors in the system possessed perfect knowledge of what the future would bring, the provision of the level of investment that would assure full employment over time was as much a matter of chance as anything else. Keynes tells some amusing stories to make this point in chapter 16 of the *General Theory*. But as long as the interest rate could not give a perfect indication of the future there was no way for changes in the relative price of capital and consumption to guarantee full employment. In fact, Keynes completely rejected this explanation of the determination of the rate of interest.

Thus the acknowledgement of a world with less than perfect information about future events, where uncertainty and individual expectations were a matter of critical importance, clinched the case against the ruling orthodoxy. Even if individuals did respond to changes in relative prices (which they probably do in the broad sense), shifts in supply and demand due to changes in expectations and uncertainty would more than offset any shift along the curves produced by relative price changes. Thus the level of investment was more influenced by what Keynes called the 'state of long-period expectations' than the relative price of capital. Changes in expectations about uncertain future sales from a current investment project could cause the marginal efficiency of capital (demand for investment) curve to shift bodily, thus swamping any effect that might be caused by changes in relative prices. The same effects were at work in consumption demand which was also subject to the vagaries of uncertainty. When there is an increase in uncertainty over future income, precautionary balances may be built up at the expense of current consumption. Changes in expectations over future income may then also cause a shift in the consumption function. Despite the fact that most econometric models built on Keynesian principles expect the consumption function to be constant over time, Keynes himself was not of this belief. The co-ordination of decisions to invest and decisions to save at a level that produced full employment of labour was a problem that the price system alone could not handle for it could neither provide the necessary information nor produce effects on expectations that might overcome this lack of information. To make any sense at all of the theory of relative prices required the *assumption* of full employment, but this is no explanation of why or why it does not produce such a state of affairs.

A PRAGMATIC CHOICE

From this point there were two directions that Keynes could have gone. Having shown the price system to be faulty, at least in producing full employment, he could have attacked the static theory of prices determined by supply and demand and changes in supply and demand determined by changes in prices. But Keynes had no time for such theoretical niceties (nor, according to Gerald Shove, the inclination) with in excess of a million unemployed. The problem was to get the system back on its feet, not pursue the frailties of the neoclassical theory of prices. Thus Keynes chose to pursue a practical remedy for bringing about the changes in quantity that prices could not: by working on factors that influence uncertainty and expectations.

Even though his approach explicitly rejects the operation of relative prices, Keynes believed that once his palliatives had restored full employment the 'Classical' mechanism would again become operative. This remark, made in the concluding chapter of the *General Theory* introduces an inappropriate dichotomy into his system and also opens the way for the neoclassicists to salve their consciences that Keynes's critique was not as basic as it actually was. Keynes thus laid the path for those who wished to reincorporate his theory (as Pigou did in *Employment and Equilibrium*)[4] as a special phenomenon that occurred in a period of time too short for the neoclassical adjustment process to operate through the Pigou effect (or the wealth effect, or real balance effect, or what you will). Thus the previous doubts about the revolutionary aspects of the 'Keynesian Revolution'. Keynes himself, in this respect, is much to blame for the rewriting of Keynesian theory in the general equilibrium framework of the neoclassical tradition he was attacking, and for the failure of his more revolutionary, if not explicit, contributions to be recognised as such outside a close circle of his students and followers.

As a final point in this respect, it should be noted that Keynes objected to the existing theory only to the extent that it did not provide the means to full employment. He was in complete accord with the *laissez-faire* principles of the 'Classical' orthodoxy.

> If we suppose the volume of output to be given, i.e. to be determined by forces outside the classical scheme of thought, then there is no objection to be raised against the classical analysis of the manner in which private self-interest will determine what in particular is produced, in what proportions the factors of production will be combined to produce it, and how the value of the final product will be distributed between them; . . . It is in determining the volume, not the direction, of actual employment that the existing system has broken down.[5]

How much of the wider reaching implications of Keynes's theory were recognised at the time is not known, probably very few of the

[4] See [70] and also the retrospective reviews of the *General Theory* in [45].

[5] [35, p. 379]. Joan Robinson has suggested that this is a short-sighted approach applicable to the limited short-run objective of full employment. The question of what type of employment should be created and the direction of government investment she has called the 'second crisis in economic theory'. See [93; 94; 79, p. 81].

implications were clearly seen, most certainly not by Keynes himself as the above quotation gives witness. It is easy now, however, to see how it was possible to be a good Keynesian in support of public investment to cure unemployment and at the same time retain an unchallenged basic theoretical position grounded on neoclassical relative price adjustments and marginal productivity theory to determine distribution. One should certainly not be surprised that more so-called Keynesians did not follow Joan Robinson in her attempts to follow the logical extensions of Keynes's theory, when their interpretation of the *General Theory*, backed with the dictum of Keynes, appeared to lead back to the theory of general equilibrium and the refinement of the theory of Walras.

Unfortunately this return to orthodoxy with good conscience left the implicit challenge to the problem of pricing unnoticed. The problem of the role of prices (more bother to Edgeworth than to Keynes) at the time, and also today, stands on the feeble explanation of the 'invisible hand' in Adam Smith and its formulation in Walras's 'tâtonnement'. Walras was trying to construct a theory of what the economists of the time *thought* the market did. The market was assumed to equate supply and demand and, in addition (or possibly as a measuring bonus) to give optimal distribution and allocation of resources by providing perfect information. To do this Walras had to tell a story about an auction market where prices were fixed *à la criée au hasard* to allocate arbitrarily given bundles of goods to be traded. Some say that Walras had in mind the Bourse de Paris. But as financial wizards know, even the stock market requires a jobber or a 'specialist' to set prices and keep them in order, that is to keep them from instantaneously equating supply and demand when the jobber considers this to be against his own interests, or his expectations about future market conditions.

In Walras's system the distribution of physical product is given in advance and the groping for the market price that equates supply and demand is something that only happens in imaginary or logical time. There is no way to handle the production of goods over time nor the movement through history that this requires. Prices are determined instantaneously and costlessly and provide to all traders all the information that they need to know to make their decisions, also without cost or elapsed time. But there is little point in criticising this story (or Edgeworth's process of recontracting) because it is not meant to be realistic. It is only supposed to be a story that reproduces the results the free market is *presumed* to produce in its own mysterious and invisible way. The point we should note, however, is that this story in no way serves as a proof that the market really functions in the manner assumed, it may be true or false without being an accurate description of what it is supposed to describe. Walras's theory makes no pretentions to being a perfectly accurate description of the workings of the market. Before and after Walras's infamous auctioneer, the 'invisible hand' remains like most religious apparitions, only seen if believed. But it is on this story that the neoclassical theory of market prices rests, and despite its modern refinements, it has not been seriously challenged up to this day with the exception of Marx (and as we have attempted to argue above, Keynes, if only implicitly).

The static results of instantaneous market clearing prices have also been accepted for the analysis of intertemporal allocation of consumption and production and dynamic analysis in general. It is finally in its application to the Neo-neoclassical model of economic[6] growth that one can see how inessential this theory is, for these models seem to behave according to market principles even when there is only one produced commodity and hence little role for relative prices to play. In this approach the decision to save determines both investment and the real wage required to produce full employment over time. In such a system the story of the auctioneer is hardly worth telling, for he has almost nothing to do.

Other attempts to deal with the problem of dynamics and of the allocation of output over time take the analogy of the auctioneer to infinite limits. In such theories the market sets not only today's prices but also future prices, somewhat like a futures market, for all possible future dates and all possible future products and events. Here the auctioneer becomes infinite and omniscient in order to fulfil the belief in the perfect information aspect of the market. I cannot say whether or not Keynes believed in the Diety, it is certain that his belief in the importance of uncertainty applied to the analysis of future events that simply could not be known, either from past experience or future projection. This formulation of the Walrasian theory, like the others, is meant to be an analogy of what the market is thought to do, not a description of what it actually does. The mere fact of unemployment was enough to lead Keynes to question it.

---

[6] Readers not familiar with the neoclassical approach are referred to [42, chapter 4].

This habit of practical thinking does not, however, seem to have caught on.[7]

All this concerns what is called the theory of perfect competition, which Keynes was more or less willing to assume throughout his analysis despite the appearance between the publication of the *Treatise* and the *General Theory* of the new theories of imperfect competition. Although these theories, stemming from Sraffa's criticisms of the Marshallian system, did not much concern Keynes (cf. [94]) they launched a sharp critique against the 'Classical' price mechanism. Joan Robinson's innovating role in these theories undoubtedly sharpened her recognition of the inadequacies inherent in the theory Keynes was attacking to an extent Keynes, satisfied with the explanation of the means to full employment, did not appreciate (cf. [73, 74, 75, 89]). It was, however, not in this line that the full implications of the Keynes theory were to result, but rather in the application of the theory to the problems of the long-period and economic growth over time.

TOWARDS THE LONG-PERIOD ANALYSIS OF EMPLOYMENT

Although Keynes's theory was primarily static in the sense of singling out the present from both the past and the future and working within the context of the existing capital stock in given conditions of expectations, the basis of the system was dynamic. Indeed, in addition to the nature of the concepts that he used which inherently took account of the links between the present and the future, Keynes left some vague hints about the application of the basic premises of the *General Theory* to a theory of the long-period theory of employment [35, pp. 46–50].

Although Joan Robinson was probably the first to follow up these hints there can be little question of Harrod's priority in the concern over the dynamic aspects of the *General Theory*. Harrod was already occupied with dynamics in general and the dynamics of the *General Theory* in particular in 1934 (cf. [18, 19, 45, 38]). It hadn't taken much time to realise that a Keynesian short-period situation with $S = I$ equilibrium and positive net saving implied a future increase in productive capacity and thus growth of output. Thus the level of investment required to produce full employment in

[7] For a fuller critique of this approach see Nuti [63]. Keynes's view on uncertainty is succinctly given in [37].

any given period will have implications on the future stock of productive capacity that results from present investments. In this respect the employment creating possibilities in the future as well as the profitability in future periods is linked to the present level of investment.

But Harrod was more concerned with the possibility that post-war investment opportunities would lag behind the potential level of savings generated at full employment and thus concentrated his analysis on the inherent instability of a closed capitalistic system. The relation between the future employment possibilities of the capital stock generated by present investment was glossed over with the assumption of neutral technical progress, allowing Harrod to concentrate on the relation between investment opportunities and the level of savings at full employment.

Although Keynes had pointed out that the distribution of income could directly effect the level of consumption and thus the profitability of investment, Harrod chose to ignore the problem of the distribution of income and the determination of the rate of profit in relation to the real wage. Joan Robinson, on the other hand, took these problems to be of crucial importance.

In reviewing and comparing the theory of Marx to existing economic theory [78] she was surprised to find that the existing theory had nothing that could be called a theory to determine the rate of profit and thus the distribution of income [81, 78, 93]. Joan Robinson thus set out to provide a theory of distribution within the Keynesian framework which, of course, required an explanation of the determination of the profit rate – both purposively lacking in Harrod's limited demonstration of the feeble hope of post-war stability with full employment.

It was at this point that the extensions of the *General Theory* took two directions. The existing (1950s) theory of distribution and profit-rate determination were based on the empirical generalisation of Wicksteed, by Cobb and Douglas, into aggregate terms, with a touch of J. B. Clark's synthesising hand. The wage of labour and the price of capital were believed to be determined by the marginal products of labour and aggregate value-capital via the Cobb–Douglas production function. Given factor prices determined in this manner distribution was determined by multiplying factor quantities by factor prices.

The working out of the theory of imperfect competition had

already raised great doubts concerning the validity of this procedure,[8] and its integration into the Keynesian framework made it even more suspect. The argument against this approach is, again with hindsight, really quite simple. If the sum of the heterogeneous capital goods is to be calculated as an aggregate comparable with profits it must be in value terms to yield a homogeneous ratio of profit to capital. But if the profit rate is then determined by the marginal product of this sum there is a logical flaw in the argument, for the prices of the capital goods must initially have been calculated at some rate of profit. Thus the marginal product of capital as given by the aggregate production function can only determine the rate of profit that is already determined and is expressed in the prices of the capital goods that have to be used to find a homogeneous measure of the capital stock.

Far from explaining *why* the rate of profit is what it is, the best this approach can do is discover *what* rate of profit is implied in the prices of the existing capital stock. It could not then be an explanation of the rate of profit, but only a tautological proof that the rate of profit is what it is. Coupling this with the fact that the marginal product of labour must cover not only the wage of labour, but also a return to the capitalist on the capital he has advanced as wages, breaks the other factor price–marginal productivity equivalence. This notion is, however, spelled out explicitly even in Adam Smith's *Wealth of Nations*.[9]

The important thing to stress is that these criticisms were levied before any of the Neo-neoclassical extensions of Harrod's model by Swan [108], Solow [101], Meade [52], et al., had appeared in the literature. It was not what is now known as Neo-neoclassical growth theory that could not be placed within the Keynesian framework (it did not at that time exist) but the existing orthodoxy that had survived the Keynesian revolution untouched, in particular the simplification of the Walrasian general equilibrium system (or Wicksteed's analysis of particular individual factors) through the

---

[8] Cf. [73]. R. F. Kahn also puts the point clearly in [23, p. 78]. The objection is first put in the modern context in [82].

[9] As well as by Marx who quotes from Smith [49, p. 74]. Another, and more important criticism comes in terms of increasing and diminishing returns, which is brought up in the first two references in the previous note. It has recently been given strong emphasis by Nell [60, 61] who points out that a real-life case of diminishing returns which is necessary for the upward sloping marginal cost curve of neoclassical equilibrium has never been produced, while real world examples of increasing returns abound.

aggregate production function relating the value of total output to labour and aggregate value-capital.

The upshot was two distinct lines of analysis, the tearing down of the existing orthodoxy that should have been the result of the so-called Keynesian revolution, and the building up of a full generalisation of the *General Theory* in its full potentiality. It should by now be obvious that this process was something that required an even longer struggle to escape than even Keynes himself had envisaged.

It is the positive side of these struggles that I want to emphasise in the chapters that follow, trying to show that the Keynesian theory of profit and distribution can be applied to the analysis of economic dynamics in general. To note that there are several alternative lines in this generalisation, we will also try to note the basic differences between post-Keynesian writers by comparing the approaches of Kaldor and Pasinetti to that of Joan Robinson in chapters 13 and 14. Along the way I will try to offer additional extensions and applications of the theory which has as its basis Keynes's *General Theory*; by which, as Joan Robinson has pointed out, one does 'not mean simply the book called *The General Theory of Employment, Interest and Money*, but the whole stream of ideas, or rather the analytical system, to which that book made the main contribution, but which is still in the process of developing the perfecting itself, finding new applications and modifying its methods to treat new problems' [79, p. 134].

Thus we have what might be called the recent history of the development of post-Keynesian theory. But the roots of Keynes's theory go back much further than that, as do those of the existing orthodoxy. We first develop the historical and theoretical background of the two approaches in order to find a definitional framework for the analysis that follows. In this way we can more clearly see the relation between post-Keynesian theory and 'Classical' Political Economy.

2 Skeletons of the Past

Some fundamental differences between the post-Keynesian and the orthodox Neo-neoclassical theories can be found by looking at the evolution of the theory of value. There we find two distinct branches, one associated with the Classical economists from the Physiocrats to Ricardo, and the other with the neoclassical economists, such as Jevons, Walras and Marshall. This difference in approach of the two branches can best be described in terms of 'physical' and 'subjective' conceptions of value. Most often, in recent times, the latter conception goes under the name of price theory in order to escape the implication that it has to do with unscientific 'value judgements' and normative theory. Whether a simple change in name is sufficient for this purpose may become clear below.

ECONOMIC PRE-HISTORY

The problem of economic growth is by no means a new one in the history of economic theory. It was the main preoccupation of both economists and men of affairs (in fact they most often co-incided) from the rise of the nation-state. Any reasonable explanation of the activities and writings of the Mercantilists must take into account their practical recognition of the value of physical resources and the necessity of using them to make a nation strong, not only in the field of trade. Strong trade balances and strong nations were both synonymous of rapid economic growth (not to say anything of geographical conquest). But this practical approach to the economic affairs of the state did not produce anything that could be called a theory in the proper sense of a system of logically co-ordinated ideas. Mercantilism was simply a general method of analysis that was worked out by applying it to specific cases as the need arose. A strong nation was more important than consistency or economic logic.

With the French 'economists', the Physiocrats, comes the first attempt to organise and understand the production of output at an aggregate level, and the role of the mechanism of exchange. The unifying conception, patterned after the discovery of the circulation of blood in the human body, was symbolised in Quesnay's *Tableau Economique*. This conception placed economic study in line with the philosophical movement of the time towards the belief in the natural organisation of the universe on simple and general principles or laws. The theory was in direct contrast to the preference for economic controls expressed by the Mercantilists, but at the same time it guaranteed results that would be at least as successful while philosophically more pleasing. Thus '*laissez-faire, laissez-passer*' became the order of the day.

The most important concept of the approach was the *produit net*, the amount of physical product that remained after the physical costs of producing agricultural output had been recovered when all products exchanged at prices calculated in terms of their values in physical terms. The fact that the Physiocrats only recognised a physical surplus over inputs in agriculture simply reflects the economic and social conditions of the time; it by no means diminishes the usefulness of distinguishing between real resources used up in production, gross output and the remaining surplus.

In terms of natural law the *produit net* was something that was left over after exchange at natural values had occurred in the system, this between the farmers, the manufacturers and the landowners. This process implied, as natural law logic must, that the real cost of agricultural output could be measured in physical terms: the produce that was necessary to provide labour and raw materials for the next season's planting. Real physical cost of production was then equal to natural exchange value. This left the surplus, which was claimed by the landlords as the natural inheritors of the fruitfulness of the soil. The approach can hardly be said to have been egalitarian, but none the less it is obvious that the problems of growth, value and distribution were all part of the larger process of the production and circulation of the national produce.

THE CLASSICAL APPROACH – THE LANDOWNERS UNSEATED

The concept of real physical cost was taken up by the classical economists who followed the Physiocrats, and is especially obvious in Adam Smith. Smith, however, made two major additions. First he took it as given that a surplus in the production of agricultural produce was a prerequisite for the division of labour which would be necessary to increase the wealth of the nation. Secondly this implied that not only agriculture was productive but also that those manufacturing sectors where division of labour could be applied could produce a surplus over physical production costs. He did not, however, employ the grand explanation of circulation found with the Physiocrats, and thus the elucidation of general abstract models was left to Ricardo and Malthus.

Ricardo went directly to distribution as the basic problem underlying the analysis of economic growth. He was more interested in the economic actions of the broad social classes as they applied to the dynamic process of growth than the technical characteristics of production (although he spent a good deal of time figuring out his position on the effect of machinery on employment). On a class basis the landlords simply squandered their rents on servants and high life, while the parsimonious capitalists invested their profits in productive enterprise. For the maintenance of growth it was obviously more beneficial to give the capitalists the greater share of the surplus. Labour really never came into the problem at this stage, the Malthusian devil assuring that the wage remained near subsistence while diminishing returns increased the proportion of the labour force required even to produce this meagre subsistence.

In order to analyse the distribution of the growing output between the social classes it was necessary to have a theory of value that provided a consistant measure of the surplus that was distributed. But the distribution of the surplus not only determined how much of the surplus was invested, but at the same time the market values of the produced goods. Thus any measure of the output based on normal market prices would be of different value with different distributions of the surplus.

This problem is something over and above simple day-to-day fluctuations in market prices, which were expected and not of much overall interest within the classical tradition of *normal* market values. The conception of a value that was determined under normal conditions and around which day-to-day prices would fluctuate was in an indirect sense related to the natural prices of the Physiocrats. The Classical economists were also strong supporters of *laissez-faire*, but had rejected the worldly relations of natural law for natural harmony based on the actions of individuals following their best interests. Thus normal values implied the prices at which goods would be exchanged by free individuals, each parting with and receiving an equal value in exchange.

The search for normal value in exchange, for Ricardo's purposes, thus implied a paradox. What was required was a value measure that was independent of the distribution of income, but this meant that the value measure could not itself have a normal value that was determined in the process of exchange. It was this type of measuring rod that Ricardo required to measure the surplus and to compare with prices in the market. Thus the search for a measure that would serve the same purpose in economics as pounds and feet serve identically as measures of weight and length as well as the concepts of weight and length in themselves.

Ricardo took the labour theory of value as the basis of his investigations.

I know no other criterion of a thing being dear or cheap but by the sacrifices of labour made to obtain it. . . . That the greater or less quantity of labour worked up in commodities can be the only cause of their alteration in value is completely made out as soon as we are agreed that all commodities are the produce of labour and would have no value but for the labour expended on them. Though this is true it is still exceedingly difficult to discover or even to imagine any commodity which shall be perfect general measure of value, . . . [71, IV, p. 397].

In taking labour as the basis of value Ricardo also introduced an important distinction into the analysis of value. His theory distinguished sharply between those goods that could be *produced and reproduced* by the application of labour and materials, and those that could not, like old masters' paintings. It was only the former category of goods that were of interest to the process of growth and which were thus taken into account in his theory of value. The latter, smaller and less interesting, group were left to the vagaries of taste of the wealthy and normal supply and demand. This sharp distinction in Ricardo's theory has led some economists to conclude that there is some inconsistency in Ricardo's framework, that he was less than convinced in the application of his labour-theory of value. That he made a distinction between reproducible and non-reproducible goods is, of course, true; but it is less an inconsistency than a realistic perception of the factors that enter into the growth process. If Ricardo had an incomplete labour theory of value, his followers proceeded to extend the analysis of those goods Ricardo excluded into an analysis of the entire output of the community. It is indeed unfortunate that Ricardo's basic distinction has all but disappeared from the analysis of growth.[1]

Thus, in Ricardo's sense, using labour as the basis and measure of output is quite sensible from the point of view of the society's overall productive potential. Labour is required to transform raw materials into products. Different amounts and combinations of products can be compared in terms of the amount of the total labour available and required for their production.

The problem that arises, however, is how to measure labour. When the quantity of labour is the measure of value it is not consistent, as Ricardo recognised [71, IV, p. 392], to value labour's real cost in terms of the subsistence wage. Indeed, this simply brings the measure of value back into the exchange process where the price of labour is determined by subsistence. As Ricardo's theory of the determination of the wage implies, labour is also producible and reproducible. Thus Ricardo's unending search for an invariable measure of value.

It is clear – as Marx later emphasised – that a sharp distinction must be made between the effort expended in the production of output (real physical cost independent of distribution) and the normal exchange value of labour power (the commodity that the entrepreneur purchases with the subsistence wage) which is determined in the process of exchange and thus unsuitable as an invariant measure of value. The possible confusion results from equating the real physical cost (effort-time) with the subsistence wage (the normal exchange value of the commodity labour that must be paid by the capitalist). It was on this distinction that Marx based his analysis of exploitation and the origin of profit in the capitalist system. He thus chose simple labour time itself as the standard of value, which would then also provide a measure of the value of labour power.

There is another, secondary problem, related to the use by both Ricardo and Marx, of a value theory based on labour. It will not, in general, be true that prices observed in the system will be directly proportional to labour embodied in the production of output, nor will relative prices tend to correspond to relative amounts of labour embodied in output. With production processes that use fixed capital there is no good reason, as Ricardo admitted, for prices to be related proportionally to embodied labour. Thus in cases where the

---

[1] It has recently been revived due to the work of Sraffa.

ratio of capital to labour is not uniform for all output, prices need not be proportional to labour costs, although Ricardo thought the assumption worked well enough for rough averages. In the more general case prices will equal wages plus profit on capital employed and will be proportional to labour costs only in the special case where the capital–labour ratio is uniform in all lines of production. This problem was, however, for Ricardo something quite separate from the problem of finding an absolute measure of value that was unchanged when the distribution of income was changed, something he did consider to be a serious problem (cf. chapter 9).

The general problem of relating values to prices is often called the 'transformation problem' and is raised as an objection to the theory of labour value as found in both Marx and Ricardo. For Marx, however, the so-called 'problem' is slightly different for his analysis of labour value, as pointed out above, is different from Ricardo's. For Ricardo, transformation was a secondary problem to that of finding a measure of output consistent with changes in the distribution of income. Marx felt that he had solved this problem with his dual definition of labour. Thus, in Marx's analysis the distribution of income between labour and the capitalists is given by the rate of exploitation in the production process (the difference between the time it takes for the labourers to produce his value and the length of the total working day the capitalists impose on labour). Thus for Marx the transformation *process* concerns the distribution of the *given* surplus amongst the capitalists so that each earns a uniform rate of profit on his capital, irrespective of size. This operation was carried out by the forces of competition in exchange and occurred because of the social relations between capital and free labour under capitalistic production, which gave a dominant position to the capitalists. Transformation was then not so much a 'problem' as a description of the process by which the capitalists divided up the profit or surplus value they derived from employing labour. Thus although transformation is similar in Ricardo and Marx, its function and theoretical basis in each is markedly different.

Ricardo's problem of measurement was taken up by Sraffa about 100 years later, and some 40 years after that the solution was published in *Production of Commodities by Means of Commodities* [107]. An outline of the solution need not be repeated here as several are readily available [2, 17, 41]. We can simply note that Sraffa, respecting Ricardo's distinction between goods that can and cannot be reproduced with labour and raw materials over time, treats capital as a produced good in the system and finds that it is impossible to speak of a value of capital (or of national output) without first having given distribution and the rate of profit. Which is, of course, what Ricardo was trying to say all along.

To sum up the classical approach it is sufficient to mark three things. First the meaning which the early economists attached to cost and value, that is in terms of the real physical cost of producing output. The second is the existence of a surplus of output over production costs measured in this way and the effect of the distribution of income on both relative prices and growth. Third is the important distinction between reproducible and non-reproducible goods. In the classical mode of thought the problems of profit, distribution and growth are all part of the same process. Any one cannot be dealt with without reference to, and solution of, the others.

Before turning to the second branch of value theory a few words must be said about Malthus, who is probably better known for his theory of population than, for what Keynes believed to be, his early contribution to the theory of effective demand. For most of the classical economists (Marx being the best known exception) Say's maxim was taken to be self-evident, in the sense of the impossibility of generalised overproduction or commodity gluts. Keynes, in the *General Theory*, picks out some choice quotations from Malthus that decry the diminishing effects of saving on demand and profitability and call for 'unproductive consumption' to avoid excess commodity production and slumps. In this way Malthus provided a justification for the existence of the landlords (under heavy attack from Ricardo) by attempting to show that profit resulted from the profligate spending habits of the landed classes. He even went so far as recommending that their spending be subsidised, as it was the main cause of profits and thus economic growth and prosperity. While there may be superficial similarities, Malthus's logical structure was far different from Keynes.

Marx is much more trenchant in his criticism of Malthus's theory of profit than his theory of population.[2] This should be obvious, for Marx was interested to show that profit (surplus-value) was created in the production process through the employment of labour.

---

[2] See Marx [50, chapter xix]. Keynes was much more kindly in his assessment of Malthus, e.g. [35 chapter 23].

Malthus's position suggested that profit could be created simply by giving the landlords enough money to spend. Profit then appeared to be something that arose outside the system of production in the economy. The difference between prices and costs thus appeared as an addition to costs that was possible due to the extra income the landlords added to the economic circulation. It was in order to escape this interpretation that Marx worked out his entire explanation of the origin of profits in Volume I of *Capital* on the assumption that all commodities exchanged at their values measured in labour time. Under such an assumption the possibility of an explanation such as Malthus proposed on the origin of profits was ruled out of existence. By demonstrating the origin of profit, even under these extreme assumptions, Marx hoped to put to rest the notion that profit was something added to costs from outside the system or was a charge that the capitalists extracted by selling output in the process of exchange. Marx's answer, of course, was that profit was created by the purchase and employment of labour in the production process, the difference between the time required for labour to produce its own value and the imposed length of the working day.

It was only in Volume III that Marx concerned himself with the circulation process and the relation between values and prices of production to show how the capitalists divided up the surplus they had already extracted from labour, a question he took to be quite separate from the origin of profit in surplus value, but crucial to the realisation of surplus value. In the sense of Marx's attack, Malthus does not fall strictly within the classical framework which is most clearly represented by Ricardo and Marx.

SUBJECTIVE VALUE – THE CONSUMER SOVEREIGN

In the following 100 years the real cost approach was replaced by a very different conception of both price and value. We will not here inquire into the causes of this shift (it was not particularly sudden) except to say that it had as much to do with the failure of Ricardo's intellectual heirs to understand him as it had to do with the liberal bourgeoisie's reaction to Marx's development of Ricardo's analysis.[3]

The new line of theory, primarily associated with the names of Jevons, Menger and Walras, concentrated on demand, relative

[3] An explanation is given in Marx [50, chapter xx], 'The Disintegration of the Ricardian School.'

prices and consumption. Productive relations, real cost and the supply side in general carried very little weight. The class aspect of economic theory was also greatly changed. In the classical tradition Ricardo had advanced the interests of the capitalists against the landlords, who were defended by Malthus; Marx took up the cause of the all but forgotten labouring classes. With the neoclassics all this changed and a man was a man for all that; class relations gave way to the analysis of equal individual atomistic decision making units and all men were created and existed politically and economically equal.[4]

By starting with the consumption decisions of individuals the neoclassical economist could cast the entire economic process in purely mental or subjective terms (the influence of Bentham is obvious). The consumer was assumed to act rationally. This meant that, given his income and the supply of goods available at given prices, the consumer would seek the greatest possible utility from the expenditure of his income on consumption. The value of each good purchased is thus determined subjectively by the individual's utility function. The value of the good is the utility it adds at the margin of consumption.

If the good is indeed purchased, market price must be equal to the subjectively determined value, irrespective of the cost of the inputs that have gone into its production. This must be true or else the purchase would not have been made in the first place. Thus market price, largely ignored by the Classicists in their emphasis on normal prices, is elevated to a position of crucial importance in the analysis in an attempt to explain the day-to-day changes in market prices as determined by supply and demand.

Not only does this method eliminate the difference between normal price and market price, it eliminates any discrepancy between value and price and with it the existence of the concept of surplus. When price equals (in fact is) value there can be no unclaimed product to be distributed among the social classes by a mechanism of distribution. In this approach distribution is predetermined (or better, post-determined) by exchange and purchase in the process of circulation. This proposition, represented more formally in Euler's theorem [73], effectively removes the whole basis of classical

---

[4] For a brilliant explanation of the relation between the theory of liberal political democracy and the assumption of individual economic equality see C. B. MacPherson [47].

theory, the best utilisation of the surplus for increased growth. In the neoclassical view, in equilibrium the summation of costs equals selling price, the surplus and the classical concern with growth both vanish. More importantly it turns all output into old masters' paintings by working with given supplies of goods and given consumer incomes at a given point in time. Ricardo's distinction, as outlined above, is completely rejected and forgotten.

The nomenclature of the neoclassical theory – production, distribution, value – was the same as the Classical (recall the rabbit and the elephant) but their point of view was obviously different. Market prices were the sole point of reference in the explanation of why individuals made decisions about specific products and factors.

Assuming given tests, given techniques of production and given supplies of factor services the question was to find which of all possible allocations of the given supplies to production and consumption would produce the greatest utility for all. With price as a direct reflection of final utility the problem was to determine the equilibrium set of relative prices with given resources. As long as each individual consumer (producer) maximised his own utility (profit) the utility of the whole would be maximised by the operation of the price mechanism in producing the equilibrium set of relative prices, without the need of any outside direction or intervention. Like their Classical predecessors, full employment was taken as given.

The real problem is that the neoclassical economists thought they were analysing and answering the same questions about distribution and growth over time as had been the concern of the Classical economists. Some of this confusion comes through the extension of the theory of maximisation to cover the supply side (demand is worked out on the assumption of given physical amounts of productive services). This is done by writing a production relation for each individual commodity produced in terms of the individual commodity inputs required to produce it. To yield a solution with optimum factor input utilisation it could be shown that specific factors should be employed up to the point where their marginal contribution to revenue was equal to their purchase price. But this is still on an atomistic level, dealing with specific commodities, individuals and factors.

To move the analysis to aggregate terms the individual units are classified in three compartments of production: land, labour and capital. Even on the aggregate level we note the shift from the three classes of society to the factors of production that are associated with them, this without leaving the realm of individual equality by emphasising the factors rather than the classes. Since each aggregate factor grouping is composed of the specific individual units it is assumed that each aggregate 'factor' can be measured by summing the individual units, and furthermore, analysed in exactly the same way as the individual factors. The relative prices of the three aggregate 'factors' will then determine the distribution of income amongst the 'factor' groupings. The prices of the 'factors' land, labour and capital are then determined by supply and demand just as the prices of individual factors and commodities are determined by supply and demand based on individual utility and profit maximisation. Distribution thus becomes a problem of the amount of revenue received by different factor services, rather than by the capitalists, landlords and labour. Ownership and class are arbitrary social conditions, and are thought to be quite independent of the economic considerations of relative prices and the distribution of income by means of the awards to 'technical' factor services.

The distinction between specific and aggregate factors appears small, but the consequences are not. To determine 'factor' prices the theory must be able to identify factor quantities. Land and labour can be conceived of quite easily in natural units, as for example land of a given quality and labour of given efficiency. But capital as a factor of production, rather than as an amount of finance or the revenue of capitalists, has no natural unit that can be aggregated to give a quantity of a productive service which can be used to determine its price. If capital is taken in terms of money, or cost or discounted expected future yields, in order to provide a quantity of capital it must first be priced to yield its quantity. This value quantity of capital as a productive service cannot then be used to determine its price or distribution of income. The 'price' of the aggregate 'factor' capital will then be affected by the distribution of income amongst the factors. What appears to be a simple 'adding-up' problem or index number problem (as it seems it appeared to Malthus viewing Ricardo's struggles) in the aggregation of specific factor inputs is something more. The summation of the individual prices of factors to yield aggregate 'factor' quantities will no longer yield a unique measure of the factors nor of the total output produced. Except, of course, in the special case where the capital–labour ratio is the same for all output produced in the system.[5] The crucial distinction between the neoclassical problem of the value of capital and Ricardo's concern with the unique measurement of social output is that for the neoclassicist capital is taken as a naturally occurring factor of production which must have an identifiable quantity to produce a market price. For Ricardo capital as a means of production was a commodity like all others, produced and reproducible over time by labour and thus part of the national output which varied with the distribution of that output.

Even recognising this inconsistency in the neoclassical approach to 'factor' prices, the analysis is static, it works with given factor supplies – a situation unlikely to be conducive to the study of a dynamic system and markedly different from the type of economic analysis envisaged by Ricardo and Marx.

We thus seem to be back where Ricardo started. On the presumption that the remaining pieces of the story of the determination of the supply of labour and capital in the neoclassical approach are well known we shall not repeat them here. What is necessary for our purposes is to recognise the difference in the two approaches and to see that the neoclassical cannot avoid, even when it changes the major emphasis, the problems associated with measurement and perpetual equilibrium when it ventures near realistic problems of evolution and growth. The basic bulwark of the theory, if we can single one out, is the assumption that the price system will always produce the proper set of prices that assures equilibrium, at a point in time and over time.

In sum, the basic differences stem from value theory. For the Classicists value was something related to the physical concept of costs, related to the application of real resources (primarily labour) to the growth of output. Resources were important, not because they were scarce, but because combining natural resources (or the 'free gifts of nature') and labour was the only way to produce a surplus.

For the neoclassicists on the other hand, value is in the mind of the consumer, there can be no divergence between value and price and thus the direct analysis of the surplus (in the Classical sense) is impossible. The static analysis of the optimum distribution of factors and consumption of goods requires a hypothetical price system that

---

[5] Keynes solves these problems for the short run by employing standardised wage units. See [35, chapter 4].

can never be out of static equilibrium. (It is in this sense that the theory can be said to be normative – it is a theory of how the market should operate to produce the desired results.) The initial amounts of factors taken at a point in time (which all but determine distribution) are never explained. Resources were scarce because they were initially assumed to be given and never seemed to be able to increase the amount of output produced. The whole point of the analysis seems to be the extension of the theory of supply and demand to determine the value of not only those goods Ricardo excluded (the old masters' paintings and the like) but all output in the system. The entire scheme was inimical to the analysis of economic growth as understood by Ricardo and the Classicists.

There is one important difference that must be further stressed. The specification of the equilibrium in the neoclassical framework is broadly similar to that found in the natural sciences. The proof is carried out by showing that equilibrium exists. The economic application then goes on to show that at any point outside of the equilibrium position there are forces that exist to drive the system back to equilibrium. This says nothing about how the system gets to equilibrium in the first place, but proves that such a position exists and that any state of existence outside equilibrium is illogical (or a result of some malfunction in the system caused by outside interference). Thus the neoclassical belief that the system, left alone for a sufficient period of time, will naturally attain the position of equilibrium at full employment. But the theory allows of no analysis outside the state of equilibrium. Thus all change (and this is actually what the concept is for) is measured against the equilibrium position (Plato called it the Golden Age; Hegel, the Idea). All changes are taken in hypothetical terms or in terms of logical, potential time: *if* supply were greater than demand at a certain price such a position could not exist for the price *would* be driven down instantaneously to the equilibrium level that equates supply and demand. Equilibrium is the only logically admissible position, historical time is not allowed to exist. This is symbolised in the concept of the auctioneer, who assures the equilibrium price in pre-time, before trading is commenced. Small wonder that changes from the *status quo* are frowned on by the neoclassicists when disequilibrium does not, for them, exist. This conception of equilibrium has restricted their thinking and produced an inherent prejudice towards change and a blind faith in the ability of the market to produce full employment.

Even neoclassical dynamic analysis is essentially static, for the static equilibrium position is preserved despite differentiation of the variables with respect to time.

The Classicists, or more precisely Ricardo and Marx, had a much different method of handling the problem. Instead of measuring everything against a position of equilibrium where nothing changed (so there was no problem of measurement over time) they chose to look for something that they could use to compare with the system – for Ricardo the unique measure of value. This approach allowed all sorts of variation in the actual system and the analysis of all kinds of different conditions. The only problem was that Ricardo didn't quite get his measure worked out properly. By the time Marx (and then Sraffa) had offered usable measuring devices that were external to the internal operations of the system economists had lost interest in *social* science and had gone off to imitate the emergent natural sciences. I invite you to reflect on the different kinds of problems the Classical approach offers and which must be expressly rejected within an analysis based on the concept of equilibrium. We will return to the problem of measurement and equilibrium later: in chapter 9 on the measure of capital.

Keynes's theory was a strong reaction against the neoclassical type of logical equilibrium analysis. For Keynes everything took place at a given point in historical time, decisions made in the past determined present actual conditions, income, available capital stock, employment potential, etc.; and the future was reflected on the present by expectations, uncertainty, contracts made in terms of money. Each point in time could not be taken *de novo* to find what the equilibrium position should be if the past had only occurred in our imaginations and the future could be perfectly foreseen. Each point in time has its own particular past and its own expectations of the future. In such conditions equilibrium in the neoclassical sense has very little meaning, and Keynes spent very little time analysing it.

Keynes was, however, highly concerned over the problem of measurement in meaningful economic theory, going so far as to refect the usefulness of prices or the general level of prices which had been the main point of his *Treatise on Money*.

Unfortunately, as has been suggested above, these implicit criticisms by Keynes have been largely overlooked, most subsequent economists trying to rework Keynes's theory in terms of the old neoclassical concepts of relative price adjustments and a tendency for these adjustments to produce equilibrium price vectors with full employment of all factors. This line reaches its peak in Samuelson's 'neoclassical synthesis' and there has been no effort to deny that this has been the purpose of many economists who have taken up Keynes's approach.[6]

To finish by drawing our relations between the past and the present, the current neoclassical theory stems directly from the subjective branch of value theory and its concept of timeless equilibrium (although the use of the aggregate production function is a unique modern addition).

The Keynesian, on the other hand, is more closely linked to Ricardo and Marx of the classical tradition, of the analysis of value in physical terms, the analysis of quantities in terms of some type of measure based on labour, and of the analysis of a system undergoing change through historical time. So in an effort to keep hold of the rabbit I urge you to remember that the post-Keynesian analysis, and most especially that of Joan Robinson, is talking and reasoning in the sense of the classical approach to value and change over time. Subjective value and static equilibrium with naturally occurring full employment have no place in this line of analysis.

We now turn to the definition of some terms we will frequently use, and which may cause misunderstanding because their meanings are quite different from those they carry in neoclassical usage.

[6] See [96] latest edition. In fact, the so-called synthesis started far earlier with [21, 22], and to a certain extent still survives in radical rethinking of Keynes' work, e.g. [44]. While governments have taken the message that a return to perfect competition and the reign of flexible relative prices can do little to remedy either inflation or unemployment a large body of academic economists still promote this regime as the only hope for a sound economy. See the statements on preferred economic policy by a board of academic economists in [109], where all recommend a return to more open competition and price flexibility.

3 Definitions and Assumptions

There are several terms and techniques that will be used in the course of the book which have meanings that are slightly different from their normal usage. The main areas of possible confusion are surveyed below.

COMPARISON AND CHANGE

The essence of the study of economics and of economic growth is change over time. Two of the most difficult problems to handle in abstract theory are time and uncertainty. In a sense they are inseparable. Combined with the problem of disequilibrium they create great difficulty in trying to discern cause and effect (determination) in the growth process.

When an economy exists in historical (as opposed to imaginary or logical) time each point in time is different from every other. Each has its own past history; the results of decisions made in the face on uncertainty, some realised some not. At the same time each point has its own set of expectations about the future which will affect individual decisions and actions in the present. These actions will have both short- and long-term consequences which may diverge in disequilibrium. Thus a change in the ruling or normal conditions and the expectations attached to them in any particular economy can have any number of consequences depending on individual behavioural reactions in the face of an uncertain future. It is the recognition of this fact that is given major emphasis in the Keynesian rejection of the neoclassical belief in perpetual full-employment equilibrium.

In fact the criticism of the neoclassical theory of price in the preceding chapter implies that that theory fails to give an analysis of change over time, although some economists claim that this is what comparative statics is about. In actual fact the most that we can say is that, given a particular economy at a particular point in time and implying a given set of past decisions, past experiences, and expectations about the future, a change in the situation could bring any of a large number of possible consequences. To find out which ones are most likely requires specifying behavioural reaction functions, which are, of course, arbitrary. (For example, the rationality postulate regarding individual behaviour.)

If each given situation is unique, is it possible to say anything about causality in general? The answer is yes, but not much. The method which is employed may be called comparative dynamics. While the nomenclature is close to comparative statics the usage is different. The procedure is to set up two (or more) economic systems that are identical except for the single variable that is under consideration. It may be higher or lower in country A than in country B. We then watch the two systems evolve over time. As they grow, each with its own past development incorporating different values of the variable under discussion, we can take any common point of time in their maturity and compare the two systems at this point. Are they discernibly different in any way? If they are then we can say that the difference in the variable under investigation was in some sense responsible for the difference. This will allow us to make a statement of the general type 'If variable X had been higher (or lower) in an economy with such and such conditions, then Y would have been higher (or lower)'. It does not allow us to say that 'If X in an economy were changed to $X + \Delta X$ at time $t + 10$, then Y will be $Y + \Delta Y$ at time $t + 20$', for we have no way of knowing what other reactions might follow on a change from X to $X + \Delta X$.

Neither can we say that if X in A (X^A) were changed to the value of X in B (X^B) so that $X^A = X^B$ that Y in A (Y^A) would adjust to equal Y in B (Y^B) so that $Y^A = Y^B$, for the set of decisions made over time relating to the current values of X^A and X^B may be different such that it might be impossible for $Y^A = Y^B$ for any subsequent value of X in A.

To take a more simple example, assume two motor-cars of exactly the same type in exactly the same condition. Put Dunlop tyres on one and Michelin tyres on the other. Put them both on a straight road, start them at the same time at the same motor r.p.m. After two hours compare their positions. If they are different we can say that the difference in tyres caused car A to be ahead of car B. That is all. We can say that 'if A had used Michelin tyres it would have been in the same position as *B'*. It does not allow us to say that if car *A* had changed from Dunlop to Michelin after two hours that it would ever achieve the same position as *B*. If fact such a statement is nonsense. So is any statement that says what would happen after the tyre change. Of course motor-cars are not economies, nor are tyres economic variables, but we sometimes try to make statements about economic change as if they were.

The comparative dynamics approach does not really allow us to say very much about causality – only 'if *X* were . . . etc.'. But we do know at least that *X* and *Y* are connected, and that, other things playing their normal role, a change in *X* should bring some effect on *Y*. Comparative dynamics thus explicitly recognises that when time and uncertainty enter the picture there are other things that will change. The comparisons are taken over a length of time so as to allow these other forces to make their effects known, looking at the system after these changes have been fully digested.

The distinction drawn here is very important. You will notice that the method is very close to comparative statics, but this is so only in the strict sense of comparison, not in the sense that comparative statics is used by some neoclassical theorists, e.g., to explain how a system moves from one static position to another, and how that equilibrium is achieved. This latter is bound up in the story of the auctioneer.

Thus we will always be dealing with comparisons, except when explicitly stated otherwise. But it is easy to forget and slip into the old mode of expression, and once this happens it is just a short step into thinking we are explaining something that we aren't.

NORMAL PRICE, NORMAL VALUES

Normal values, as noted in chapter 2 above, find their beginning with the Classical economists. They are also used extensively by Marshall to try to eliminate the small random changes in the economic system that the Walrasian theory elevated to a *raison d'être*.

When an economy has settled down in a state undisturbed by chance events, wars, sharp shifts in technology and so forth, the repetition of events will tend to make them expected. The values of certain variables will become established as norms. Sets of relative prices and the price level will also be established, which will allow expectations to be satisfied and the continued growth of the system to be achieved. There is nothing unique about these magnitudes, and small deviations would not be surprising. Normal values have as much to do with expectations as with any conception of their uniqueness in achieving equilibrium.

For example, ruling rates of interest for borrowing are now in the range of 7–8 per cent. A rate of 6 per cent or 9 per cent would not cause great surprise. A rate of $2\frac{1}{2}$–3 per cent would create panic, yet within the past century rates nearly this low were considered common (or normal) and a rate of 8 per cent would have appeared just as fantastic then as 4 per cent does now.

The conception of what is 'normal' thus applies to both the objective conditions and the expectations of the magnitudes of the economic variables that those conditions engender. Thus a certain proportion of aggregate investment for each period produces a certain revenue that covers costs and produces an excess in given proportion to the amount of investment per period of time. In his *Treatise on Money* Keynes calls this the normal income of entrepreneurs, or normal profit. When normal conditions prevail the entrepreneur does not desire to change any of the contracts he has entered into (for labour, raw materials, intermediate inputs, etc.) on a binding basis. He is earning normal (expected) profit at the given rates of wages, input and commodity prices. This is just another way of saying that experience confirms expectations and that individuals are satisfied with this existing state of affairs (cf. Tranquillity below). Movements in investment come about in the *Treatise on Money* when profits depart from normal. Thus excess or 'windfall' profit encourages investment. For each level of investment there is an amount of profit that would be considered normal. From the point of view of the satisfaction of expectations one is no more optimal than another, nor, in its particular circumstances, is one any more 'normal' than another. Thus we say that the normal values of the variables are the ones that would be established in a system that has settled down into a state where all large changes have been digested and no further sharp corners have yet been encountered.

Normal price in this sense bears very little relation to the price as determined by the day-to-day movements of prices in the auction market, for normal prices and values refer to an economy in which goods are produced over time in a system that distinguishes and recognises present and future, linking the two through contracts denominated by money.

EQUILIBRIUM CONDITIONS

The conditions of equilibrium that we will be talking about are also of a different nature than the neoclassical variety. Equilibrium is usually shown to exist and in only one unique combination of variables (this is usually called 'uniqueness and existence').[1] The proof that the system can attain equilibrium is achieved by showing that forces exist to drive the system back to equilibrium if it should happen to stray a short distance away from it (this is in fact part of the uniqueness condition), i.e., there is no equilibrium state of rest possible other than the one initially posited. If the system were in any other position it would instantly find forces at work that forced it back to the initial equilibrium state.

This, of course, takes the argument from the point of assuming that the system is initially in equilibrium and then showing that it could not logically be any place else. But straying away from and moving towards an equilibrium become very different things when we allow decisions to be made in historical time and acknowledge the fact that outside logical time non-equilibrium values of variables may rule.

The notion of equilibrium that we will use involves setting up a combination of variables and seeing if they can establish some kind of a coherent pattern as they evolve over time. So pick up our motor-car example, to see if the cars can always move forward in a more or less steady fashion (if there were no petrol stations, for example, they would soon stop). So we are looking to see what

[1] Unfortunately the word equilibrium is still used for both (and other) approaches. Within the neoclassical context which refers to the state of supply and demand equality at full employment of all factors such as is produced by the Walrasian auctioneer, the problems of uniqueness and existence take full stage. That is, the neoclassical theorist is interested in finding out if one and only one equilibrium price vector exists as a possibility, taking it on faith that the system will somehow get there. (In some versions e.g. [7] only existence is claimed, so there may be more than one equilibrium position, and the problem becomes not only how the system will get to equilibrium, but how it will get to which one.)

This conception was, of course, implicitly challenged in the *General Theory* with the demonstration that there is little chance for a free-enterprise economy to reach full employment, and that far from tending to full employment equilibrium, the system was perfectly capable of bumping along from slump to slump, never settling any where.

combination of variables or what *structural relations* are necessary to keep the system moving. Joan Robinson likes to call these the 'rules of the game'. They may not always be harmonious (trade union pressure for higher wages) or optimal or moving to a constant value, but practically they may operate to keep the system from grinding to a halt.

Equilibrium conditions in this sense function in a world that is uncertain, and in which decisions, once taken, are unalterable without great cost. Recontracting is logically impossible in such a system where time moves in one direction, ever forward.

The neoclassical proof of equilibrium, as well as being modelled on the science of mechanics, rests on the assumption of perfect knowledge, i.e., that the price system signals buyers and sellers in the direction of equilibrium. This, as was pointed out above, is always assumed, never proven (except for the case of the auctioneer).

Let us take an example of a number of traders with given amounts of goods, say apples, oranges and pears. There will be some set of relative prices (physical exchange ratios) at which the market clears. But how do the traders know what it is? With no auctioneer and no normal established price they don't know where to start. But let us assume that a trade takes place. Say four apples exchange for two oranges, but that this is not the equilibrium price. It is too high from the point of view of the apple producer. The apple producer has given too many apples for the oranges that he received. He will thus have fewer apples left to exchange for pears. The price of pears will thus be lower than that required for equilibrium. On the other hand the orange producer gets the apples he wants at a lower price and thus has oranges left over. He may buy more pears because their price is lower, but that leaves the pear producer with more oranges than he wanted and fewer apples. The differences only cancel out if there is unit elasticity of substitution and demand for all traders. Otherwise once a trade at a non-equilibrium price is contracted the original set of equilibrium prices (exchange ratios) can never be reached.

The problem is that the relative prices will also determine how much each trader can buy. The apple producer does not know how much he can demand until he knows the price of apples and the prices of the other products. If the prices are known the system is in equilibrium, but no amount of groping in the market can move it towards equilibrium. Without recontracting or an auctioneer to provide this information the price system cannot produce equilibrium; the system is always there from the start, or it never gets there except by chance.

The problem becomes even more complicated if the analysis is allowed to move from day to day and if accumulated stocks come into the picture. In this case the auctioneer must indeed take on the functions of the stockjobber, actively entering the market with his own stocks and demands to make sure there are no excesses from day to day that might upset the market. This problem is, however, usually treated by taking only perishable goods, or having trading sessions only at the end of production cycles.

Taking another aspect of the problem. If one trader, say the apple producer, brings more apples to the market than on the preceding day, he has no way of knowing if he has more, the same, or less purchasing power. If the demand for apples is equal to unity, he is no better off. If it is elastic he is better off, and if inelastic worse off: the relative price falls more than quantity sold has increased (compare with the decision of a monopolist who operates on the elastic portion of his demand curve as close as possible to the point of unit elasticity). In this case more does not always mean better in terms of what his income can buy. The problem is that he must know what his income will be before he can decide how much to produce and demand. It is easy to see why the neoclassical analysis usually starts by assuming equilibrium to exist and then showing how it will be preserved, rather than showing how it is achieved.

In the following analysis, if equilibrium of any sort is assumed, it is assumed from the beginning of time. There is no question of the system tending towards it. These states of existence are not in any sense positions that cannot be left, but are those which may have incompatible forces that produce a certain stability, usually not as a result of relative price adjustments. The degree of difference may appear subtle, but it allows for a much different scope of analysis.

FULL EMPLOYMENT – TRANQUILLITY

Analysing a system growing steadily over time implies, in a sense, that it is employing all its available labour or a constant, high proportion. If it were not, the reserve army of the unemployed would be growing and it would require a complicated system of income transfers to keep it from becoming explosive (at least politically). Keynes taught us that there is no reason to expect the free-enterprise system that we are discussing to produce full-employment equilibrium in the short run. There is thus no reason why we should expect this result in the long run (*per contra* the neoclassical models yield full employment as a necessary result of equilibrium in both the long and short run).

This creates a problem, for we want to concentrate on long-run equilibrium positions and comparisons. If the system is always falling into a slump normal prices and values will never be established and comparisons cannot easily be made. One way to solve this problem is simply to say that if equilibrium exists at all, then full employment must prevail. One implies the other. This is roughly Kaldor's method and is tantamount to assuming full employment and being done with it.[2] In actual fact Kaldor provides a logical proof of his assumption (cf. [28, 30]), but this hardly makes the problem any easier to handle. The problem, to a certain extent, boils down to how one can have a post-Keynesian analysis and at the same time work in a system with more or less full employment. The neoclassical economists instantly enter and wonder what all the fuss is about, for don't they after all have a theory that works on the same assumptions?

Joan Robinson approaches the dilemma differently. She employs what she calls the tranquillity assumption, attributed to Kalecki [80]. This involves giving each entrepreneur autonomy in making decisions in an uncertain world, but the decisions are set up such that they are mutually compatible, i.e., the entrepreneurs' expectations are usually justified. This satisfaction leads them to continue making decisions more or less along the same lines, so that in conditions of tranquillity expectations are never upset to such an extent that the system falls into a slump. This, as Joan Robinson points out, allows free will to prevail with a high level of employment without assuming it to be predestined, and does not require full employment. In other words, the system could at any time plunge into a slump, but there are no major disturbances that might panic entrepreneurs so as to discourage them from carrying out the amount of investment required to produce stable growth (cf. Harrod's concept of the warranted rate of growth). Thus stable growth can be analysed at less than full employment. This way out of the problem is slightly

[2] For a slightly more pessimistic assessment see [15].

more pleasing than Kaldor's as it does not require full employment for the analysis of growth, although there is not much to choose between the two. There seems to be little harm in accepting either solution as long as one remains aware that there is nothing in either approach that says stable growth or full employment *must* occur as a natural result, and that in fact in most circumstances it will not. But if the major tendencies, the 'rules of the game', are to be derived, some concessions have to be made. This is one of them.

Growth that produces full employment in tranquil conditions is called a 'golden age' in Joan Robinson's analysis. It is a golden age more in the sense of Plato than anything else, that is, a position that the actual world will never achieve, and will never be naturally or constantly tending toward. It is set up to see what conditions would be required for it to exist, and thus why the actual world does not exist in such conditions. It is not set up to show why the system will always be tending toward it. Joan Robinson very pointedly calls it a Myth. In fact there may not be anything particularly desireable about it, although Plato was obviously convinced to the contrary.

COMPETITION – IMPERFECT COMPETITION

Competition is not taken in the sense of the normal theory of pure or perfect competition. Competition simply implies sufficient labour mobility for wages to be uniform over all occupations (or types of occupations, allowing differences among them), and for the return to capital to be uniform. In this sense profit rates provide a guide to capitalists as to profitable investment opportunities. This does not deny the existence of imperfect competition in the sense of decreasing costs or product differentiation within an industry. Neither does it deny the existence of monopoly (although monopolists need not earn a higher rate of profit than other firms as is often, wrongly, assumed). The main contention is that over time capital will move to those occupations that provide a higher rate of profit. The degree of monopoly, in the sense of Kalecki, can easily be introduced into the analysis on the aggregate level (91). In actual fact, the types of market conditions faced by individual firms and industries (as found in the neoclassical microeconomic theory in terms of oligopoly, bilateral monopoly, pure monopoly, etc.) do not play a significant part in the analysis of prices, more emphasis being given to general market conditions (e.g. buyers' and sellers' markets) and the movements of other aggregate variables in the system. A possible method of introducing firm structure will be given in chapter 10, which deals with firm price determination.

The main burden of the assumption of generalised competition is to bolster the assumption of a uniform rate of profit on capital. This assumption was the result of the logic of capitalism for Marx, and an unchallenged fact for Ricardo. It has recently been challenged on a theoretical level by Leon [46] and introduced into the discussion of the analysis of dynamic growth processes by Pasinetti [67]. There seems to be no crucial reason for maintaining the assumption, but neither is there too much restriction if we retain it. The point that must be stressed is that although competition is assumed it is indeed of a very imperfect variety amongst firms which are not perfect competitors and do not abide by the rules of price equal to marginal costs, and thus operate with excess capacity as a normal state of affairs.

LONG-RUN – SHORT-RUN

The problems of the terms long-run and short-run are bound up with the problem of time, and therefore with uncertainty and expectations. Economic time is made up of an infinite number of short-run decisions and situations. Decisions have short-run and long-run consequences. In equilibrium (or without historical time and uncertainty) these consequences are mutually compatible.

For Marshall, the long-run was a limit to a kind of decision making, or over periods of manoeuvre. The long-run marked the limit for decisions that were not solely influenced by the fluctuations of market sales and prices. The neoclassicists, however, have turned the 'long run' into an actual state of existence where one can exist as a god-like omniscient being. It is the place where there are no wrong decisions, no mistakes (they can always and instantaneously be made good), no uncertainty and no disappointed expectations. History does not exist and time moves in two directions, not in a one-way continuous process where the past can never be re-lived. It is what the world would be like if the price system operated in the way it is presumed to (complete with infinite horizon futures markets), by Walras and his followers. But this is just another dodge around the real problems of time and uncertainty.

In the theory that we will present the long run is not a place where one can exist or actions can take place. If anything it is a representation of the fact that, 'Best of all that we should know the future', but we don't. So the term long-run is always a descriptive term, it describes a type of action or a type of decision. All action takes place now – in the short run. As Joan Robinson says, today is a break between an unchangeable past and an unknowable future. This is the only place where decisions can be made and executed. It is, however, the very nature of a production economy that these actions will have consequences well outside the immediate and, thus known, present short run.

DETERMINATION

This is probably the point that causes the most confusion between the post-Keynesians and the general equilibrium theorists. Joan Robinson originally set out to look at the effects of distribution on accumulation and found that there was no existing theory to explain the profit rate. She thus set about to find out what 'determines' the rate of profit, that is, why the rate of profit is 15 per cent rather than say, 7 per cent. This was necessary in trying to find out what factors determined the long-run rate of accumulation of capital. At the same time she set about attacking the existing explanation because, in her view, the theory of marginal productivity did not provide an *explanation* of what *determines* the real wage and the profit rate. The marginal productivity theory was at best a statement of an equilibrium relationship, a requirement that a general equilibrium solution, properly defined, would satisfy.

The more knowledgeable Walrasians, of course, should never have claimed more than this. When driven back from the facility of the aggregate production function and its marginal product implications into the fully specified Walrasian (or Dorfman–Samuelson–Solow type programming[3]) model, they could logically claim that they couldn't understand what the 'determination' argument was all about. As long as there were enough equations to cover the unknowns in the system, the question of determination was nonsense to them. In a true general equilibrium model nothing is 'determined', everything is solved simultaneously. To say that one equation or variable is more important than another has no meaning. If one

[3] This is what is often called the neoclassical model in its fullest generality, see [97, 8], as well as [1, 7].

equation drops out there is no solution, but this is true of every equation. Likewise changes in any one variable affect all the others in the system. In such a system it is very difficult to talk about direct causality, for everything determines everything else, determination cannot be discussed outside the scope of the entire system. Thus a somewhat justified bewilderment was the response to Joan Robinson's question of the determination of the rate of profit.

When pressed on the point of what 'determines' the rate of profit in the general equilibrium model Solow responds with the equation for social time preference, unable to see that this fails to answer the question in the spirit in which it is posed. Rabbits and elephants cannot exist simultaneously. In the Keynesian theory where saving and investment are independent acts carried out by different people for different reasons we find a useful starting point for answering the question. On the other hand, the general equilibrium theorist will say that in full-employment equilibrium $S = I$ so that savings are always invested and thus what people want to save (time preference) will be offset by net investment which implies some rate of growth of output. Nothing 'determines' anything else in this scheme, but what results is what is consistent with the given initial conditions of the system. If any one of them had been different the equilibrium solution of the system would have been different. Picking any one of them can be nothing more than arbitrary.

This is a very marked case of rabbits and elephants. In the post-Keynesian approach we are trying to find out both what conditions are required to produce an equilibrium rate of accumulation and why that rate is what it is and not some other rate. The answer cannot be that no other rate would solve the set of equations for the static equilibrium of the system.

THE RATE OF PROFIT

The determination of the economy-wide rate of profit in an economy growing over time is a basic part of the post-Keynesian theory. The rate of profit is a pure number representing the rate at which the employment of the capital stock produces profits over costs, both taken net. With profits in money terms capital employed must also be taken in money, i.e., value terms. In tranquil conditions the forward-looking expected rate of profit on capital and the profit actually earned in respect to the value of capital actually employed come to the same thing. When expectations are disappointed conditions are not as they were supposed to be, the rate of profit in the *ex-post* sense cannot be calculated, for the value of the capital stock is different than it would have been had expectations been confirmed. Similarly the expected ratio of profit to the costs of capital currently being introduced has no relation to the profit earned on existing investments.

This has lead some economists to reject the usefulness of the concept because conditions are never tranquil such that a rate of profit can be meaningfully defined. However, the use of the rate of profit in economics has a long history. The post-Keynesian approach first allows us to specify under what conditions we can talk about the concept. That these conditions are not very general should not mean that we should be uninterested in what they actually are. Secondly the expected rate of profit on new investment will always exist as a factor in the investment decisions of the economy. Thus the explicit determination of the conditions under which we can talk about a rate of profit in both senses give us a guide to the broad, overall movements of the system. The rate of profit in its short-period, expectational sense continues to have usefulness. What we do find, however, is that the rate of profit as the price of capital used by the neoclassical theory has a very limited use, if any at all.

SUPPLY AND DEMAND

In the historical review of the preceding chapter it was suggested that the classical economists were more interested in the supply side of the economy while the early neoclassicists elevated demand to the prime position. This is something of an overstatement, made to emphasise underlying differences in approach, and we might do well to recall Marshall's reasoned position as exemplified in his analogy of the two blades of the scissors.

At the same time it has been suggested that the neoclassical theory of relative price adjustment based on supply and demand could not produce equilibrium, at least in the sense of the full employment of all factors. If supply and demand does not produce equilibrium then can we say that supply and demand determines prices? In what follows we will occasionally speak of supply and demand determining a pattern of prices for goods sold, but in the sense of an equilibrium condition or a confirming relationship. In the first sense we do not enquire into how prices are actually determined, but assume that they are such that supply and demand are equilibrated at those prices. By this we mean that there are certain underlying forces that produce a flow of goods and a flow of income that results in market clearing at a certain set of prices, that is that supply and demand confirm the consistency of these underlying forces. In chapter 10 we will introduce a method of price determination that is not determined by supply and demand, but by oligopolistic firms' behaviour functions. Thus we would still be able to talk of supply and demand as the manifestations of these decisions without actually making the assumption that prices are 'determined in the market by supply and demand'; but supply and demand in the sense of the overall quantity of goods available exchanging for the income available to purchase them continues to be a confirming relationship.

Thus in the earlier sections when the structural relations of the system are being derived we talk of prices that must rule if aggregate supply of consumption goods is to equal the quantity of income spent on them. This is not to imply that we are letting the neoclassical price mechanism in through the back door, so to speak, with prices determined in the market or by some invisible auctioneer. Prices are never determined in this way. This is, of course, to demote relative prices to a relatively minor role, consistent with Keynes's view of their importance. It would be possible to allow simple supply and demand to determine relative prices, but there are strong indications that even relative prices can be explained otherwise,[4] and thus the break with the neoclassical approach on the functioning of supply and demand is complete. Thus the difference in the utilisation of the term should be kept in mind, and will be pointed out in the text where there are possibilities of confusion.

SOCIAL RELATIONS

The neoclassical theory is often presented as a theory that is perfectly general in dealing with the 'economic problem of scarcity' and thus valid for all kinds of economies and social organisations. Taken on an individual basis with given factor endowments the

---

[4] Cf. below, chapter 10, Leon [46, pp. 125–31] suggests that it may even be within the power of the capitalists to control the income elasticities of the commodity bundle they choose to produce.

problem of distribution is sometimes described as a process of free bargaining. Each factor has something that the other has not and thus has an interest to bargain for it. Thus capitalists with capital and organisational know-how, workers with labour, and landlords with land, all engage in free market bargaining to determine the prices and returns to the factor services that each owns. All are presumed to be on a equal footing.

This is not the case in the post-Keynesian theory. Social relations are important and explicitly taken into account. Workers are not in the same position as the capitalists, for if workers cannot find employment they must cease eating, whereas the capitalist has, at the very least, a wealth position that insures that he need never face this possibility. The social relations are much as Marx saw them, in terms of the class struggle between free labour and capital; that is, capitalism as primarily a social relation rather than merely an economic one.

Thus the distribution of income is not determined by freely conducted bargaining between equal partners, who must submit to the law of scarcity in the determination of their factor rewards. Harmony is not the underlying force for stability in the system, which is instead based on conflict between the interests of different classes. Unfortunately these implicit power relations have not always been emphasised in the working out of the logic of the Keynesian mechanism. They are, however, a basic framework for the analysis that follows and we do well to keep them in mind.

SOCIAL CLASSES AND FUNCTIONAL INCOME CLASSES

While the analysis takes explicit account of social relations and social classes, it also distinguishes between purely economic classifications and social classifications. It is standard in economic analysis to distinguish between types of income by function, that is to distinguish between income that is earned through the sale of labour power, and income that is derived from ownership in the means of production which combines with labour to produce final output. In this sense we can distinguish between wage and salary incomes (or simply wages) and profits incomes.

At the same time social relations distinguish between two types of social classes, workers and capitalists (or, in primarily agrarian times, a third – the landlords, more recently replaced by rentiers).

Only under certain specific conditions can we identify strictly the social classes with the functional income classes, and by speaking about one imply the same thing for the other. In all other cases social classes must be sharply distinguished from the economic categories of functional income.

Much confusion has been caused in recent economic analysis from a failure to adequately mark this distinction. In the following analysis we will hold closely to the distinction, most of the analysis, for example of the determination of the rate of profit, being concerned with functional income categories. Only when social and economic classes coincide, for example under the assumption that all labour income is spent, will the two be used simultaneously. The possible problems will become apparent as the book proceeds, and will be discussed at more length in chapter 11.

With all these differences in definitions and terminology in mind we can now approach the building blocks of the post-Keynesian reconstruction of political economy.

Part Two

4 The Basic Model – the Consumption Sector

The logic and operation of the post-Keynesian model is actually quite simple. It only appears difficult because we may not be accustomed to its method of analysis. The general approach presented here is founded in Joan Robinson's 'generalisation of the General Theory', especially [85].

It was a basic tenet of Keynes's theory that the wage bargain was made in money terms. In a system in which wages were paid in terms of money labour could not bargain for the real wage. The real wage was not determined in any particular market, but as a result of the aggregate relations of the system. The real consumption value of the money wage was determined by the prices that labour had to pay for wage goods. The present chapter concentrates on the consumption sector and the prices of consumption goods in order to determine the relations that affect the real wage, taking the relations with the investment sector, for the moment, as given. In the next chapter we take up the relations between the two sectors, and the determination of aggregate distribution, the rate of accumulation of capital, and the rate of profit on capital.

CLASSIFICATION AND THE GENERATION OF INCOME AND OUTPUT

First of all we take as given the physical resources available. These include the potential labour force, natural resources, and the state of technical knowledge. The money wage of labour is determined by the wage bargain, and taken as given. Later we will introduce forces that may cause it to change, but for the moment it is given in money terms. Next we apply a method of classification to the uses to which resources are put in production of output.

In the *Treatise on Money* Keynes used a broad division between *available* and *non-available* goods. Available goods are those that can be potentially consumed by the population; they are available to be purchased for consumption. When only labour consumes output they correspond to wage goods.

Non-available goods cover most everything else: capital equipment, liquid capital, work-in-progress, research and development, etc. We can then divide the economy into sectors associated with the two types of output. The consumption goods sector is concerned with the production of available output (wage goods) and the capital (or investment) goods sector carries on the production of non-available output.

This of course does not imply that the economy is in reality divided into these two sectors. Firms producing consumption goods will have work-in-progress, etc., which at any point in time is part of non-available output (in this case soon to become available). We are thus dividing the economy in terms of resource utilisation rather than actual point of production. We can, however, think of the two sectors as if they were definable units, each employing labour and means of production to produce its specific type of output.

At any point in time the employed labour force will be divided between the two sectors of production. Given the production technique in use this division of labour will determine the total amount of output that can be produced each period as well as the relative amounts of available and non-available goods. The supply of labour is taken to be appropriate to the amount of employment offered by the two sectors.

We start by assuming that only labourers demand consumption goods and that they spend all of their money wages for consumption goods. This implies that the marginal and average propensity to save out of wages is zero. Assuming that the money-wage rate paid to labour is the same irrespective of the sector in which it is employed, the total demand in terms of money for consumption goods by labourers in both sectors is equal to the economy's total wage bill. If w is the money-wage rate, N_i the number of labourers in the investment sector, and N_c the number of labourers in the consumption sector, then aggregate money demand for consumption goods is

$$D = wN_c + wN_i \qquad (4.1)$$

This is the sum of aggregate money demand that will come forward to purchase the consumption goods per period and thus represents the gross sales value of production in the consumption sector. Let us symbolise the output of consumption goods by Q. This symbol can be taken to represent a vector of all the different consumption goods in the system. It may be conceptually easier, however, to think of it as a bundle of consumption goods with fixed proportions of particular goods, produced under constant returns, which is purchased all at once at a single price. We can then simply look for a single price for the composite bundle of consumption goods, rather than a vector of prices to match the vector of particular consumption goods. On the simplifying assumption of a consumption bundle, its price becomes something like a general price level (or index) for consumption goods.

If all labour incomes are used to purchase the existing consumption goods then there will exist a price, p, which equates total sales proceeds with total wage incomes and allocates the consumption goods produced amongst the labour force

$$pQ = D = wN_c + wN_i \qquad (4.2)$$

Assuming vertical integration of all firms in our economy (thus cancelling out all intermediate input costs), the prime costs of producing consumption output Q will be the wages cost of producing the consumption output or wN_c.[1] Total receipts gained from selling output Q at price p are equal to pQ. Net revenue on consumption sector sales is then equal to gross sales minus prime costs or

$$R_c = pQ - wN_c \qquad (4.3)$$

Since $pQ = wN_c + wN_i$, net revenue is also equal to

$$R_c = wN_c + wN_i - wN_c = wN_i \qquad (4.4)$$

The net profit earned on the sales of consumption goods is just equal to the wages paid to the investment sector workers or the wage bill in the investment sector. The real wage of labour (no matter the sector in which it is employed) is then determined by the relation between the money wage, w, and the price of consumption goods, p.

Let us look more closely at this relation by making some mental comparisons. Assume that total employment had been higher, again

[1] Vertical integration simply implies that each firm produces all its required intermediate inputs and thus takes care of problems similar to those of double counting in national income calculations. It also makes things somewhat easier in terms of price determination, for difference in the determinations of prices at intermediate levels are standardised when they are all calculated in a single production unit. Keynes solved the problem by standardising on the wage unit which allowed the calculation of an economy-wide aggregate supply curve, see the *General Theory*, chapter 4.

with the supply of labour adequate to employment offered. Let us also assume that the increase in employment is proportionally higher in the investment sector than in the consumption sector so that the ratio N_i/N_c is higher under the new conditions. The capital stock is appropriate in each sector to provide the new amounts of employment, but output per man is unchanged. The output of the consumption sector, Q, is now higher, but total employment, and thus aggregate money demand for the output of the consumption sector, has risen in a greater proportion than the output of consumption goods is higher. The price of consumption goods that will satisfy relation (4.2) will now be higher. With a given money-wage rate and a higher price of consumption, the real consumption value of the money wage is lower.

The consumption goods producers now have greater production costs (their wage bill is higher due to the higher employment) but their gross receipts have increased by a greater proportion than total costs. Their net revenue is thus higher in the same proportion that N_i/N_c is higher than it was in the original situation. Their total profits are higher, but still equal to the wage bill in the investment sector (as in (4.4)). When wages incomes are fully spent, under these assumptions, profit in the consumption sector is equal to the wage bill in the investment sector. The real wage of labour is inversely associated to the ratio (N_i/N_c) or more simply the ratio of investment to consumption output (or the ratio of investment in total output which comes to the same thing). Thus a higher ratio of investment to consumption sector employment or a higher ratio of investment to consumption is associated with a lower real wage for labour, a higher price level for consumption goods and higher total profits on the sale of consumption goods.

Looking at it in another way, a price must be established so as to share the consumption goods between those who produce consumption goods and consume them and those who earn incomes that are spent on consumption goods but produce non-available or investment goods. To effectuate this 'sharing' process prices must be higher than costs. If there had been no investment, and thus no employment in the investment sector, relation (4.2) would have been $pQ = D = wN_c$. There are only consumption sector workers to produce and buy consumption goods. In such a case receipts minus costs (relation 4.4) are $pQ - wN_c = 0$, sales proceeds just equal prime costs and profits are zero. The workers would be able to buy everything they produce with their wages – they do not have to share the consumption output with anyone else.

In this case (admittedly unrealistic to make a simple point) the real wage of labour (the amount of physical goods that can be bought with the money wage) is just equal to the output of consumption goods per man. When some workers are employed to produce non-available goods the real consumption and thus real wage is lower (some of the consumption goods are now purchased by investment sector workers) even though the real product per man employed is the same. Thus the relation between the proportion of labour employed in the sectors and the real wage of labour and profit in the consumption sector.

CONSUMPTION BY CAPITALISTS

So far we have ignored the capitalists by implicitly assuming that the propensity to save out of profits is unity. Now let us assume that the capitalists spend some of their profits and use the rest to purchase capital goods. Spending out of profits (by both consumption and investment sector capitalists) will add an additional item to the demand for consumption goods at any given ratio of investment to consumption. To take account of the expenditure out of profits for consumption ($s_p < 1$) we can write c (where $c = 1 - s_p$) as the propensity to consume out of profits, P (since we will not be able to define total profits in the system until the next chapter, we take them as given, cP representing expenditure out of profits by capitalists in both sectors). The relation of the sales value of consumption goods to total expenditure (4.2 above) now becomes

$$pQ = D = wN_c + wN_i + cP \qquad (4.5)$$

Now the price level, p, that exhausts total demand for consumption goods output must be higher than in (4.2) for the goods must be rationed amongst more demanders. At the same time as spending from profits is related to higher prices it also affects the excess of receipts over costs so that $R_c = pQ - wN_c$ is now also higher. Relation (4.4) now becomes

$$R_c = wN_c + wN_i + cP - wN_c = wN_i + cP \qquad (4.6)$$

Expenditure by profit earners out of profits increases pQ by cP which causes R_c to be higher by cP. In the aggregate exactly the amount that is spent from profits comes back as profits. Keynes called this the 'widow's cruse' [33, p. 139]. Kalecki put it this way: 'the workers spend what they get, the capitalists get what they spend'. (In the next chapter we see how profits are shared among the capitalists in both sectors.)

Thus consumption out of profits will be associated with higher prices for consumption goods and thus a lower real wage and real consumption for labour. We thus have two forces that act on the real wage of labour, the ratio of investment to consumption (or N_i/N_c as we have symbolised it) and the propensity to consume out of profits. The higher is the share of investment in national income, the lower is the real consumption value of the money wage. The higher is the consumption out of profits for any given value of N_i/N_c, the lower is the real consumption value of the money wage.

SAVING OUT OF WAGES

Now there is no need to assume, as we have done so far, that there is no saving out of wage incomes (although this is not as unrealistic as it may seem when contractual saving is left out of account). We merely have to correct relation (4.5), reducing wage expenditure by the amount of savings out of wages. The relation now becomes

$$pQ = D = b(wN_c + wN_i) + cP \qquad (4.7)$$

where b ($b = 1 - s_w$) is the propensity to consume from wage incomes and $b > c$.

If we look at the effects of the savings by workers we have to keep in our minds the paradox of thrift. When workers save aggregate expenditure is lower for a given level of employment, and the margin of receipts over costs is lower. In such a case we have to strain our imaginations to believe that the capitalists will continue to carry out the assumed level of investment and employment, for profits on a given level of employment will be lower. There is no easy way to tell what level of profits the capitalists will look upon as necessary – in any actual case it depends on how the economy has developed over time. As a logical point workers cannot save so much that profits fall to zero. This would be the case if savings from wages exceeded the wage bill in the investment sector plus consumption out of profits. This would mean that $D - wN_c \leqslant 0$ and the firms' receipts would fail to cover costs of production. The point at issue is how low capitalists will allow profits to fall before cutting back on investment in new equipment. There is no reason why the system must have a minimum amount or rate of profits, it depends more on what the capitalists are used to (recall the discussion of normal values), while a sharp change in workers savings at a point in time producing a sharp swing in profitability will produce disastrous effects whether the original rate was high or low. At the same time, as we have seen, these effects on profits can be offset to a greater or lesser extent by differences in capitalists' investment or consumption. In fact, it will be argued below (chapters 5, 11, and 14) that under certain conditions concerning long-run, full-employment growth the existence of saving out of wages has no effect on the rate of profit or the distribution of income between wages and profits, but that it does effect the amount of profits earned by the capitalists and the distribution of income between workers and capitalists.

The counterpart to the minimum profitability that the capitalists consider acceptable is the minimum real wage that labour considers to be acceptable. When higher proportions of investment to output eat into the level of consumption that workers consider to be a minimum subsistence consumption we cannot assume that labour stands idly by without attempting to remedy the situation. Since there is no direct means by which labour can affect the real wage their only effective means of action is stoppage of work and demands for higher money-wages. Thus our assumption of a given money-wage is only viable if the overall conditions of the system produce a real wage that labour considers acceptable. If not the result is either cessation of production or rising money wages (or both), followed by rising prices and a spiraling inflation. Such a situation may produce a slump just as easily as anything else that disturbs the confidence and tranquillity of the capitalists. As long as the system remains viable, the success (in terms of increasing real consumption) of labour's bid for higher wages depends on the ability of labour to change the proportions of output committed to investment and consumption goods (or reduce capitalists' consumption). In modern capitalism the balance is weighted against them, as claims for higher wages usually result in unemployment, lower output, rising prices, and low or zero growth rates rather than an increase in the real wage or labour's share in national output (we return to this process in chapter 10). The limit on the combination of the ratio of investment to consumption and the consumption of the capitalists which effect the real wage is thus a real one, which Joan Robinson calls the 'inflation barrier'.

We have thus considered two possible limits on the values of the variables considered for consumption sector prices and production in relation to the system as a whole. The limit on profitability is primarily a psychological one to the extent that it effects 'animal spirits' and the desire to invest, while the limit on real wages has a psychological aspect as well as a real, biological lower limit.

PRICES AND OUTPUT

In the relations that we have drawn above between expenditure and output for the consumption sector we have assumed that, somehow or other, the prices of consumption goods were established such that all goods were sold at prices that exhausted aggregate expenditure on them. These are not 'market-clearing' prices in the sense of Marshall's market period (Saturday night fish market) nor prices 'determined' by the forces of supply and demand, but prices compatible with the underlying forces that produced the supply of goods and the income to buy them. They confirm the underlying forces in the sense that they allocate consumption to the labourers in the same proportions that labour produces available and non-available goods.

For manufacturing industry, where stocks can be run down or built up to meet changes in demand at given prices, or the level of capacity utilisation can be increased or decreased to meet changes in sales at given prices, market-clearing prices or supply and demand determined prices have little meaning. It seems more reasonable to assume, in a world of less than perfect competition, that manufacturing firms set prices by adding a margin to prime costs, allowing capacity utilisation to adjust to the level of sales that is produced at these prices. On this view it is the level of capacity utilisation that adjusts to changes in demand, not market-clearing prices in the short run and the amount of plant, always working at full capacity, in the long run, as in the neoclassical theory of perfect competition.

The relations that we worked out above showed us that when investment is going on or there is consumption out of profits, prices will exceed prime costs of production for goods sold. This gives us an easy way to introduce Kalecki's theory of the 'degree of monopoly' to determine prices in the consumption sector and the consumption value of money wages spent on them at these prices. Thus we could say, for example, that if the ensemble of consumption-goods producers, at a given level of capacity utilisation, produced an output of Q, with N_c labourers, and marked up their prime costs by the proportion R_c/wN_c they would sell this output produced at desired capacity utilisation only if N_i labourers were employed at money wage w in the production of investment goods. The price produced by this mark-up of prices over costs would then be the same as the price p that appears, for example, in relation (4.2). Putting it another way, we could say that this mark-up added to prime costs by the consumption producers was compatible with the existing ratio of N_i/N_c at the ruling utilisation of capacity output (and the employment that this implies) in the consumption sector. We would then have a relation that runs directly from the degree of monopoly to prices, real wages, capacity utilisation and employment.

If, for example, the consumption-goods producers had chosen a higher mark-up, the price charged for consumption goods would have been higher than the price p in relation (4.2). The amount of goods that they would then have sold, given aggregate money demand from relation (4.1) would then have been less than Q, the output produced with N_c labourers. The only way they could operate without excesses of unsold goods would be to reduce output by reducing capacity utilisation and thus employment. This implies a reduction in N_c and a higher ratio of N_i/N_c.

Alternatively, output Q could have been sold at this higher mark-up and original utilisation of capacity and employment if additional workers had been employed in the investment sector (i.e., if N_i had been higher in relation to (4.1)). This, of course, also implies a higher ratio of N_i/N_c, but now by increasing N_i rather than reducing N_c. This resembles our mental experiment with a higher ratio of N_i/N_c (see above p. 56). Our general results are the same, but now we tell the story somewhat differently. Here a higher overall mark-up in the consumption goods sector is compatible with a given utilisation of capacity only if the ratio of employment in the investment sector to employment in the consumption sector is higher. The higher mark-up then corresponds to higher prices and lower real wages just as in our earlier example.

It may be helpful to set out some simple numerical examples in order to trace out the relations that have been developed between mark-ups, prices, investment and the real wage. We take the money-wage as one unit and a relation of production where one unit of labour produces one unit of output. Prices and costs are also measured in our 'unit' of money, and the real wage is thus the money-wage in units divided by the price level in units.

We represent the degree of monopoly or the ruling mark-up in each example as the numerical value of price per unit over prime costs per unit of output or aggregate receipts as a proportion of total prime costs. Thus a situation where price is just equal to prime costs (and costs are not marked up at all) is represented as a mark-up index of 1. Then, as in example I, where receipts are just equal to

EXAMPLE I

	Consumption sector	Investment sector
Labour (N)	100	0
Wage bill (wN)	100	
Output	100	
Prime cost	100	
Sales value	100	
Profit	0	
Mark-up $=1$	price $=1$	
Real wage $=1/1=1$	$R_c = 100 - 100 = 0$	

prime costs $100/100 = 1$. A mark-up of 100 per cent (unit cost of 1, price of 2) then has an index value of $2/1 = 2$. We indicate the index value of the mark-up in this way because, under our assumptions of the money-wage being equal to one 'money' unit and one unit of labour working with one machine unit producing one unit of output, prices will correspond directly to the mark-up which allows us to see directly the effect of a higher mark-up on the price and thus on the real wage. It should, perhaps, be stressed that it is not the absolute values, but the proportions that they represent that are important in the examples.

We can think of the examples below as representing distinctly different economic systems, each with its own past and its own expectations about the future, existing in tranquil conditions. The capital stock in each is then appropriate to the employment conditions assumed to rule in each. The technique of production used is the same in all of them. The supply of labour is appropriate to employment offered, but need not imply full employment. Firms are operating plant at desired capacity utilisation, with more or less constant costs per unit produced.

We then enquire as to the differences in mark-up and real wage that would be compatible with differences in investment, thriftiness, etc. Again we stress that the absolute values shown are only indicative, and that it is the proportions that are important. The absolute values used are thus arbitrary.

Example I is our extremely unrealistic case, with no employment in the investment sector. Here, as we might expect, there is no profit earned on the production of consumption goods. The wages paid, when fully spent, are just sufficient to cover the prime costs of production with no mark-up of prices over prime costs. The real value of the wage (the wage unit divided by p) is equal to one indicating that real consumption purchased with the money-wage unit is in the aggregate equal to the real output of labour.

This example does, however, allow us to see clearly the effect of the mark-up and the degree of monopoly on the real wage. If, for example, the degree of monopoly had produced a mark-up over prime costs of 2 the price charged for consumption goods would have been 2. In this case only 50 units of consumption goods would have been sold for 100 units of money receipts. The money receipts of the capitalists are unchanged, but the real wage of labour is lower by one-half at $\frac{1}{2}$ instead of 1. We thus see that the degree of monopoly directly effects the real wage, but does not effect capitalists' receipts. By the same token, if the capitalists had been earning profits, a higher degree of monopoly would effect the real wage, but not profits earned, so that with a given capital stock a higher degree of monopoly producing a higher mark-up reduces the real wage but does not change the profit on capital. We will return to this relation below.

Now let us assume that there is employment in the investment sector, and that the employed labour force is divided equally between the two sectors. In this case the 50 units of labour in the consumption sector produce 50 units of output for a wage bill of 50 units. The higher mark-up of price over prime costs is now compatible with the production of 50 units of investment goods by 50 labourers, so that in this case the higher mark-up is compatible with higher investment as well as a lower real wage. The 50 units of profit produced by the given mark-up can now buy 25 units of investment goods from the capital sector, capital goods also selling at the same mark-up. The overall saving–investment equality is maintained, for with no savings out of wages and no consumption out of profits, all profits are saved and the total profit in both sectors equals the value of investment goods produced.

In our analysis of the equational relationships above we said that a higher mark-up would be compatible with either (or both) a higher proportion of N_i/N_c or a higher consumption out of profits, in example III we look at a higher proportion of investment to consumption and then in example IV consumption out of profits.

In example III the capitalists in the consumption sector set a higher mark-up of prices over costs than in example II. To sell the

EXAMPLE II

	Consumption sector		Investment sector
Labour	50		50
Wage bill	50		50
Output	50		50
Prime cost	50		50
Sales value	100		100
Profit	50		50

Mark-up $=2$ price $=2$
Real wage $=\frac{1}{2}$ $R_c=100-50=50$
Consumption sector buys 25 units from Investment sector for 50 money units.
Investment sector exchanges internally 25 units valued at 50 money units.
Value of investment (100) = Savings (profit) $50+50$.

output they desire at their desired capacity utilisation the proportion of investment to consumption must be higher (this corresponds to our mental comparison, see above p. 61). Here, with a higher ratio of N_i/N_c that allows sales of 65 units at the higher mark-up the real wage is lower than in example II, falling from $\frac{1}{2}$ to approximately $\frac{1}{2.15}$. We thus see the relation between a higher degree of monopoly and ratio of investment to consumption and a lower real wage for labour.

We also see that if the degree of monopoly had been still higher, say three, actual sales of consumption goods would have been only $46\frac{2}{3}$ leaving unsold stocks at the degree of capacity utilisation and employment that produced 65 units. Sales receipts would, however, be unchanged although the real wage would have been lower at $\frac{1}{3}$. Thus for a given capital stock the ratio of profits to capital is un-

EXAMPLE III

	Consumption sector	Investment sector
Labour	65	75
Wage bill	65	75
Output	65	75
Prime cost	65	75
Sales value	140	161
Profit	75	86

Mark-up $=2\cdot15$ (approx.)   price $=2\cdot15$
Real wage $=\frac{1}{2\cdot15}$ $R_c=(65+75)-65=75$

changed with a higher degree of monopoly, but the real wage is lower. To produce the same proportion of profit to capital employed at the same employment without unsold stocks would require a technique of production that used more capital per man and unit of output. This is a question of the techniques of production in use, which we have taken to be given. The choice of technique will be taken up more fully in chapter 7. We thus stay with the simple proposition that a higher degree of monopoly, with given employment effects the real wage in a downward direction without effecting the rate of profit.

We now look at the effects of consumption out of profits. In example IV we see the other side of the two forces that effect the real wage. Here we return to the proportions of investment to output of example II, but find that a higher mark-up will be compatible

EXAMPLE IV

	Consumption sector	Investment sector
Labour	50	50
Wage bill	50	50
Output	50	50
Prime cost	50	50
Sales value	125	125
Profit	75	75
Capitalists' consumption	12·5	12·5

Mark-up $=2\cdot5$ price $=2\cdot5$
Real wage $\frac{1}{2\cdot5}$ $R_c=(100+25)-50=75$
Consumption sector buys 25 units from the investment sector for 62·5 money units. Value of investment goods exchanged internally in the Investment sector $=62\cdot5$.
Value of investment (125) = Savings = Profit (150) less consumption (25).

with not a higher ratio of N_i/N_c, but with consumption out of profits. Here also the degree of monopoly and the mark-up is higher with the real-wage lower, but now this combination is compatible with a positive consumption out of capitalists' profits. Thus examples III and IV show our two general forces working on the real wage. A higher degree of monopoly and mark-up of prices over prime costs and thus a lower consumption value for the real wage can be associated with either a higher ratio of investment to output (N_i/N_c) or a higher consumption by capitalists out of profits. Thus we see that both the proportion of investment to consumption and consumption out of profits, and the mark-up associated with them, effect the real wage, but in distinct ways. For our last example we look at savings out of wages.

In this example (example V) we assume that labourers save 0.2 of their wages. We continue to use the proportions of investment to consumption of example II. The ruling mark-up that allows all the consumption goods to be sold at the desired level of capacity is here lower than in example II. The real wage is thus higher. We must remember that if there had been consumption out of profits this would have been associated with a higher mark-up, which would have offset this higher real wage. It must also be assumed that the capitalists continue to carry on the investment to provide the employment postulated in the example. Employers in the system represented by example V are earning lower profits than those in the economy of example II. If they have the same capital stock, they are earning a lower rate of profit as well. If this effects the demand for investment goods there is no reason why the ratio of investment to consumption, nor the level of total employment, profits and mark-ups should

EXAMPLE V

	Consumption sector	Investment sector
Labour	50	50
Wage bill	50	50
Wage saving	10	10
Output	50	50
Sales value	80	80
Prime costs	50	50
Profit	30	30

Mark-up $=\frac{8}{5}$ price $=\frac{8}{5}$
Real wage $=\frac{5}{8}$ $R_c = (1 - 0.2) \, 100 - 50 = 30$
Value of investment (80) = Savings = Profits (60) + wage savings (20)

stay the same. But this brings us directly to the relations between the consumption and investment sectors. Up to now we have held the operations of the investment sector to one side to emphasise the relations between investment, capitalists' consumption, and the mark-up of prices over costs on the level of employment and the real wage. We deal directly with the investment sector in the next chapter.

We should, however, make two final points of warning. First, in actual fact, the introduction of workers' savings is not quite as simple as we have here made it out. If workers are saving and if they use these savings to finance investment then they will have income from the profits on these investments. This is true whether they actually carry out investment, lend to the capitalists, or simply put their savings in the banks. Thus labour will no longer receive only wage incomes and our simple exercises have to be redone. This problem was first discussed by Pasinetti, and will be explored further in chapters 11 and 14 below.

The second point of warning, as we shall see, is related to the first. In example V, by deflating the wage unit by the price index, we were able to say that the real wage of labour was higher when a lower mark-up was associated with savings out of wages. This should have struck some readers as paradoxical, for the amount of real consumption in examples II and V is 50 units. How can we say that the real wage has gone up when the real consumption has stayed the same? The answer to this paradox is related to the difference between the functional and social income categories that we stressed in chapter 3. We will return to the problem in chapter 10. For the moment, however, we must stress that we are looking at functional classes and wages and profits – on the provisional assumption that workers do not save.

The examples given thus far are, however, sufficient to show that, subject to the restrictions set out above, savings by workers can be allowed in the analysis without changing the basic mechanism, emphasising the relation between the degree of monopoly, the ratio of investment to consumption, and consumption out of profits to real wages and profits. Thus having looked at the effect of differences in aggregate mark-ups in the consumption sector on the real wage, we can now relate this to the production of investment goods and the price relations in that sector.

5 The Basic Model – the Capital Goods Sector

The capital goods (or investment) sector will be producing capital goods for its own use and for use in the consumption sector to produce consumption goods. The first claim on capital goods in a growing system will be for replacements in both sectors. If the system is to keep its overall productive capacity constant, it must continuously provide replacements for those capital goods that have reached the end of their useful life. This may be because of simple physical wearing out, because of obsolescence due to the recent existence of more productive machines, or the result of rising real wages in line with overall rises in productivity, as in a vintage model.[1] Depreciation and the scrapping of capital equipment cause a number of technical problems that will not concern us here.[2]

In addition to replacements, capital goods will also be demanded to increase the productive capacity of both the consumption and capital goods sectors. From the previous chapter we know that once the proportion of labour employed in each sector is known, given the technique of production in use, the quantity of each capital good produced is also known. This follows simply from the technical relations of production ruling in the system. We must thus determine the prices at which the capital goods producers will sell their capital goods output to the consumption goods producers and how they will value the capital goods that they exchange amongst themselves. Capital goods tend to be use-specific or industry-specific. They are seldom produced in quantity without a firm idea of the potential buyer and the potential selling price. This is a result both of their

[1] Such a scrapping procedure is set out in [31].

[2] For an explanation and application of the scrapping rule to non-competitive situations see Nuti [62], more general problems associated with depreciation and replacement in the post-Keynesian model are treated in [64]. The simplest method of dealing with the replacement problem would be to assume a fixed proportion of the capital stock to be replaced each period. This would not, however, be correct, for depreciation will itself be a function of the ruling rate of profit, cf. Kahn and Champernowne in the appendix to [85] and Sraffa [107, chapter 10].

high overall costs of production and their specificity. It is obvious that we have in mind here the analysis of fixed capital equipment, which is proportionately greater in money terms than the 'nuts and bolts' that are also produced in this sector. The role of 'nuts and bolts' is further diminished when we realise that much of such production is linked specifically to larger capital equipments.

To take an extreme example, it is not usual to find several firms willing to supply, on demand, a fully operational petro-chemical plant. Petro-chemical plants are not 'thrown on the market' to see what price they will fetch. We thus extend the approach of mark-up pricing of the previous chapter directly to the pricing of capital goods. While it may be true that some types of consumption goods (like primary products) are determined more by elements of supply and demand than by degree of monopoly, there are hardly any examples in the case of capital goods that would justify trying to tell a story about supply and demand effecting their prices.

Neither are there any very well developed second-hand markets for capital equipments (as distinct from financial assets that may represent the ownership of an organisation of such equipments) so that the value of existing installed equipments cannot be easily determined by their second-hand sale value, which is usually close to zero except as a tax dodge through a take-over bid, so that reservation demand will be the primary factor.[3] Thus without any well defined markets in the neoclassical sense the necessity of assuming prices fixed by a mark-up over prime costs for the sale of capital goods is confirmed.

Considering our overall capital mobility assumption from chapter 3, capital goods producers will expect to earn a rate of profit on their operations as least as high as that ruling in other industries in which they could have made investments. On the simple, two-sector approach we have presented, the capital goods producers will expect a rate of profit as least as high as that earned in the production of consumption goods.

Prices for capital goods will then be calculated such that the margin of selling prices over prime costs of production will be sufficient to cover any other costs and will yield the appropriate rate of profit on capital employed (fixed capital plus working capital

[3] In financial parlance these would be called 'thin' markets. The concept of reservation demand to indicate the prices of installed capital goods is employed in P. Davidson [5].

which includes the wage fund), i.e., similar to the rate being earned in the consumption sector. We continue to look at this margin as a mark-up in terms of a margin over total prime costs of production, for in reality costs per unit of product (or type of product) may be difficult to discover.[4] So it may be more reasonable to think of prices being set to yield a certain sum of profit over costs in relation to total capital which is being employed at some normal rate of capacity utilisation. These are then the prices that the consumption sector must pay for the capital goods it buys from the capital goods sector, and the prices at which capital goods exchange in the capital goods sector. On the assumption of overall competition the mark-ups are then set in each sector such that the proportion of profit to capital in both sectors is uniform.

The consumption sector then uses the profits it earns on the sale of consumption goods to purchase capital goods from the capital sector, which leaves the consumption sector with capital goods instead of money profits. These earnings for the capital goods producers cover the cost of labour in the capital goods sector (recall that in the previous chapter the profit in the consumption goods sector was just equal to the wage bill in the capital goods sector when $s_w = 0$ and $s_p = 1$). The remaining capital goods, valued at the same prices then represent the profits of the capital goods sector, and also represent the investment in new capital for the increased production of capital goods. Thus each sector has new capital goods to increase its productive capacity in the next period. Abstracting, as we have done, from the replacements of old capital goods, the net profit for the system per period is then equal to the capital goods purchased by the consumption sector plus the remaining new capital goods in the investment sector. The mark-up over costs in the capital goods sector thus determines the amount of productive capacity the consumption goods sector can buy with its profits, or more simply the distribution of the net capital accumulation between the two sectors. Thus for the rate of expansion of productive capacity to be compatible in the two sectors the mark-ups in the two sectors must be such that the profits in the consumption sector can purchase enough capital to keep its productive capacity expanding at a steady rate. *If* the relations between men, machines and output in the two sectors are the same, steady expansion at the same rate in both sectors requires a uniform mark-up in both sectors. In such a case

---

[4] Cf. below chapter 10, and [83, part IV].

the demand for new capital by the consumption sector (the growth of its total profits) just keeps step with the increase in the capacity of the capital sector to produce new capital due to the investment in new capital of its own profits.

Thus, for example, in example II of the previous chapter the capital sector would sell 25 units to the consumption sector for 50 money units, representing a price of two money 'units' per unit of capital good output. The remaining 25 units of capital goods valued at the same price yield an additional 50 money units of revenue so that total revenue equals 100. With wage costs of 50, net profit is equal to 50. The ratio of receipts to costs (100/50) is thus the same in both sectors. At a mark-up higher than this the capital goods sector would be increasing its capital and productive capacity at a faster rate than the consumption sector and the level of capacity utilisation would have to change in the capital sector or the capital goods producers would find that they had an excess of capital goods to sell at the given mark-up and desired rate of capacity utilisation. *In general* the mark-ups in the two sectors will not be similar because of differences in techniques of production or capacity utilisation in the two sectors, i.e. when capital-labour ratios are not uniform.

When the mark-ups in the two sectors are compatible it is not necessary to calculate profit in money terms, for when all profit is used for investment in new capital net profit per period equals net capital accumulation, taking the system overall.

When we work with the assumptions that the workers do not save and that the capitalists do not spend, the real wage (for workers in either sector) is equal to consumption output divided by the number of labourers employed. Total net profit in the system is equal to the gross output of the capital goods sector less replacements in each sector, or the net accumulation of capital. Profits are then equal to the net output of the capital sector and consumption is equal to the net output of the consumption sector. The ratio of profits to wages thus corresponds directly to the ratio of output (or employment N_i/N_c) in the two sectors, which explains why we have chosen to divide the economy in this way. In such a position the workers do not have to share consumption output with the capitalists, who consecrate all their profits to the construction of capital equipments. This is sometimes called 'golden-rule' accumulation for it gives the highest real wage for a given accumulation of capital.

Equally when profits are identical with the accumulation of capital per period, the proportion of profits to capital, and new capital to existing capital, will be identical. This is just another way of saying that the rate of profits (P/K) is equal to the rate of capital accumulation (g) so that $\pi = P/K = g = I/K$.

Kalecki has a handy way of expressing these relations between profits, real wages and the level of activity in the investment sector. Dividing the system according to income and output we have

Income	*Output*
gross profit	gross investment
	capitalists' consumption
wages and salaries	workers' consumption
Gross National Income $=$	Gross National Output

When workers consume all their income, workers' consumption is equal to wages and salaries, so they cancel each other out. The above relation then becomes

gross profits = gross investment + capitalists' consumption

This relation should be recognised as just another way of saying that savings equals investment. Under the assumption that only capitalists save, whatever investment happens to be the capitalists must receive enough profits so that after the capitalists consume part of them enough is left to equal the amount of investment they have chosen to carry out. Thus if s_p is the propensity to save out of profits the savings–investment equality must be $s_p P = S = I$ (cf. example IV, above). In the case where capitalists do not consume their profits, but invest them all (as in the 'golden rule'), $s_p = 1$, and the relation is $P = S = I$. Thus both investment and the propensity to consume of the profit earners affect the level of profits and the distribution of national output between wages and profits. The simple relation between wages and consumption output, and profits and the net accumulation of capital, breaks down where there is consumption out of profits. As we saw in the preceding chapter, consumption out of profits will be associated with a higher mark-up of prices over costs. Thus the real wage is lower, for prices of consumption goods are higher when consumption out of profits is associated with any given rate of accumulation. In such a case the golden-rule relation is lost, so that $\pi \neq g$ and $P/K \neq I/K$, and the simple relation between profit as a share of income and capital as a share of output is also destroyed. The consequences of this are taken up again in chapters 11 and 14. The relation must now be written $\pi = g/s_p$. This new equation follows directly from the fact that the savings–investment condition (as seen above p. 72) now becomes $s_p P = I$, so that the amount of profits remaining after the capitalists' consumption provides enough saving to equal investment. Thus when $s_p = 1$ and $s_w = 0$, $S = I = P$, and $\pi = g$; but when $s_p < 1$ and $s_w = 0$, $s_p P = S = I$ and $\pi > g$, as given by g/s_p. This way of looking at things causes no particular problems except that P/K loses the simple meaning in physical terms, and now in order to calculate the ratio in common units capital must be valued in money terms for profits have no measure in physical terms. We return to this problem later.

The equation for the rate of profit is not, however, effected when workers savings are introduced, and the workers receive profits from the capital they finance with their savings (cf. [66]). This is so as long as $s_w < s_p$ (recall that s_w is the propensity to save out of wages).

As simply as possible the argument goes like this. We compare two economies, each with its own past and its own future, moving along in tranquil conditions. In one $s_w = 0$, while in the other $0 < s_w < s_p$. In the second economy workers give their savings to the capitalists who invest them and pay the workers the ruling rate of profit on these investments. The amount of total investment carried out in the two positions is the same. Some of the profits that would have gone to the capitalists if s_w were 0 now go to the workers. The workers save less out of these profits than the capitalists would have ($s_w < s_p$). But at the same time when $s_w = 0$, savings out of wages were zero, but when $s_w > 0$, savings out of wages is positive so that the savings out of profits in the second system is lower by ($s_p P_w - s_w P_w$) where P_w is the amount of profits now going to workers. This amount is just equal to the new savings out of wages by workers so that total saving in the system is unchanged.

$(s_p P = s_p P_p + s_w W + s_w P_w,$ where $s_w W$ is net savings out of wages).

If saving is unchanged then investment is the same, as are the ruling mark-ups, prices and profits. Thus the rate of profit is the same in both positions and the formula $\pi = g/s_p$ still holds even when there is saving out of wages. The valuation problem that we spoke of above does not concern us, for since prices are unchanged, however we chose to value capital, it will be unchanged, so that the rate of profit on capital continues to be expressed by the rate of accumulation divided by the propensity to save out of *profits*. (A fuller explanation of this argument is given in chapter 14.)

The problem that does arise, however (refer to the last section of chapter 3), is that once $s_w > 0$ we are no longer in a world where income categories (wages and profits) are strictly related to social categories (workers and capitalists). It is no longer possible to talk of real consumption as being the real income of the workers (for they now also receive profits). It still remains true that the rate of profit is equal to the rate of accumulation divided by the saving propensity from profits (as a functional income category). It is easy to confuse the two relations as is evidenced by Samuelson and Modigliani's failure to fully recognise the distinction [99]. It cannot be sufficiently stressed that the equational relation that has been derived for the rate of profit refers only to the functional categories of wages and profits income in a system where there is positive savings out of wages. Statements about workers and capitalists under this assumption are more complicated as will be seen in chapter 11.

To look back, we now have a level of mark-up that determines the prices for the output of both sectors to ensure that their output at expected levels of capacity utilisation is sold, given the initial conditions. We also have a rate of capital accumulation ($\Delta K/K$ or I/K) and a rate of profit (P/K or π). As long as the system stays on a steady path the valuation of the capital stock is no particular problem for there will be nothing to encourage the producers to change their mark-ups over costs, and thus prices ruling in the system will be unchanged. In such a case the value of capital goods can be easily calculated as the prices of all consumption and capital goods (as well as the goods themselves) remain unchanged; if the system strays off its steady path this is no longer the case. But in the case of non-steady growth the difficulty in calculating capital values so that the rate of profit can be calculated is not the most pressing problem. In such cases neither the value of capital nor the rate of profit being earned on it have any meaning, for the conditions that were expected to rule when the investments were made have not materialised, and entrepreneurs must make what they can out of the current conditions; the return on mistaken investments provides no guide to the present or the future, or what the present would have been like if things had been as expected.

CAUSALITY AND DETERMINATION

The aspect of the above relations that we have not yet explicitly discussed, and this is perhaps the most important, is causality and determination. So far we have simply looked at relations that must hold if steady growth is to be attained in the sense of expectations being fulfilled. This is not a simple matter. It is based on the Keynesian contention that decisions to invest are independent from decisions to save, that decisions to invest are by and large autonomous, and that investment determines saving. More practically this approach emphasises and recognises that the basic source of not only increasing output, but any output at all, is investment. The primary causal relation then runs from investment to output. In our rather unrealistic example I of the preceding chapter we postulated that there was no expenditure on investment. In such a case labour claims and consumes all its output, but at the same time it fails to replace the capital stock. The system could not survive for any length of time without exhausting its capital and running into a slump where both labourers and capitalists would be forced into handicraft production. Capitalism as an ongoing process is a contradiction in terms without investment being carried out by the owners of the means of production to at least preserve those means of production.

Investment decisions enter in on both sides of the aggregate supply and demand relations in the system. First, investment determines the proportion of capital to consumption goods, and thus the supply of both types of goods produced. It also provides demand for consumption goods through the wages paid to labour employed in the capital goods sector as well as the possibility of consumption out of profits that this investment generates. Demand generated by investment is then tempered by thriftiness conditions in terms of the propensity to consume out of wages and profits incomes. Thus investment and thriftiness determines the flow of income to purchase consumption goods, while investment decisions determine how much of a given total output is available as supply of consumption goods. This conjuncture will be compatible with a certain mark-up of prices over prime costs, level of capacity utilisation and rate of profit in the system.

If the proportion of investment to consumption for any given level of total output is higher then the ruling mark-up, prices and rate of profit will be higher. If the propensity to save out of profits is lower the rate of profit is higher. This relation is symbolised in the equation $\pi = g/s_\mathrm{p}$ and allows us to say that the rate of profit, π, is determined by investment and thriftness. If g were higher, π would be higher and so forth.

But this is only an explanation of the mechanism of causality in the system. The crucial statement is that investment decisions determine the proportion of investment to consumption or non-available to available output. This statement involves a power relationship as well as a belief in the logic of the capitalist system where investment determines saving. As long as investors are able to obtain finance from the banking system in excess of their net proceeds they will have the ability to increase their appropriation of resources for investment purposes. This, of course, is not to say that they will always do so, but that they have the ability to do so if they desire.

The consumer has really very little to say in the investment decisions of either small family firms or the large impersonal corporations. It is the firms' decisions that determine both the level of employment and output and how the output will be divided between investment and consumption. The consumer can do little else but battle over the consumption goods that are available. This remains true even at less than full employment, but then the battle is between those who have incomes and those who do not. The system appears to be set up so that the group that has the most to gain from combination spends its time fighting amongst themselves over a given amount of national output, instead of fighting with the capitalists over the size of the pie and how it should be divided between investment and consumption.

It is through the assumption that by size and finance, investment decisions take precedence in both time and power over consumption decisions that the model derives its causality. To consume and save, one must have income; income only results from positive invest ment The proof of the assumption that capitalists control investment decisions is not a matter to be denied by logic or philosophy but by reference to actual capitalism.

The statement that the rate of capital accumulation is determined by individual time-preference only makes sense in a world where investment is determined by the decisions of savers. It is this Say's Law view of the world that the post-Keynesian analysis explicitly rejects by emphasising that investment determines income and employment and therefore saving. It is not the individual household savers that control the decision to invest in such a formulation.

6 Golden-Age Growth and Neutral Technical Progress

The aggregate economic relations that we have considered up to now have been looked at with a given ruling technique of production and without respect to their movement over time. Part of the process of looking at things in terms of comparisons implies making assumptions about past accumulation. Thus for each possible proportion of investment to consumption considered in the preceding exercises we also had to assume that the existing accumulation of capital in each sector was appropriate to the labour force employed in that sector. A simple increase in employment in one sector will change very little unless the appropriate capital equipment for the extra labour to work with is also provided. This is what we mean by looking at systems, each with his own past record of accumulation and its own prospects of the future. The systems have had enough time to digest, so to speak, any large shifts or changes in conditions.

Likewise we have said very little about how the new capital equipment produced in the investment sector will be used. Will there be enough labour available to man it when it comes into use? Or, on the other hand, will the new capital that is produced provide enough employment for the labour that is seeking employment in the period when the new capital is put into use? It is to these very important questions that we will seek answers in the next two chapters, trying to identify the conditions of accumulation that will be necessary to assure that the capitalists will be willing to carry out the investment necessary to provide employment for the available labour force. Since the technical relations between labour input and means of production are crucial to the determination of the quantities of consumption and capital goods produced in each sector we will also have to take into account the changes that will result in the basic model when there are changes in the technical relations governing production, that is, technical progress.

TECHNOLOGICAL CHANGE

In the preceding examples we have taken as given the physical resources available at a point in time in the history of a single economy. Over time the resources available will be changing. This primarily refers to the size of the labour force available for employment. It also, however, applies to raw materials as well as the re-arrangements of raw materials. Changes in scientific knowledge do not change the actual raw materials that exist, but the form and use of raw materials will be affected by changes in knowledge. We must not forget that the progress of man's understanding of the physical universe not only changes the conditions of labour production, but it also changes the form of the raw materials that are used in the production process. It is indeed tempting to reduce all of technical progress to changes in man's understanding of the operation of the material universe.

Thus labour and natural resources form the limits of possible production in an economic system. The application of labour sets the limits of the conversion of resources into commodities. Many of the observed changes in technology can be explained in terms of deficiency of labour, deficiency of labour at a given cost, or in the uncertainty that labour will be continually available at predictable costs.

The maximum possible rate of growth is then limited by the combination of the rate of increase of employable labour and the rate at which technical knowledge changes the form and amount of raw materials with which labour works. Thus depending on the state of technical knowledge there will be different particular techniques of production for different goods at any point in time, as well as different goods thrown up by the changes in knowledge. None of them will be the same, and it is very difficult to find a consistent means of comparing or equating them.

To attempt the introduction of changes in technology into the abstract analysis of the growth process, we assume that particular states of technical knowledge can be classified and identified. These states will represent a number of different particular techniques both within and between groups of products. Thus a spectrum of techniques will represent both a continuum of techniques for different classes of products and also alternative techniques (other than the one actually in use) for the production of the particular products.

Thus, as technology changes, a new spectrum of techniques represents a new set of alternative technical methods of production for each product. Imagine, say, the new techniques made possible by the application of steam power, or cast iron, or steel, or light metals (aluminium, molybdenum, etc.), or carbon fibres, or computers, or atomic energy as possible cases; as well as the new products that these discoveries suggest.

To simplify the complexity caused by looking at individual products, some of which will be disappearing and being replaced by others, let us revert to our simple classification of products in terms of consumption goods and capital-investment goods. To distinguish the effects of changes in the spectra of technology we can represent each spectrum in terms of the output per man employed that each yields in each sector. The emphasis is thus placed on changes in the processes of production, rather than in terms of the products produced. Superior techniques, represented by a new spectrum, will yield a higher output for a given amount of labour employed, than those techniques previously in existence.

To analyse the contribution to growth of a growing labour force and more advanced technology (which may normally occur simultaneosly) it is necessary to analyse them separately.

GROWTH OF LABOUR, TECHNIQUE CONSTANT

When the spectrum of techniques is unchanged, output per man is constant. If the number of men employed is also constant, total output per period is also constant. If there is no unemployed labour in the system, any capital good produced in excess of those required to replace equipment wearing out will not have any labour to work with it and will lie idle. When the investment sector produces just enough equipment to provide replacements the system is in a stationary state with a constant number of men employed. Output per man and total output per period is also constant. All labour not employed in the investment sector must find employment in the consumption sector. This implies a certain number of machines in both sectors in order to provide full-employment of the labour force. If this condition is met, and if the capitalists are willing to continue to offer employment under these conditions the system can continue over time with a constant capital stock and a zero growth rate.

If the labour force is growing, new capital goods will have to be produced each period to equip the new labour coming available each period. With unchanged technology the level of output per man is constant. If the capital stock in the capital sector is appropriate to produce an amount of machinery that will provide replacements, as well as employment for all the new labour becoming available, the growth in output per period will be directly related to the increase in the labour force. Thus, if the labour force grows at X per cent per annum, total output will also rise at X per cent per annum, since the output per man employed is constant. The rate of growth of output is equal to the rate of growth of labour. The capital stock thus must also grow at the same rate, if the labour force is to be fully employed over time.

CHANGE IN TECHNOLOGY, CONSTANT LABOUR FORCE

We now reverse the situation and take the labour force as given, allowing the spectra of techniques to change. We assume that new techniques are assimilated into the existing stock of capital in a smooth fashion, fully realising that this is *usually not* the case, and that a host of assumptions about capitalists' expectations, etc., are required for this to occur. Some of these problems will be treated later.

As each new spectrum raises output per head it likewise raises total output produced from a given labour force. Thus when output per head rises at a steady rate due to the occurrence of new types of technology, total output per period produced in the system also rises at this rate, with the amount of employment unchanged. If output per head rises at, say Y per cent, total output will also rise by Y per cent per annum, when the existing constant labour force remains employed over time. If the rate of increase is to be a steady rate, technical progress must be of a very special variety such that it raises productivity in all activities equally. This type of technical change is called neutral technical progress because it has a neutral effect on the relation between capital and labour and capital and output. We will deal with this concept in more detail below. Thus when the capitalists are willing and able to carry out the investment necessary to keep the constant labour force in employment over time and are also prepared to invest in the new techniques as they arise the system expands at the steady rate Y per annum.

LABOUR AND TECHNOLOGY – THE GOLDEN AGE

When the labour force grows at X per cent per annum and neutral changes in the spectra of technology raise output per man employed by Y per cent per annum, the maximum rate of growth in output possible is the combination of the two effects, or $g = X + Y$ (neglecting the cross product). If the capitalists in the system are willing and able to carry out the amount of investment required to produce full employment and introduce the neutral techniques as they occur, the system is in what Joan Robinson calls a 'golden age'. This condition is called a golden age in order to indicate a mythical state of affairs which no real system is ever likely to achieve in practice. The actual rate of growth, as was stressed above, depends on the willingness and ability of the capitalists to carry out investment. The ruling rate of investment combined with the conditions of aggregate demand (thriftiness) will then determine the rate of profit and real wage associated with the ruling growth rate. This may or may not be the rate associated with the conditions of the 'golden age', although it may be a steady rate.[1]

NEUTRALITY

Above we cited neutral technical progress as a condition for the 'golden age'. The determination of the real wage and profit rate in chapters 4 and 5 was carried out in terms of the exchange relations between the capital and the consumption sector. We have chosen to retain these divisions in terms of identifying different types of change in technology. If a change in the spectra of techniques of production is to leave the rate of profit and the real wage unchanged then it is obvious that it must not disturb the factors affecting the prices of consumption goods and capital goods. Depending on how we look at the determination of prices, aggregate mark-ups must be left undisturbed or the expectations of profit on investment and normal capacity levels must be unchanged.[2]

To eliminate the effects on the pattern of prices that may result from changes in technology we identify as a norm (or as a myth – just as in the golden age) the concept of neutral technological change.

---

[1] Several possible combinations of actual growth in comparison with golden-age growth are spelled out in Joan Robinson [86].

[2] An alternative approach is sketched out in chapter 10, below.

This is the type of technological change that leaves the relations between the two sectors unchanged. More specifically we can say that neutral change in the spectra of techniques increases the output of productive capacity per man for labour employed in the production of capital goods in the same proportion as output per man increases in the consumption sector when working on the new capital equipments produced by the capital sector. Thus output of productive capacity per man and output of consumption goods per man rises in the same proportion.

Since the basic determinant of the distribution of income and the ruling pattern of market clearing prices is the ratio of investment to consumption (or N_i/N_c), the idea is to leave this ratio unchanged while allowing technological change to occur. If, for example, the increase in the output of productive capacity per man in the capital sector were less than the increase in output per man employed on the new machines in the consumption sector, the capital producing sector would be unable to produce a sufficient quantity of the new machines of higher productive capacity for its own use and for use in the consumption sector. More labour would then be required in the capital sector to produce the required capacity. This would imply a change in the ratio of capital to consumption sector employment (N_i/N_c), different prices, profit rate, and probably a different rate of growth. Irrespective of the final outcome, the system would no longer be in conditions of steady growth at the same sets of prices and distribution of income. It is precisely to avoid these complications that we assume a type of technological change that leaves the ratio of investment to output unchanged.

We shall not enquire further into these changes for the moment except to note that we can distinguish capital-using technological change as those changes in technique that require a higher proportion of resources employed in the capital sector producing productive capacity, and capital-saving as requiring a lower proportion.

This highlights the assumptions that we must make about the structure of the capital stock in existence being appropriate to the assumed conditions. When changes in technology are neutral, the existing capital stock is always evolving in the manner required for the smooth assimilation of the new processes of production. There are no mistakes embodied in the stock of capital in the sense of machines produced in anticipation of events that never materialised, and thus there are no machines inappropriate to current conditions.

Such mistakes will, however, always be embodied in the capital stock whenever there are sharp changes in the spectra of technology and are even more bothersome with non-neutral changes in technology, for these are certain to change profit rates and expectations.

THE REAL WAGE WITH TECHNOLOGICAL PROGRESS

As a corollary to the necessity of maintaining the relations between the capital and consumption sector constant we also require that the consumption and capital goods markets continue to clear. Recall the case where the labour force was constant and output per man was increasing due to technological change. The amount of output is increasing over time, but the number of men to consume it is not. Therefore if the system is to remain on a steady growth path, either the prices of consumption goods as a whole must be falling as labour costs per unit of output fall with constant money wages, or the money wage must be rising in tandem with increasing productivity so that the prices of consumption goods are unchanged. We say that one or the other must occur, for if not the labour force could not buy the increasing output and unsold goods would pile up, soon causing the system to dive into a slump. With the prices of goods falling at the same rate as their quantity is increasing an unchanged money-wage bill is sufficient to purchase the increasing amount of consumption goods produced. If the prices of goods, on the other hand, are unchanged, the money-wage bill must increase at the same rate as the quantity of goods so that aggregate money demand keeps step with the aggregate supply of consumption goods.

In either case, everything else (consumption out of profits, saving out of wages, etc., if they exist) remaining the same, the real wage is then rising at the same rate as technical progress raises output per head. Either of the two assumptions will do to make sure that the increasing output can be sold. We will choose to leave the money-wage constant, and allow prices to fall, thus reserving rises in money-wages for the results of labour's reaction to the inflation barrier.

The rate of profit in these conditions, however, remains unchanged, for the decrease in price is just offset by the increase in goods sold so that the difference between proceeds and prime costs still produces the same ratio in respect of the value of capital employed. From the point of view of the employer the cost of labour is the same proportion of his own produced product price, thus leaving his total profit unchanged.

Likewise the share of money wages in total output remains constant, as does the proportion of consumption goods in total output when taken in money terms.

Since the capitalists taken together do not appear to increase their return on capital with the introduction of new technology it would appear that there is little incentive for them to make improvements in production techniques. This would of course be true if the capitalists acted as a group and each individual capitalist could rely on his competitors to take similar views. If no one introduces the new technology there is no reason for anyone to do so, but once one producer has done so, all must follow to survive. Within the degree of competition that we have assumed there is little choice but to apply all new techniques as they arise.

If, for example, a competitor introduces a new technique he can reduce his prices without lowering his profit rate, thus taking a larger share of the market. The other firms then must either accept the reduction in their sales and rate of profit (or match the reduction in prices which also reduces the profit rate) or introduce the new method of production as soon as possible to try to minimise the loss of sales and profit due to their laxity. Thus, unless the firms combine to block the applications of new techniques (which can often happen) the force of overall competition will provide the impetus for all firms to introduce new technology and thus at least preserve their existing profit rates, although the new techniques may do nothing to increase them.

CHANGING MONEY WAGES

The existence of technical progress also introduces the role that can be played by the trade unions. If we take the alternative assumption for the moment and assume that the prices of consumption goods are held constant, steady growth requires that the money-wage must rise at the same rate as that at which technical progress increases output per head.

For reality, as opposed to abstract analysis, this assumption is probably more reasonable. But, for the employer, any increase in the money-wage is an increase in costs, and thus a prior claim on the revenues from the new technique of production. From the point of view of the employer's costs, he wants his own wages to be as low as possible. From the point of view of his sales, he wants the wages paid by all other employers to be as high as possible. Thus, any concerted effort by employers to hold down increases in money-wages (which it is in each individual's interest to do) will result in purchasing power growing more slowly than the quantity of goods that they want to sell at current prices. This would result in falling sales volume, lower profits, and the eventual possibility of lower prices once the slump has got into full swing and the capitalists' confidence in their ability to sell anything at all has long been shattered.

But the capitalist employers are saved from this suicidal course to the extent that the trade unions continually push for higher money-wages. Union pressure can thus help to squeeze the purchasing power required to buy the goods out of the stingy employers. In this sense the unions help to preserve stability by making sure that some of the increased productivity accrues as higher money-wages, higher purchasing power, and higher sales. This prevents increases in productivity from running the system into a slump due to lack of purchasing power to buy the greater output produced due to more productive techniques of production. This is not the only example of extreme paradox in the analysis of growth in free enterprise capitalism.

There is however, another side to the story. As we have seen, the system can move along a steady path with constant prices as long as purchasing power keeps pace with output; money-wages rising in step with productivity. But when money-wages outstrip the increases in productivity, the capitalists enjoy what is called a sellers' market. In such conditions they can raise prices as they like to take up the gap between the rise in wages and the increase in the supply of goods; or they can run down stocks and try to increase delivery times. Such conditions make sales more profitable and investment more attractive. In such a case the consumption goods producers may feel that they would like to increase the rate at which they add to their productive capacity and so they place increased orders with the capital goods producers. The capital goods producers are happy to oblige by lengthening delivery times at the same time as they attempt to increase their productive capacity. But an increase in investment goods production implies more labour employed in the capital sector (if it can be found, if not it will have to be bid away from the consumption sector) and an increase in the proportion of investment to output (N_i/N_c rises). This shift implies that the real wage will be damaged, and may start off additional demands for higher wages after the fashion of the explanation of the operation of the 'inflation barrier' above. It will also be most likely that, in this case, the capitalists will be happy to meet the wage demands and the ground is then laid for a spiralling inflation at the same time that steady growth and tranquillity are lost for the system.

The economic logic behind the utilisation of an incomes policy for the control of inflation should now be obvious. An incomes policy seeks to limit wage rises to the rises in productivity, precisely the conditions that we found necessary for the steady growth of the system with constant prices of consumption goods output. The social implications behind an incomes policy are, however, not so straightforward, nor is its successful application. The logic of the policy, however, as well as its appeal to economists interested in preserving steady growth with little change in prices, should be obvious.

To return to our initial mythical point of a golden age, where the capitalists provide investment in neutral improvements sufficient to employ the existing labour force, output grows at a rate determined by the combination of the rate of productivity growth and growth of the labour force; the real wage rises in step with productivity, and the rate of profit and shares of wages and profits in national income are constant in tranquil conditions over time. It really does look to be a myth, not unlike Plato's golden age. But, as Joan Robinson often says, the sole reason for working it out is to find out why it is not attained in reality, not to believe that we will ever approach such a state as a result of natural forces.

We are now ready to enquire into the effects of changes of technique as a found within one individual spectrum.

7 The Choice of Technique within a Spectrum

Up to this point we have assumed that each spectrum of techniques of production has contained a number of different specific techniques associated with the state of technical progress ruling at a given period in time. We have looked at the effects of changing degrees of technology in the sense of changes in the overall spectra of techniques, but we have avoided the analysis of which particular technique on an existing spectrum the economy (or more appropriately the entrepreneurs in the economy) will choose.

Each technique within a spectrum can be identified by a different set of engineering blueprints. These blueprints comprise the specific capital equipments associated with a technique, the specific labour requirements, and the amount of work-in-progress required for the construction of the associated machinery, as well as to put it into operation to produce final output.

In choosing amongst the existing techniques on a spectrum, we assume that the entrepreneur knows (and expects to continue into the future) the cost of the final product, the ruling money-wage, and the cost of capital associated with each technique (or alternatively the expected rates of change of these variables). The available techniques within a spectrum can then be ranked in terms of their costs of capital per man required. Feasible techniques that require a higher cost of capital per man at given prices and wages yield more output per man employed and can be said to be more *mechanised* than those which require less capital per man employed.

With a given amount of finance to invest in a new process of production, a feasible technique of higher mechanisation will employ fewer labourers and produce a smaller amount of total final output. This may sound a little bizzare, but it is really quite easy to see. Compare two techniques of different mechanistion, one more mechanised than the other. If the technique of lower mechanisation with its greater employment requirement and thus greater wages bill produced a smaller total output it would be absolutely inferior to all other techniques of both higher and lower mechanisation and thus would not be under consideration as a feasible technique. This is so because it will produce both a lower total revenue (the given product price times its lower output) as well as a higher wages bill (the given money wage rate times the higher total labour requirement), and thus both factors combine to decrease profit per man employed. Thus, given the money sum to be spent on a new technique, those techniques of higher mechanisation will have lower labour requirements and lower total output if they are to be considered as realistic possibilities.

The techniques of higher mechanisation under consideration then yield a greater amount of profit per man, but at the cost of a lower total sum of revenues; but also with the benefit of a lower total wages bill to be paid out of the lower total revenues. There is thus both a gain and a loss associated with a technique of a higher degree of mechanisation. The positive aspects of the technique of higher mechanisation are (a) the lower total wages bill, (b) the higher output per man, and (c) the greater profit per man employed, given the money-wage rate and the expected product price.

The negative aspects are (a) the lower total output, and thus (b) the lower total revenue at the given price for final output, and (c) the higher costs of capital per man. The entrepreneur must decide whether the combination of these factors, positive and negative, will cause the total profit he earns in respect to his *given amount of finance* to be greater or less if he adopts the technique of higher mechanisation.

If, for example, the technique of higher mechanisation would reduce the wage bill by *more* than it would reduce the total revenues expected from operating the technique, the total amount of profit earned with the more mechanised technique would be greater. The entrepreneur could then earn a higher rate of profit on his invested finance if he chose to invest in the technique of higher mechanisation. If, on the other hand, the reduction in total revenues were greater than the reduction in the wages bill, the technique of lower mechanisation would produce the higher rate of profit given the money-wage rate, the price of final output, the money sum available for investment, and the costs of capital associated with each technique of a different level of mechanisation.

From this point of view one can see that higher wage rates will push entrepreneurs to introduce higher degrees of mechanisation in order to try to reduce the increased cost of labour by utilising techniques that require less labour, and increase the amount of output per head produced by each unit of labour employed.

It has been customarily assumed that higher wages are associated with lower profit rates, thus generating the broad general rule that techniques of higher mechanisation will be chosen when profit rates arc lower (and wages higher), and vice versa. This, we recognise, is very close to the neoclassical proposition that associates a high rate of profit with low capital intensity (a low capital–labour ratio) because a high price (rate of profit) for capital means that the 'factor' capital is scarce and entrepreneurs will want to minimise its use in production by substituting cheaper 'factors' in its place.

We should instantly recognise that the propositions that we have presented are different in the sense that they have no application in terms of a process that occurs in a single economy over time, but can only be used in the sense of making comparison of steady positions over time. Thus our general proposition is that an economy which is growing steadily over time in a state of tranquillity with a higher rate of profit and a lower wage would be using a technique of lower mechanisation than a similar economy with a lower profit rate and higher wage rate, when both choose techniques from the same set of engineering blueprints, subject to each economy's unique history of past development. In fact, it is most likely that the history of past development of an economy will indeed affect the kinds of techniques that will be available at any point in time, these being related to particular needs. Thus our ability to apply the general proposition in real situations is severely limited by the assumption of similar available techniques. But this is not the greatest problem with the general proposition.

WAGE RATES, PROFIT RATES, AND THE COSTS OF CAPITAL

There is, however, another way in which the approach differs from the neoclassical analysis of the choice of techniques in relation to relative factor costs. Up to now we have assumed that the costs of each of the existing techniques is known and unchanged for different rates of wages and profits. It is now necessary to see if the simple relation between degrees of mechanisation and the rate of profits will remain valid when we take into account the costs of constructing the different techniques at different wage and profit rates.

We first notice that the costs of an outfit of capital goods (and its requirements of work-in-progress) associated with each feasible technique should include a notional rate of profit reckoned on the finance committed to the new technique from the time its construction is commenced until its costs are fully amortised through the production and sale of final output over its producing lifetime. The decision concerning the choice of technique concerns both the effect of differences in the wages paid to labour constructing and operating the technique as well as the notional rate of profit included in the financing of the construction and utilisation of the technique.

So far the argument has been taken with a given level of wages, prices of final product, rate of profit, and cost of capital required by the technique. It explains why entrepreneurs would prefer a particular degree of mechanisation under given conditions, *on the assumption* that at a lower profit rate the notional interest cost entering the cost of construction of each technique would be lower and thus the relative differences between the costs of capital per man of different techniques is undisturbed.

But the effect of a notionally different rate of profit in the calculation of total costs (and thus the costs per man) of the techniques may not affect all techniques within a spectrum in the same proportion. If, for example, a technique of a lower degree of mechanisation has a longer period of construction, or a different time pattern of inputs over the construction period, its costs of construction (and cost per man) may be affected to a greater extent by a notional difference in the rate of profit used to calculate costs than another technique of a higher degree of mechanisation (this can be thought of as different amounts of labour applied at different dates during the construction period, a device first suggested by Sraffa [107, chapter 6], and which is exploited in the example given in the Appendix to this chapter). In such a case it may be possible that the reduced wages bill associated with a more mechanised technique will be more than offset by the lower capital costs (from the lower rate of profit used to calculate the costs of the technique) of the less mechanised technique. Then the capital costs per man of introducing the less mechanised technique are lower in *greater* proportion than its output per man (and thus profit per man) is lower. Thus when a lower rate of profit is applied to the finance committed to the construction costs of a less mechanised technique this may cause its costs per man to be lower in a greater proportion than the profit per man associated with the more mechanised technique is higher. In such a case the technique of lower mechanisation is more profitable than the technique of higher mechanisation, comparing the two at a notionally lower rate of profit.

Let us recall the positive and negative aspects that we listed above for the comparison of techniques of lower and higher mechanisation when the money sum available for investment is given, and wage-rates, product prices, and capital costs (and the profit rate used to calculate these costs) were assumed known. The positive aspects of the technique of higher mechanisation were (a) the lower total wages bill for labour required to operate the technique; (b) the higher output per man employed with the technique; and thus (c) the greater profit per man. Against this we posed the negative aspects: (a) the lower total output, which at given prices produces (b) a lower total revenue; and (c) higher costs of capital per man. We then said that the main advantage of the more mechanised technique would be its ability to reduce wage costs in greater proportion than it reduced total output and total revenue, thus increasing output and profit per man in greater proportion than it increases the cost of capital per man. Now we are adding the effect of notional differences in the rate of wages and rate of profit to these relations, and especially on the relative differences in the capital costs per man of different techniques.

Under certain assumptions about the gestation periods or the time pattern of inputs in the construction of the competing techniques, it becomes possible for the profitability of the two techniques to be reversed when we calculate the positive and negative aspects at a notionally lower rate of profit and higher wage rate (or if the decision had been taken in an economy that had evolved through time with a lower rate of profit and higher wage rate). Thus at the lower notional profit rate (and higher wage rate) relative capital costs may change in a greater proportion than the difference in the required wage bills caused by the higher wage. This serves to diminish positive aspect (a) which also diminishes positive aspect (c), while it increases negative aspect (c), so that the cost per man of introducing the more mechanised technique is higher in greater proportion that its output per man and profit per man (positive effects (b) and (c)) are higher, the effect of higher wages on the relative wage costs (positive aspect (a)) not being sufficient to offset this difference.

Thus the notional change in the profit rate is enough to make the technique of lower mechanisation more profitable.

Looking at this in terms of two economies facing the same spectrum of techniques, we would find that an economy with a lower profit rate ruling through time chooses a less mechanised technique on the critereon of profitability than that chosen in an economy with a higher profit rate ruling over time. Thus the possibility arises that our general relation between the degree of mechanisation and the profit rate may not hold, and that lower profit rates may be associated with lower degrees of mechanisation when the effects of differences in the rate of profits on capital costs are taken into account. This phenomenon was explained by Joan Robinson in [85] and was dubbed a 'curiosum'. It is now more commonly known as 'capital reversal' as it contradicts the neoclassical maxim that capital intensity is inversely related to the rate of profit. It is called a 'reversal' because it suggests that the relation may indeed be positive, and thus the reverse of the relation predicted by the neoclassical maxim.

These conclusions enforce Professor Robinson's insistence that economic analysis, expecially of capital accumulation and technical choice, should be initially carried out in terms of comparisons of systems in steady growth over time where the rate of profit prevailing undisturbed over time is known and is confidently expected to remain unchanged over time, i.e., in conditions of tranquillity. The problems to be sorted out are difficult enough under these seemingly simple assumptions and must be understood before we can approach change in a single economy over time.

In an economy that is changing over time (or in the analysis of movements along a production function) the value of capital can never be calculated with surety, for the capital stock will not be appropriate to the current conditions, for it was constructed in anticipation of events and conditions that were never actually realised. In such a situation the ruling rate of profit has no meaning in respect to the capital stock (either to its costs of construction or its earnings) in existence or to its profitability in the future in which it must operate. It is thus impossible to make valid or consistent comparisons between any past or future points of time, either between or within economies. It is not possible to say definitely whether any particular economy is using more or less capital per man to produce its output, or whether labour is better or worse off in one set of conditions or another.

It is the result of the possibility of capital reversal (and the associated concept of 'double-switching'[1]) that causes one to question the neoclassical analysis of capital in terms of supply and demand for a scarce resource. When we recognise that capital is not a natural element in the process of production, but is itself a produced means of production, we can also see that differences in the costs of the inputs used in its construction (specifically the effects of differences in rates of wages and profit) will effect any nominal measure of the 'quantity' of capital. It is thus impossible to speak of a quantity of capital (or to specify the capital intensity of a technique of production within a given spectrum) without reference to either the rate of profit or the real-wage rate. It is in no way possible to logically derive the rate of profit by means of the supply and demand for a 'quantity' of capital or by taking the marginal product of a 'quantity' of capital entering a production function, for in both cases the rate of profit must be known before the quantities to be analysed can be determined.

One must also be careful to note that this problem concerning the quantity of capital is not unique to capital goods, but applies to all produced output in the system; to all output that Ricardo considered as could be produced and reproduced by means of labour and means of production over time. Thus you may also recognise in this context Ricardo's problem of the valuation of the economy's national product under different distributions of the national product (and thus differences in wages and profit rates); or Marx's contention that the measurement of a social relation requires a social measure, one that is not determined with the process of exchange in the system of circulation. Thus the result not only challenges the neoclassical analysis of capital, but the entire theory of prices, in terms of supply and demand, utilised in the neoclassical economic theory (again excepting, of course, the old masters' paintings and the like).[2]

[1] The concept of switching and its relation with capital reversal is taken up in the Appendix to this chapter.

[2] See [85, pp. 411–30], for a diagrammatical representation of the 'perverse' case of capital reversal. These relations are generalised, and compared with Sraffa's approach in Robinson and Naqvi [95].

APPENDIX: THE TIME-PATTERN OF INPUTS AND THE COSTS OF A TECHNIQUE

We can take a simple example to illustrate the effect of different rates of profit on the construction costs of techniques, as suggested on page 90, above. The example used here was originally proposed by Sraffa [107, chapter 6].

Let us assume that we can calculate the input costs of the construction of techniques in terms of the accumulated labour applied over the construction period. Thus we could assume, say, that labour begins the construction process with free raw materials and produces means of production that are used in later stages of the production process. The contribution to the total cost of the construction of the technique of any unit of labour at any period before the end of the construction period is the cost of the wage paid plus the rate of profit on the wage paid from the time it is paid until the technique is ready for use. If, for example, one unit of labour is required n periods before the completion of the machine it will contribute to costs its wage times the rate of profit (r) over n periods, or in general if L is the quantity of labour and w the wage this sum can be represented as $wL(1+r)^n$.

Let us take two techniques, each requiring 20 total units of labour, but applied in a different time pattern. Technique A requires that all 20 units of labour be applied 8 periods before the end of the construction period. Technique B spreads the application of labour, requiring one unit 25 periods before completion and the remaining 19 units one period before completion.

This can be translated into our general cost equation in the following manner. The cost of construction of A will be

$$A = w0L(1+r)^1 + \ldots + w20L(1+r)^8 + \ldots w0L(1+r)^{25}$$

and for B

$$B = w19L(1+r)^1 + \ldots + w0L(1+r)^8 + \ldots w1L(1+r)^{25}$$

For technique A the zero entries show that no labour is required in periods 1 and 25 and thus add nothing to costs, whereas these are the periods in which B uses labour, and vice versa for period 8.

Taking the wage as equal to one unit, when the rate of profit is zero, both techniques have the same value, 20 units. As the rate of profit rises, the wage unit falls (recall the effect of a positive ratio of

TABLE 7A.1

Rate of profit (r)	Real wage
0	1
5	$\frac{4}{5}$
10	$\frac{3}{5}$
15	$\frac{2}{5}$
20	$\frac{1}{5}$
25	0

N_i/N_c on the real wage in our examples in chapter 4). Thus there will be a value of the real wage associated with each rate of profit above zero, until the wage itself falls to zero;[1] and again the two techniques have equal cost, namely zero. The relations between the rate of profit and the wage are given in table 7A.1. Thus for a rate of profit of 5 per cent and a real wage of $\frac{4}{5}$ the costs of the two techniques could be calculated from our general equations

$$A = \tfrac{4}{5}w \cdot 20L(1 + 0 \cdot 05)^8$$
$$B = \tfrac{4}{5}w \cdot 19L(1 + 0 \cdot 05)^1 + \tfrac{4}{5}w \cdot 1L(1 + 0 \cdot 05)^{25}$$

The results of such calculations for the combinations of r and w given in table 7A.1 on the costs of A and B are given in Table 7A.2.

We can now see that the *relative* costs of the techniques change at different rates of profit, B being cheaper at low profit rates, then becoming more expensive at higher rates of profit. Thus thinking back to our example in the text where the relative costs of construction of techniques of different degrees of mechanisation caused a less mechanised technique to be associated with a lower rather than

TABLE 7A.2

Technique	Rate of Profit (%)					
	0	5	10	15	20	25
A	20	23.6	25·7	24·5	16·5	0
B	20	18·7	19·0	21·9	20·7	0
$A - B$	0	4·9	6·7	2·6	− 4·2	0

[1] This is based on the relation that when the wage in excess of subsistence is nil, the profit rate is at its maximum possible value. Alternatively when profit is zero the wage is at its maximum, here symbolised as equal to 1. The maximum possible wage and profit, of course, depends on the production structure of the system which determines its ability to produce a surplus over necessary inputs (cf. chapter 2). The complete relation is found in Sraffa [107].

a higher rate of profit, we can see, through the present example, the process at work. Thus if we called B the less mechanised technique its cost is relatively cheaper at notional profit rate 10 per cent than at notional rate 15 per cent. It is this relative change that brings out the possibility of negative aspect (c) (cf. p. 91 above) outweighing the positive aspects of the technique of higher mechanisation, the difference in relative capital construction costs. This example also supports the contention that the valuation of capital, or the determination of capital intensity, requires that the rate of profit must be first specified, and that such calculations be carried out at a given rate of profit in a given system. We cannot make statements about what would happen when the rate of profit changes, only about what would have been the case if the rate of profit had been different. As we noted above, the phenomenon we have been talking about has been called 'capital-reversal' because value capital and the rate of profit may move in the same direction, the reverse of the 'normal' inverse relation.

REVERSAL AND SWITCHING

We can look at the relationship of reversal to switching by utilising a diagram presented by Harcourt [17, p. 126]. This diagram follows Sraffa's approach and takes single techniques at all possible wage–profit rate combinations in a stationary state. Thus each point on the curve for a single technique shows the possible profit rate associated with a given wage rate. The relation of the value of capital per man for the technique to different rates of profit is shown in the lower portion of the diagram. In the diagram we have two techniques, a and b, with k_a and k_b representing the value of capital per man for the techniques at different profit rates. Note that technique b, represented by a straight line in the upper portion of the diagram, has a uniform ratio of means of production to labour for the production of both capital and consumption goods, and thus its line representing the value of capital per man, k_b, is the same despite differences in the notional profit rate. (This proposition comes up again in chapter 9).

Thus taking the two techniques shown in figure 7A.1, we can see that for real-wage rates above w_1 technique b yields a higher rate of profit; between w_1 and w_2 technique a is most profitable; and below w_2 technique b again becomes most profitable. Thus the choice, on

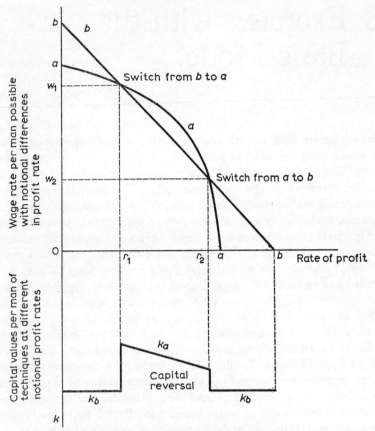

Figure 7A.1 Harcourt's Diagram showing Capital Reversal
and Double Switching for two techniques

grounds of profitability, of technique *b* at two different combinations
of wage and profit rates represents the reappearance of the same
technique at different rates of profit, or 'double switching'. The
lower portion of the diagram then shows the value of capital per
man of the technique chosen at different rates of profits and wages.
The two vertical shifts in the solid line then represent 'switching',
while the drop in the line on the right represents 'reversal', for the
capital value per man is higher when the rate of profit is higher.
(Note that moves down the page from 0 represent increases in *k*).

8 Exercises with the Basic Model

Remembering that we are always talking about comparisons between economic systems in steady tranquil conditions we can make some simple statements about the effects of different variables on the performance of the economic system. The systems we will be considering realise conditions of tranquillity as outlined above. The accumulated stock of capital equipment is appropriate to conditions actually ruling and, most importantly, expectations are continually being realised. Technical progress, when it exists, is assumed to occur at a steady rate so that large shifts in the spectra of available techniques do not disturb expectations or tranquility. New techniques are introduced in the gross investments being made each period. Thus at any point in time in the system where technical progress occurs there will be a number of different machines existing which were produced at different levels of technical knowledge. This causes no particular problem for the analysis as long as technical progress is, on balance, neutral, and the real wage per man rises in step with increasing output per man. These assumptions assure that the proportion of investment to total output is unaffected by technological progress, and therefore the ruling pattern of prices and rate of profit will be constant as the system moves along the path of steady growth.

In such conditions the rate of profit calculated on the results of past investment or on the present value of expected future yields of present investment come to the same thing. This is just another way of stating the tranquillity assumption.

Last, and most importantly, we assume that the capitalists in each economy considered are willing and able to carry out the rate of investment necessary to produce growth at the steady equilibrium rate postulated. Thus the capitalists have bouyant animal spirits and confident expectations, both of which are shared by the banking system which may from time to time be called upon to help finance the entrepreneurs investment desires. On the side of finance there is no 'fringe of unsatisfied borrowers'.

To start with, the steady rates of growth of the economies we will consider need not be 'golden age' rates of accumulation, but we must keep in the back of our minds that the 'golden age' sets a broad maximum (depending on how exogenous we assume technical progress to be) to the attainable rate of accumulation.

Taking our simple formula, $\pi = g/s_p$, we can outline the general factors that will be of major importance in analysing the process of growth:

(1) g: the rate of accumulation;
(2) s_p: thriftiness conditions – this is in reality the relation more commonly known as the consumption function;
(3) technological progress: the rate at which it occurs, its nature (capital saving or using), and whether it is exogenous or endogenous.

The different combinations of these variables will give different results in terms of different steady growth paths possible in a given economy.

We also note that the rate of growth of population will effect the 'golden age' growth path attainable. At the same time a rate of growth of employment that does not keep up with the rate of growth of population implies rising unemployment which may effect the ruling level of the money wage. We will, for the moment, assume the problem is non-existent by postulating a given rate of growth of population and a given money-wage rate, unaffected by the unemployment rate.

Each economy is assumed to be closed, with no government sector. This is not to deny the importance of international trade or government policy on the possible growth path of an economy, but simply to allow us to work out the structural relations on a simple level before introducing complications. The effect of international trade will be briefly discussed in chapter 12, and the government will make brief appearances below as well as in chapter 10.

We can now compare economies in similar circumstances concerning their supplies of natural resources, population, etc., experiencing steady growth by taking each at a point in the history of their development. For the moment we ignore the relation between the existing growth rate and the 'golden age' rate, assuming that any rate we consider does not conflict with the 'golden age' rate or cause any additional problems (such as excessive unemployment, etc.). These problems are stored away for later analysis.

THE INVESTMENT–CONSUMPTION RATIO

Let us start with a very simple case in which there is no technical progress. Two countries A and B have the same technique of production (because it is the only one available) and their capitalists have the same attitude toward thriftiness. Labourers consume all their income. The money wage is the same in both economies. The only difference is that in economy A the capitalists have a more positive attitude towards investment. Their 'animal spirits' are higher. They therefore desire a higher proportion of available resources for investment than their counterparts in economy B.

Thus in A at each point in time the ratio of investment to output is higher than in B; the higher rate of investment produces a higher rate of accumulation. If the rate of growth of the labour force is greater than the rate of accumulation in A there is unemployment in both economies. Unemployed labour is being taken into employment at a faster rate in A than in B, and its unemployment rate is growing less fast. If the rate of accumulation in A is just equal to the rate of population growth it is either in a 'golden age' or, if there is some existing unemployment its unemployment rate will be constant while it rises in B. If the rate of accumulation is higher than the rate of growth of population in A it will eventually reach full employment as a ceiling, the rate of accumulation it is trying to carry out being greater than the 'golden age' rate which is the maximum it can enjoy. In such a case the assumption of constant money wages no longer seems practical, and it is unlikely that the system can adjust to the proper rate of accumulation without inflation.

The higher rate of accumulation in A, however, implies that there is a higher ratio of money income to consumption goods there. This causes gross margins over prime costs, and thus prices to be higher than in B. The rate of profit is therefore also higher in A.

With the given money wage rate, higher prices mean lower real wages. We can look at this relationship in another way. The consumption sector workers in A have to supply consumption goods for the extra investment sector workers who contribute to the higher rate of accumulation (consumption by the capitalists aside). Thus, under these conditions, a higher rate of growth entails a higher rate of profit, and a lower real wage (remember that if we assume $s_D = 1$, the rate of growth is just equal to the rate of profit).

Since the technique in use in both economies is the same, with constant returns, the marginal product of labour should be the same in both of them. Yet the real wage is different when both are experiencing steady growth in their own conditions.

Neither can we say that the higher rate of growth in A is due to a higher preference of future over present consumption, for the workers who have no choice in the matter have to accept a lower real wage than their comrades in B who have a higher standard of living because their capitalists are less vigorous. Neither can we say that it is the time preference of the capitalists that accounts for the higher rate of growth, for as we have seen the capitalists can increase their consumption without diminishing their profit or the rate of growth. Here we can recall Kalecki's apt phrase, 'the workers spend what they get, the capitalists get what they spend'.

On the other hand, if the rate of growth in economy B is below the rate of growth of the labour force (as indicated above) then unemployment in B is growing at a faster rate in B than in A and some of the higher wages in B may be used to provide transfer payments to the unemployed; thus they may not be better off after all.

This example is not very useful, for it ignores the effects of technical progress. It is sufficient, however, to make the point that, other things being equal, a higher level of expectations on the part of the capitalists, producing a higher rate of growth, implies a higher rate of profit and a lower real wage. It also shows us how easy it is to confuse comparison with change and cause with effect. Here time preference explains nothing – at best it can describe a state of affairs (higher profit rates with lower overall consumption) – not explain why they occur.

THRIFTINESS CONDITIONS

We can now move to another example. This time let us assume that the capitalists in both countries have similar expectations and desire the same rate of accumulation. They differ, however, in their consumption desires. The capitalists in economy A, being more bent on social prestige, spend more of their profits on consumption goods and therefore save less.

Thus the rate of growth, g, is the same in both systems, but at each point in time aggregate demand is higher in A than in B. Therefore the aggregate mark-up and prices will be higher in economy A than in economy B and gross margins over prime costs will therefore be higher. The real wage is thus lower in A and the rate of profit received by the consumption-conscious capitalists is higher, allowing them to support their social consumption. The rate of growth is the same in both systems, but the workers in A have to content themselves with a lower real wage on account of 'socially necessary' consumption by the capitalists.

If the capitalists react positively to the rate of profit – higher profit rates increase the desire to invest (which we may well imagine) – then the rate of investment might be higher in A. We have assumed, however, that this is not the case. If there is an attempt by the capitalists in A to *raise* investment, our steady growth path is lost, for the stock of capital is different from what it would have been if the new expectations had prevailed initially. Such a case moves us outside strict comparisons.

At the same time it is, of course, not possible to say that if the capitalists in A suddenly developed great fellow-feeling for their workers and decided to reduce their consumption to the level prevailing in economy B that the workers in economy A could enjoy the higher level of real wages prevailing in B. Such an act of benevolence would most likely lead to an acute crisis in those consumption good industries which cater for capitalists' consumption, forcing them to lay-off labour, and the eventual generation of a slump in the economy as a whole.

Again in this example, since the rate of growth is the same in both economies but the rate of profit is different, it is impossible to say that the 'rate of time preference' determines the rate of accumulation or the rate of profit, for the former remains a result of the investment expectations of the capitalists and the latter is strongly affected by the social consumption that is expected of them.

This example has also assumed that techniques of production are constant. If there had been a choice among a number of available techniques it is most probable that the technique in use in economy A would have been different from that in B since the cost of labour in terms of the ruling real wage and the rate of profit required and expected on capital are different in A and B. If this were the case, it would make it even more difficult for A to reduce its consumption to that ruling in B, for then not only the composition of consumption goods, but also the techniques used in all production would be different from those required in the new, desired situation.

GROWTH RATES AND PROFIT RATES

Now we move on to a more complicated situation. This time we start by posing the question: 'Is it possible for the rate of growth to be different in two economies that have the same rate of profit?' We can answer this question by combining the two exercises above.

If the capitalists in economy A have a greater desire to accumulate, the rate of growth in A will be higher (this from the first example). If at the same time the capitalists in A have a lower propensity to consume out of their profits income than their counterparts in B, it is possible for the difference in thriftiness to offset the difference in desire to accumulate. From the second example we know that a higher degree of thriftiness produces a lower rate of profit for any given rate of accumulation. Thus it is possible for the higher thriftiness in A to cause the profit rate to be lower in A by just the amount that the greater desire to accumulate causes it to be higher.

This allows the rate of profit to be equal in both A and B (as well as the real wage) while A grows at a faster rate than B. The situation from the point of view of the workers is preferable in A for they get a higher rate of growth while enjoying the same real wage as the workers in country B. This is on account of the capitalists in A being more thrifty. If there is a system of transfer payments at work to provide unemployment benefits then the workers in B are even worse off for more and more of the wages go to supporting the unemployed labourers that result from its lower rate of accumulation (and thus lower rate of growth in employment).

The limiting case of such an example would be what has been called the 'golden rule' of accumulation. In such a case the capitalists invest all their profits which leaves all the consumption goods to the workers. Apart from the benefits this gives to the position of real wages, it also gives the maximum rate of increase in employment, thus diminishing the necessity of transfers to the unemployed. This proposition reaches its *summum* when it provides new employment opportunities at the same rate as the employable labour force is growing, or in other words a 'golden age' with $s_p = 1$, and $s_w = 0$.

There are distinct problems of course when it exceeds the rate of growth of labour. One solution to these problems is technical progress, which we now finally introduce into our simple exercises.

TECHNOLOGICAL PROGRESS AND STEADY GROWTH

Up to this point we have assumed that the technique of production in use was unchanged over time. This meant that higher or lower rates of accumulation required a greater or lesser utilisation of the available labour force, since total output could only grow at a faster rate if more workers were employed to produce machines of given output per man to provide employment for additional labour. We have thus had to assume that the rate of growth of the labour force was always sufficient to allow the rate of accumulation postulated. This also implied the existence of unemployment (of an increasing amount) when the same rate of growth of the labour force ruled in two countries with different rates of accumulation.

Changes in the spectra of technique have their most important effect on this margin of unemployment, and on the position of the inflation barrier. We recall that a new spectrum raises output per man employed on the new technique in respect to the previously existing technique, and that neutral progress is such that it does not disturb the proportions of investment to consumption, and thus leaves the pattern of prices and the profit rate unchanged.

We now assume that technological change is a matter of course in the economies that we have under consideration, and that it occurs at a steady rate over time. Thus, with a higher rate of neutral technical progress occurring in economy *A* than in economy *B*, the rate of increase in output per man will be higher in *A* than *B*. The rate of growth is also higher by this difference, assuming that both are alike in all other respects. If *A* is on a steady path of growth, the rate of increase of the real wage is also higher in economy *A* than in economy *B*.

The higher rate of growth in *A* comes not only without penalty to the workers in terms of decreased consumption, but indeed allows the rate of growth of consumption to be higher. Thus, if there is some readily determined level below which the trade unions will not allow the real wage to fall without a fight (the 'inflation barrier') it will occur at a higher proportion of investment to output in *A* than in economy *B*. The capitalists in *A* have more leeway to increase accumulation (or less happily, increase consumption) than their brothers in *B*.

In economy *A* every combination of investment to output implies a real wage higher than that found in *B* for similar conditions. This is a result of the higher rate of increase in productivity per man when both are assumed to start experiencing technical change at the same level of technology.

If the 'inflation barrier' occurs at a physically determined amount of consumption per man this amount will correspond to a higher rate of accumulation (or higher capitalists' consumption) in economy *A* than in economy *B*. There is no reason to believe, however, that the 'inflation barrier' will be the same in both or that it will be a fixed amount in economies in which the real wage is continually rising over time.

Within the terms of our present example, when the two economies are the same in respect of the capitalists' desires for accumulation, consumption, etc., a higher rate of neutral technical progress implies that *A* will have a higher rate of growth as well as a higher rate of growth of real wages for its labour; the real wage of labour rising at the same rate as productivity per man in order to provide purchasing power over the more rapidly increasing quantity of goods. Thus the rate of rise in the real wage is higher in *A* in the same degree as its rate of productivity growth is higher. At the same time there is thus less risk of the capitalists in *A* trying to accumulate at a rate that bumps the inflation barrier causing the workers to demand higher money-wages, for the inflation barrier, if the same in both economies, will come into play at a higher rate of accumulation in *A* than in *B*.

TECHNOLOGICAL PROGRESS AND UNEMPLOYMENT

The influence of technical progress on the inflation barrier suggests another example. Is it possible for the capitalists to take advantage of the potential rise in real wages by increasing their desire to invest? Putting the question differently, is it possible for an economy with a higher rate of technical progress to have the same rate of change of the real wage as the economy with the lower rate of technical change? The answer is to be found in the relation of purchasing power. If a given amount of employment can produce an increasing amount of output due to the rise in productivity, then a smaller amount of labour can produce the same amount of consumption goods, leaving labour consumption unchanged and additional labour to be used in the investment sector. Thus we see that it would be possible for economy *A* with its higher productivity to support a higher rate of investment to output than in economy *B*, but at the same time pay its labourers the same real wage. Thus the benefit of the higher productivity can be turned into higher profitability. If at the same time this higher profitability is an encouragment to investment, economy *A* may be increasing its employment of labour at a faster rate than economy *B*, and thus its unemployment rate will be falling. If this is the case, higher technical progress may effect the rate of unemployment for a given rate of growth of the labour force. But this is only strictly true if the capitalists' desires for accumulation had been consistently higher *over time* in *A* than in *B*, so that *A* combines a higher rate of investment with its higher rate of productivity growth, thus giving it a higher overall rate of growth and rate of increase in employment (and a further impetus to searching for more productive techniques to the extent that technical progress is influenced by the rate of accumulation).

Thus higher productivity allows a higher rate of accumulation without damaging the real wage of the labour force. As can only too easily be seen, the same story could also be told for a higher propensity to consume by the capitalists, but without the same beneficial effects to the employment situation.

In a more realistic light, technological change causes some knotty problems in terms of assuring that the capitalists maintain investment at a level high enough to preserve steady growth over time.

TECHNOLOGICAL PROGRESS AND NECESSARY INVESTMENT

Consider the capitalist making his investment decisions when technological change is occurring over time. If he considers only his productive capacity he can maintain a constant amount of productive capacity with a diminishing number of machines, for the productive capacity of machines is rising. He can also maintain a constant rate of increase in productive capacity without increasing the number of machines that he has in operation. If each machine employs the same amount of labour, irrespective of its productivity, in either case the rate of increase in the demand for labour falls as technical progress increases productivity. Thus the capitalist would be required to accumulate machines at an increasing rate if the same rate of accumulation and employment on the economy-wide level is to be maintained with a growing population. If the population is constant he must keep a constant number of machines and maintain his rate of growth of productive capacity.

We can, of course, postulate this type of behaviour for the capitalists in our economy, but we must realise that such behaviour need not always be the case, for increasing productivity appears to the capitalists as falling costs per unit of output, and thus appears as a higher rate of profit. But appearance becomes reality only if investment is kept up.

The increase in output potential due to rising productivity thus cannot be viewed as a simple addition to the analysis as worked out in its absence. It changes the objective conditions the capitalist faces at each point in time. With technical progress going on new machines will be available which produce different amounts of output at different costs, and with different profitability, and probably with different input costs. The world he faces never stays the same and is always changing, expectations will become more volatile, the future less certain. Changes in output and employment due to small changes in investment thus may have greater effect and consequence.

When the financing aspects implied in the above very simple sketch are added (in combination with either (a) falling prices, or (b) rising wages in money to assure that purchasing power grows with productivity) then the decisions faced by the capitalists become even more complicated and less certain. We see that our assumptions about the capitalists always having the 'animal spirits' necessary to carry out the investment necessary to preserve the steady growth path is in reality rather extravagant. Thus tranquil conditions, far from being the normal state of affairs, will be an exception. This becomes especially obvious when we introduce technological progress into these simple exercises. And further, we have only looked at the case of mythical 'neutral' technical progress within the realm of our abstract analysis.

We are thus warned of the extremely unrealistic nature of our analysis. That even this simple approach raises difficult problems for the maintenance of steady growth tells us that any actual situation will be even more difficult. The exercises presented here are of the most elementary nature, not having touched on the problems of bias in technical progress or the effects of choice of technique, which as we saw in the preceding chapter is extremely complicated.

There are many other less complicated exercises that the student can construct by simply changing the conditions of the comparisons with which he works. One possibility is in terms of the relation of the actual to the 'golden age' rate of growth. Such exercises, as well as those of increasing difficulty are to be found in R. F. Kahn's 'Exercises in the Analysis of Economic Growth' [24], and essay 2 in Joan Robinson's *Essays in the Theory of Economic Growth* [86].

Some suggestions for simple exercises that could be worked out on the basis of those presented above might include taking neutral technical progress and working out the effects of changes in the length of the working day rather than changes in money wages or falling prices as a means for producing steady growth with rising output per man. Another might involve introducing the costs of capital expenditures by firms for the treatment of effluent wastes in the production process, looking at the effects of such expenditures on the ratio of investment to consumption, and the share of wages and profits. One should not be surprised if he finds that the costs of improving the environment fall mainly on wages. Finally, on the simple level, the introduction of income taxation and government purchase or production of consumption and capital goods can be simply introduced along the lines shown above.

The important thing to learn from these exercises, however, is (1) the method of using comparisons rather than changes as a starting point for the analysis of the effect of different variables on the long-run growth path, (2) the ease with which causes can be confused with effects in relations drawn from the comparative static analysis used by the neoclassical theory, and (3) the operation of the income flow mechanism of the model, following the effects of changes through to the relations between the consumption and capital goods sectors, finding the resulting differences in aggregate supply and demand for consumption goods, the difference in the mark-ups, pattern of prices, profit and real-wage rates, etc., between the systems being compared. The exercises first give us a method of thought and analysis which we can then apply to the resolution of questions and contradictions involved in the process of expansion of an economy that exists in history.

Part Three

9 Value, Distribution and Measurement

The Problem of Capital

As we shall see the measurement of capital is in one sense a new problem and in another a very, very old one. It is also in one sense the same problem as that of measuring all output in the economic system, and in another sense a problem associated with a particular approach to economics. In particular it is associated with the way value, distribution and time are explained. Thus we will find that the approach to measurement in general and to capital measurement in particular will differ between the classical and neoclassical theory just as their explanations of value and distribution differ. The two theories thus approach measurement in different ways and for different purposes.

As a general proposition the problem of measurement over time is common to all disciplines. It appears to have been first introduced by the Greek philosophers, especially with Heraclitus' theory of flux. In a world that moves through time, in which nature continually changes, it is rather difficult to make general statements about that world. If one can never step into the same river twice it is difficult to make general statements about any river, much less the one you thought you stepped in twice. This leads directly to the necessity for some kind of standard, some measure against which one can measure the things that are changing, in order to be able to make specific statements about the changes.

Without some such measure one is reduced to simple description: at a certain time, on a certain day, in a certain place, under certain specific conditions, such and such happened (I stepped into a river). It may happen again, it may not; it is impossible to say.

Measurement is thus a general problem for all types of science. Plato sought to resolve the problem by postulating the existence of the Idea, which could only be imperfectly known by imputing its nature from existing forms. One could then measure movements in society in terms of deviations from this norm of Idea. It was the goal of society to stay as close as possible to the norm, although Plato believed that we were always moving away from it. It was left to the philosopher kings to arrest the deterioration.

The same problem of measurement through time exists in the science that we call economics (in Germany it surfaced in the hotly contested *Methodenstreit*, and in America with the Institutionalists, both long before its present revival in another guise). The problem is first taken seriously by the Classical economists, Ricardo in particular (cf. chapter 2, above).

Political economy, from Ricardo's viewpoint, was primarily concerned with the explanation of the distribution of income among the three classes of the community in 'different stages of society' [71, I, p. 5]. But in order to be able to make statments about the distribution of the national income over time it was necessary to have a distinct measure of the product that was distributed. Ricardo 'was troubled by the fact that the size of this product appears to change when the division changes. Even though nothing has occurred to change the magnitude of the aggregate, there may be *apparent* changes due solely to change in measurement, owing to the fact that measurement is in terms of value and relative values have been altered as a result of a change in the division between wages and profits' [71, I, p. xlviii].

This can be seen by taking an economy in which the proportions of labour to means of production are different for different outputs. In such a case a higher share of profit (and rate of profit) would require a higher price for those industries employing a higher proportion of means of production to labour than those employing a lower proportion of means of production to labour, when competition is assumed to drive the rate of profit to equality in all industries. In such conditions the relative price of all goods produced by labour and means of production would not change in the same proportions, but would rise more than proportionately for those goods with a higher proportion of means of production to labour, and less than proportionately for those with less than average means of production to labour. In such cases the sum of prices for the same amount of physical output could be different when the distribution of income between wages and profits was different. This meant that one could not unequivocally say whether a higher or lower portion of the surplus of output over inputs was actually being received by a given class when the money sum of its distributive share changed.

As Ricardo was interested in promoting growth by distributing more real resources to the capitalists who would invest them in productive enterprise (rather than to the landlords who would squander them on high living and unproductive servants) it was important to be able to determine whether the capitalists were indeed receiving more resources when distribution changed. The only way to be sure was to have a measure of the social product that was independent of distribution, or an invariable measure of value; something like height or weight as used in the natural sciences.

The measurement problem for Ricardo was then directly concerned with measurement over time and was not restricted to the measurement of any particular commodity or group of commodities, but to the output of the system as a whole.

It is a great desideratum in Polit. Econ. to have a perfect measure of absolute value in order to be able to ascertain what relation commodities bear to each other at distant periods. Any thing having value is a good measure of the comparative value of all other commodities at the same time and place, but will be of no use in indicating the variations in their absolute value at distant times and in distant places [71, IV, p. 396].

We also note that the problem of finding an invariable standard of value was in no way related to Ricardo's explanation of the changes in the distribution of income over time. The evolution of the shares of landlords, labour and the capitalists is tied up with the increasing difficulty of producing subsistence for the labour force as less and less productive land is brought into use. Thus with social forces keeping the wage at subsistence the real wage is constant, but with the increasing difficulty of producing the wage on inferior land the share of rents would rise at the expense of the profit on capital. Thus the story of the eventual possibility of the stationary state. Whether or not one accepts this theory as realistic, it does not depend in a crucial way on solving the measurement problem. The difficulties with measurement only affect the ability to talk about the magnitudes of the changes that will be taking place.

Thus the problems associated with Ricardo's labour theory of value in deriving a measure of value do not impinge on his explanation of the process of distribution. Likewise the assumption of uniform ratios of labour to means of production that is necessary for labour embodied in commodities to bear the same ratio as their relative exchange values.

As Sraffa points out, 'Ricardo was not interested for its own sake in the problem of why two commodities produced by the same quantities of labour are not of the same exchangeable value. He was concerned with it only in so far as thereby relative values are affected by changes in wages', and that the problem of differences between relative exchange value and relative labour embodied has no place in the search for an invariable measure of value [71, i, p. xlix].

Ricardo realised that his measure in terms of labour time did not meet his requirements for an invariable standard, as the paper written just before his death makes clear [71, iv, pp. 361–412]. The main problem, however, was not that prices did not correspond to labour values.

We note, however, that Ricardo was looking for a measure that was in some sense independent of the relations of distribution and circulation in the actual economy, in an effort to provide statements about changes in distribution among the classes of society over time. For Ricardo steady movement in the system was specified in terms of the prices and values that would be established in a system that could reproduce its inputs that had been used up in production with a remaining surplus. Normal values of prices and profits were those which allowed the system to expand over time in a more or less steady manner, with market prices moving above and below normal values in accordance with the day to day changes in market conditions; but always tied loosely to the normal values required for reproduction with a surplus. Ricardo's concern for the conditions necessary for reproduction in the system, and his emphasis on the surplus over inputs as the main source of accumulation and investment thus ties directly into his restriction of the labour theory of value to only those goods that could be produced and reproduced over time with labour and means of production and the product that he was interested in measuring through time. This conception of the economic system and its measurement is, as we shall see below, quite different from that of the later neoclassical economists.

MARX AND THE LABOUR MEASURE

For Marx, the measurement problem was superficially the same as for Ricardo, but Marx approached the problem from a different angle and, in a sense, changed the question that had bothered Ricardo.

From Marx's point of view Ricardo had made an error in combining a labour measure of value with the value of national output measured in terms of prices. To translate labour into value terms it was necessary to use the wage of labour as the measure of the quantity of labour. This brought the problem back into the sphere of circulation and distribution (as Ricardo realised [71, IV, p. 392]) and thus labour measured in terms of the subsistence wage could not be invariable to changes in distribution.

Marx distinguished the double nature of labour, first as the basic element in production and reproduction, and secondly as a commodity that was bought and sold like any other commodity and thus with a price (the wage) like any other commodity. The amount of labour effort and the price of labour were different things.

The wage (as effectively used by Ricardo) was determined by the production and circulation relations in the system and was thus subject to change with changes in these relations. Labour, in terms of the wage, could thus not be used to measure anything except as an indication of the amount of necessary labour time required for labour to produce its needs of subsistence in any given period of historical development. The difference between the amount of labour time necessary to produce subsistence and the total amount of time worked by the labourer (because the capitalist had purchased the worker's labour power) was the measure of surplus labour time, or the exploitation of labour.

Simple labour time was the measure of value created by the labourer, the wage was the measure of the value of labour power (the amount of goods necessary to reproduce the commodity labour power) that the capitalist purchased with the wage. The two concepts were quite different, one being determined by the specific production and social relations ruling at a given point in the process of the development of capitalism, the other, external to those relations, could be used as a measuring device reducing labour to simple abstract labour time. Thus Marx was not primarily interested in the consistent measure of total output in terms of prices, but in a characterisation of social relations that gave an insight into the comprehension of the social division of output under capitalism as a social relation. Here the use of labour time as a measure external to the forces of distribution gives a direct insight into the problem of distribution. Simple labour time thus becomes the unique measure of both the value of the commodity labour power and the value of all output produced in the system.

It is also important to add that the divergence of actual prices of production (similar to Ricardo's normal prices including the rate of profit on capital) from values in terms of labour time in Marx's scheme differs from the similar problem found in Ricardo. The divergence of prices from labour values, however, was not viewed as being of prime importance by either of them. In Ricardo's search for the invariable standard of value the problem arises with different distributions of the national output, thus a given quantity of labour corresponds to a different measure for total output in terms of prices when the wage and profit rate are different.

For Marx the problem of the transformation of labour values into prices of production was taken up with the distribution of income given (by the rate of exploitation determined on an aggregate scale in the class struggle between free labour and the owners of the means of production) and it explained the operation of the capitalist system under conditions of private ownership of the means of production and free labour. Transformation was then not a problem, either in finding an invariant measure of value, nor in relating relative quantities of embodied labour to the relative prices of particular products. It was instead an explanation of the method by which the system of circulation under capitalism distributed the created surplus-value amongst the capitalists in proportion to the money value of the means of production each capitalist contributed to the production of output.

We can sketch the problem quite simply on the aggregate level. With the rate of exploitation determined by the overall class struggle between free labour and the owners of the means of production, each labourer is exploited to the same degree whether he works for a capitalist who utilises more or less than the average amount of capital in his production process. This, however, implies that capitalists using the same labour force with a higher than average amount of capital have a lower ratio of surplus value per unit of capital since the amount of surplus they can extract is the same as that for the capitalists using a less than average capital. Surplus is the result of employing live labour, not capital.

It is the operation of the competitive system of circulation that assures that prices of production are higher for capitalists using more capital, so that surplus value produced in industries with lower amounts of capital per man is transferred to the capitalists employing a higher amount of capital per man. In this manner surplus value becomes capitalists' profit which is higher for capitalists using more capital and vice versa such that the ratio of profit to the value of capital is equalised for all capitalists irrespective of the amount of capital they actually employ.

Thus the transformation process only occurs when privately owned means of production exist in an economy with free labour, and it explains how the capitalists divide up the surplus value that they have extracted from labour among themselves such that each receives the same rate of profit on his capital, despite differences in capital per worker.[1] Thus the fact that, under capitalism, prices would diverge from labour values did not cause Marx any problems in valuation (nor would the fact that the value of output changed with changes in the distribution – a problem Marx ruled out by taking distribution as determined by the rate of exploitation) because he could see no use in measuring in anything but labour time – it was certainly of little interest that this did or did not correspond to price measures.

Aside then from the use to which Marx puts his labour theory, we can see that he has created a truly external measure of the size of output in the system, and that it in no sense depends on the internal distribution relations of the system. In addition, it can be used to make statements about those relations precisely because it is independent of them. The basic difference from Ricardo is the dual concept of labour and the explanation of transformation, given the distribution of income as determined by the rate of exploitation. Like Ricardo, measurement in Marx is not crucial to his theory of

[1] It is interesting to note that Samuelson [98] has recently accepted the possibility of using labour time as a measure of value, but at the same time seems to believe that the transformation relation is equally valid in Adam Smith's beaver and deer example as it might be on the moon. Without recognising the specific production and circulation relations necessary for the problem to exist it is impossible to grasp the meaning Marx gave to the proposition or analyse it in a meaningful way. Samuelson thus reaches the odd conclusion that Marx's model is founded on a given subsistence wage, rather than on the determination of the rate of exploitation under capitalism.

distribution; it is, however, necessary to see through the surface phenomena of capitalism to get to the basis of distribution (and exploitation) in the relation between capital and labour in the process of production.

SRAFFA AND THE REVIVAL OF RICARDO

Piero Sraffa has recently revived interest in Ricardo's problem of an invariant standard of value by providing a solution in terms of the 'Standard commodity'[2] which is a combination of all the commodities produced in the system, given in such proportions that relative prices are invariant overall to changes in the distribution of the surplus of the system between wages and profits.

The derivation of the Standard commodity is a rather complicated procedure and we will not attempt to explain it here. Sraffa's approach follows Ricardo's concern with those commodities that can be produced and reproduced by means of labour and means of production. The 'Standard system' that produces the 'Standard commodity' is thus composed of commodities that enter as inputs into the production processes of all commodities produced in the system (and are thus also inputs for the next round of production). The Standard system is derived from the actual processes of production in such a manner that the resulting system of production equations uses commodities as inputs in the aggregate in the same proportions as it produces commodities as outputs.

Thus any difference in the wage and the rate of profit (between zero and the maximum rate of surplus which occurs when the subsistence wage rules) produces changes in commodity prices of goods produced with a higher proportion of means of production to labour that are offset in the aggregate by opposite changes in goods produced with lower than average proportions of means of production to labour. When any price change up or down is offset by a change in the price of another good in the opposite direction the Standard commodity will be invariant to changes in the distribution of a given surplus between wages and profits, i.e., the same value sum will always be associated with the same physical sum of output no matter how the surplus is distributed between wages and profits.

[2] For further explanations of Sraffa's system the reader is directed to [17, pp. 177–204; 2, or 41, chapter 2.]

Sraffa makes no attempt to explain how distribution is determined, and the use and creation of the invariable measure sought by Ricardo is compatible with any explanation of the distribution process. This supports the contention above that the problem of finding an invariant measure was independent of Ricardo's theory of distribution.

In the sense that Sraffa's Standard commodity requires specification of the processes of production actually used and the distribution of surplus actually ruling (independent of why it is so), the analysis is similar to Marx's insistence that economic analysis must make reference to the specific relations of production actually in existence at a point in historical development.

This, however, is where the similarities stop, for Sraffa does not comment on the determination of the rate of profit or say anything about the social relations of production. Neither does he make any reference to change through time, the entire analysis is carried out at a specific point in time. Sraffa strictly limits his analysis to comparisons of different distributions of product and never speaks of actual changes occurring through the passage of time.[3] In this sense Sraffa notes that it is impossible to make any statements about a quantity of capital or a quantity of output as a whole without prior reference to the rate of profit prevailing in the system (or alternatively the wage).

Finally, we note that Sraffa's solution to Ricardo's problem of measurement applies to all output in the system, and is achieved by referring to an external device that is an imaginary construction of the actual production relations in an economy capable of producing and reproducing itself over time with a surplus to be divided between capital owners and labour. These factors are uniform in all purely classical approaches to the problem of finding a measure for the performance of the economic system over time.

NEOCLASSICAL DISTRIBUTION, EQUILIBRIUM AND MEASUREMENT

A different method of measurement is offered by the neoclassical economists as a result of their rejection of viewing economics from the point of view of production relations in terms of real physical

---

[3] Samuelson [98] seems not to have noticed the significance of this methodological approach and appears to believe that the construction of Sraffa's Standard commodity and Marx's analysis of transformation are similar propositions.

costs of production. With given endowments of factors this theory sought to demonstrate that the price system would produce a vector of equilibrium prices through the forces of supply and demand that would produce the full employment of all factors. At the same time the forces of supply and demand would determine the distribution of income, not between social classes, but between factors services by determining the prices of the factors through supply and demand in the market. Assuming the operation of the price system in this manner, price became the measure of all value (price was equal value) and of factors quantities; the equilibrium vector of factor prices became the standard by which movements in the economy were measured. This explains to a certain extent the neoclassical preoccupation with existence and stability analysis.

Thus in actual fact there are two distinct measurement problems in the neoclassical approach. The first concerns the measure of the quantity of factors that are priced in the market, the second the measurement of changes in factor quantities over time. In difference to the Classical analysis, however, the first problem (which was not considered to be a problem by the neoclassists) is crucial to the theory of distribution that they propose, and thus reflects directly on the usefulness of the second as a measure over time. This difference exists for, as pointed out above, the Classical problem of measurement was independent of the theory of distribution; in the neoclassical it is not.

If distribution is to be explained in terms of supply and demand for factors on the aggregate level (as for the 'factors' land, labour and capital, cf. chapter 2, above) the factors must first have a measure, and for the aggregate analysis of 'factors,' must have a homogeneous measure to allow aggregation. Now land and labour have natural units and are more or less naturally occurring units. Capital, on the other hand, is a produced means of production – it requires labour and means of production to be produced, and is thus not a naturally occurring factor. If its return is to be determined by supply and demand its quantity must be measured in some units – at both the level of specific capital goods and as an aggregate 'factor'. The neoclassical method was to measure capital goods in terms of their price, the aggregate quantity was then the sum of the value of capital goods. But this is logically impossible if the quantity is to be measured before the price is to be determined by supply and demand in the market for capital. As we have seen in chapter 7, and in Sraffa's analysis, it is necessary to have a prior determined rate of profit (price of capital) to be able to determine a quantity of capital in value terms. Without such a measure of quantity independent of price it is impossible to say that the 'price' of the 'factor' capital will be high or low when its quantity is in short or plentiful supply. Neither can the price of capital then determine the return or share of capital in output.

Thus, in the neoclassical theory, the measure of a particular type of output in the system – capital – is necessary; and the ability to measure this quantity is crucial to the theory of distribution (and price) that it proposes. Whereas neither of these problems were of importance in the Classical theory, they are of crucial importance to the neoclassical. Thus our opening statement to this chapter. The measure of capital as simply part of all produced output was part of the Classical problem, but it is a new problem as required for the neoclassical theory of distribution in the sense of the measurement of a particular type of output (capital) in order to identify a quantity that can be priced. The reader should instantly recognise that this neoclassical problem is unrelated to measurement over time (the principal Classical problem) and directly related to the 'perverse' case of chapter 7, where it was found that there is no way to make a statement about the relation between the value of capital and its price as required by supply and demand because capital is a product and not a naturally occurring means of production. Thus the prices of inputs will affect the quantity of capital, and the price of capital may vary positively or negatively with its quantity in value terms (i.e., measured in terms of the prices of capital goods).

By accepting the theory of distribution in terms of supply and demand the neoclassical theory did not recognise the problem of the measure of the quantity of capital and they therefore accepted as fact that prices, as determined by the market could be used as measures of value, at a point in time or over time. Thus for the neoclassical theory there is never a thought of a problem of measurement over time in the sense of Ricardo, for all changes over time can be taken in relation to the equilibrium position as established by the market forces of supply and demand. The moving equilibrium position, in terms of an equilibrium price vector, thus replaces the external measure sought by the Classics. This removes the vexing problem faced by Ricardo, for in equilibrium prices are assumed to be equal to values (cf. chapter 2, above) so that if equilibrium is achieved, prices can be used to aggregate total output and the sum of prices times output quantities gives a measure of the change in output over time whatever the distribution of income produced by the market. Establishing the existence and the uniqueness of the equilibrium vector of prices then becomes the measurement goal of the neoclassical theory. If the vector exists, and is unique and stable, it is also a unique standard of measurement. The difficulty in proving uniqueness (cf. [1, 7]) then appears to be the only problem faced by this type of measurement.

In fact, of course, it remains true that changes in the distribution of income will affect relative prices, and thus any measure that uses them to measure output, but this problem is hidden away by the acceptance of a theory of distribution based on supply and demand which produces the equilibrium position which is the sole requirement for neoclassical measurement.

Once it is recognised that the price of capital cannot be used to provide a measure of the quantity of capital (in the specific or aggregate) which is not a naturally occurring commodity, but a produced means of production, it is no longer possible to simply refer to the existing equilibrium prices in order to determine the quantity of capital or the rate of profit (its price) that it earns, or changes in overall output in time.

The utilisation of the unique position of equilibrium also casts a strong shadow of conservatism over the neoclassical analysis as well as impeding its analysis of the growth process. If there is only one possible position of equilibrium to be used as a measuring rod, any change from this position is automatically viewed as something suboptimal. In fact, any change from the existing situation represents a deterioration from the existing state of affairs. Under such conditions it is easy to see how the *status quo* can be consistently defended as the only preferable position, all others representing disequilibrium, i.e., a state of affairs that is undesirable and that can be shown to soon revert to the initial equilibrium state. The use of the strictly internally generated equilibrium position as a measurement device thus makes the analysis of any change in the system extremely difficult, as all changes are of a momentary, logical nature that do not change the basic structure of the system, which always finds its way back to the desired equilibrium.

To preserve the concept of equilibrium in a dynamic context thus requires that all variables change at a predetermined rate over time (the model is differentiated with respect to time), leaving the equilibrium proportions unchanged. It is thus impossible to introduce changes in production techniques, economies of large scale production, or simple increasing returns into the analysis in a meaningful way, for such phenomena change the given proportions in the equation system; each change producing a new set of equilibrium prices, uncomparable with the preceding. If such economic aspects of economic change are introduced the property of uniqueness ceases to have distinct meaning and the concept of the equilibrium position as represented by a vector of prices is of no use as a measure of the system's performance. The equilibrium position is thus only meaningful in a system whose basic structure remains unchanged over time, or in which such changes produce no effect on the equilibrium achieved. The theory remains, as it was initially set up, to show what the equilibrium position should be under given conditions with given bundles of resources distributed amongst a given number of traders. In such circumstances the equilibrium serves only to show that some such position can exist, not that the system will be there, but as a normative statement that it should. In terms of a measure of dynamic change in a system the equilibrium position is of limited usefulness, serving mainly to show that any change that might disturb it is non-optimal, providing no means for making statements about any other position which may be thrown up through changes in technique that are not Harrod neutral or returns to scale that are not constant. In fact, the common assumption of constant returns to scale in most dynamic neoclassical models serves to forbid the analysis of any economic change that would change the basic structure and thus the equilibrium of the system.

In sum, we see that there are two related problems of measurement in the neoclassical approach. The measure of the quantity of capital is a particular problem for the neoclassical theory and is directly related to the neoclassical explanation of distribution. For the Classical approach the measure of capital as such was no more a problem than that of the measurement of all output over time and was in no way crucial to the theory of distribution that was posited in the Classical theory. Thus the assumption of a uniform ratio of capital to labour in all processes of production (e.g. [97]) serves a very different purpose than in the Classical approach. In the neoclassical theory it allows the theory of distribution to be divorced from the problem of measurement by making the value of capital independent of the rate of profit, thus allowing capital to be valued in such a way that price varies inversely with quantity (cf. technique b in Figure 7A.1 above where the value of capital per man, k_b, is constant for all rates of profit). For the Classical theory it solves the problem of relative prices being different from relative quantities of labour embodied in commodities. For Marx this was not a problem, but an explanation of a fact of life under capitalism, and the assumption is thus neither desirable nor necessary. For Ricardo, as Sraffa indicates, the difference between prices and labour values, 'has no counterpart in an investigation' of the effect of a change in wages on relative values which necessitated the search for an invariable measure of value [71, i, p. xlix]. The assumption of a uniform ratio of capital to labour is thus crucial for the neoclassical theory of distribution and the use of prices for unique valuation of quantities at a point in time and over time; it is not so in the Classical approaches to the problem of measurement over time and has no relation to the Classical explanation of income distribution.

The distinction between an external measure of output and change in the economic system, and an internal measure in terms of prices established in a unique equilibrium position is crucial to understanding why the neoclassical economist is so puzzled by the valuation questions raised by the post-Keynesian writers, of which Joan Robinson was the first in recent times.

THE MEASURE OF CAPITAL

It is with Professor Joan Robinson that the problem of the measure of the quantity of capital in the neoclassical theory is first raised. In trying to derive a theory of the determination of the rate of profit she found that she could make no sense out of the concept of capital as used in the aggregate production function. She thus demanded of the production function practitioners just exactly what they meant when they wrote C for aggregate capital in the production function.[4]

Secondly, in order to focus on the problem of capital accumulation and the determination of the rate of profit on capital, she carries out her own analysis on the assumptions of a consumption basket of commodities of given proportions produced under constant returns. It thus only remains to value capital produced in the systems

---

[4] Joan Robinson [82]. It should be noted that this was well before the first appearance of models of neoclassical economic growth based on the aggregate production function, e.g. [52, 101, 108].

under consideration in her analyses of economies growing and accumulating capital over time.

In terms of actual measurement Professor Robinson takes a pragmatic if almost nihilistic position, believing that the problem is absolutely insoluble in practice. She considers Ricardo's search for a natural measure, similar to height and weight, misintended, for height and weight correspond to the natural units to which they apply; but economics is a social science and thus there is no reason to believe that concepts that exist in natural science will have like counterparts in social relations. Value is, for Professor Robinson, a social relation, while capital viewed from the point of view of producing output is a technical factor of production.

She likewise rejects Marx's labour measure as both without practical application and unnecessary to the rest of the analysis of the structural relations of a capitalist economy.[5]

Despite this strong scepticism in the efficacy of a measure of value, Professor Robinson does attempt to provide some type of measure in order to be able to make statements about changes in the economic models that she analyses. She offers four possible alternative methods of measuring the capital stock: (1) in terms of specific physical aspects of capital goods; (2) in terms of the productive capacity of capital goods; (3) in terms of the value of capital goods measured in units of the consumption basket; and (4) in terms of the labour time embodied in the production of capital goods.

It is obvious enough that the first measure is only consistent if capital goods are all physically identical. If techniques of production are not identical (as represented by say, a change in the division of labour where a single machine combines two processes formerly carried out in two single steps with labour and hand tools) the capital goods will not be physically similar, so this measure fails without further enquiry.

The second measure also fails under the possibility of differences in technique, for a difference in technique in itself implies a difference in the productivity per man of a given expenditure on capital equipment. Thus if the physical resources (labour and means of production over similar time periods) required for two different

[5] Cf. [78, 79, 81]. Professor Robinson is, perhaps, too harsh in her judgement of Marx's attempt at measurement when it is accepted that Marx did not try to derive labour values from prices. Indeed, one might think that Marx's labour measure represents just the type of social measure that might correspond to natural measures in the natural sciences.

techniques are the same, the same amount of productive capacity may be associated with widely differing amounts of resources embodied in the capital stock when the capital stock represents different techniques of production and thus different productivity per man.

The last two measures Professor Robinson finds of slightly more promise. Measurement in terms of commodities can be looked at in terms of the commodity selling price of the capital unit, i.e. the amount of profit in terms of commodities expected from the machine over its useful life discounted at the ruling rate of profit, or in terms of the commodity costs of construction of the equipment less any profit earned discounted at the ruling rate of profit up to the point in time when the measurement is taken. This measure closely resembles the use of productive capacity, but instead focusses on the costs or value of the equipment in terms of the given commodity bundle that the capital equipment must aid in producing. The measure is thus in terms of the commodities it will produce over its life, or the commodities that must be used to support the labour force over the construction period, suitable discounts being taken for the time commodity values are tied up in the equipment before full amortisation.

To enable the first three measures to produce the same measurement results a system (or two like systems) would have to be in steady equilibrium growth (at the same rate for two systems) with a uniform rate of profit, for then prices, profits and real wages would all be uniform over time and would be the same no matter what point in the life of the economy was chosen for measurement. But even this situation is subject to imperfections, for it is always possible for an economy to be at a real-wage rate that represents a transition between two possible techniques of production, and thus both techniques will be in use at the same time. Another economy, just starting the transition or just finishing the transition, will be using one technique or the other uniquely.

Thus even when the value of capital is the same in both economies, the first economy with both techniques of production in use will have a different total productive capacity than the second economy with only a single technique in use. It is also obvious that the physical specifications of the capital in use in each economy will be different.

The fourth measure can be constructed by going one step further and dividing the value of capital in terms of commodities by the commodity wage rate. This gives a measure of value in terms of labour time required for production standardised in terms of the commodity bundle. But it is impossible to completely reduce capital to labour time in this manner, for even in the earliest pre-capitalist times some means of production were necessary to produce subsistence, and in a capitalist economy at least a wage fund is necessary to employ labour in production.

Thus two machines requiring the same amount of labour time will have different values if a different rate of profit is calculated on the wages fund used to employ labour in the production of machines. Professor Robinson thus rejects all four measures, reaching the conclusion (similar to Sraffa's) that it is impossible to measure capital irrespective of a given predetermined rate of profit. Only if the rate of profit is constant can one measure the existing capital stock in a single system; and only if the rate of profit is uniform and constant can one compare the value of the capital stock in different systems.

Since this is, in reality, a most abnormal condition, Professor Robinson suggests a combined measure called the 'real-capital ratio' which she defines as 'the ratio of capital reckoned in terms of labour time to the amount of labour currently employed when it (capital equipment) is working at normal capacity,' because, 'this corresponds most closely to the conception of capital as a technical factor of production.' [85, p. 123] Thus this measure combines both the past history of the development of the system in terms of the labour time it has committed to the production of capital in existence (compounded at the ruling rate of profit over its existence) and the current commitment of labour that is required in the present to operate the capital stock at its specified normal (or engineering) capacity. It thus represents, as closely as possible, the economy's utilisation of its labour force over time and the current utilisation that this past accumulation requires.[6]

This does not imply that the other aspects considered in the

[6] There are strong similarities between this method and that employed by Keynes in choosing the wage unit as his measure in [35, pp. 37–45]. Keynes was well aware of the measurement problem and a comparison of Keynes's position with Joan Robinson's concern over the problem is striking. Keynes viewed the quantity of output as a whole, the quantity of capital equipment as a whole, and the general price level as 'vague concepts' capable of only 'imprecise and approximate' comparison. The dynamic conversion of Keynes's wage unit by Professor Robinson has a complement in Sraffa's [107] approach of 'reduction to dated labour'.

first four measures are not important to the analysis of a growing economy, but to emphasise the aspect of labour time, which can be most easily handled with respect to the other aspects.

When an economy is growing at full-employment with productive capacity increasing in line with the increase in the labour force (i.e., a golden age), capital *per man* in term of commodities rises as the real-wage rises with increasing output per head. At the same time capital, measured in terms of commodities, *per unit of output* is constant. Thus the rate of growth of employment is constant and equal to the rate of increase of labour used for the construction of machines. The ratio of labour embodied in the capital stock to current employment on the existing capital stock at any point in time (the real-capital ratio) is then constant. To summarise, in a golden age with rising productivity and labour force growth, the proportion of capital per man in terms of commodities is rising, the proportion of capital per unit of output in terms of commodities is constant, the ratio of output per man employed is rising, with the real-capital ratio constant, and the rate of profit constant.

Differences in the real-capital ratio as between economies will thus be a result of effects of differences in technological change and change in technique. That is, non-neutral technological change, which effects the proportions of investment to output; as well as different positions on the given spectrum of techniques (differences in the degree of mechanisation), will produce different values of the real-capital ratio either through the effect on labour embodied in the capital stock (as with capital-saving or capital-using technological change) or on the labour offered by a given stock of capital (due to the capital stock being composed of machines of a different degree of mechanisation). The measure thus makes possible comparisons of different golden age equilibrium systems exhibiting differences in the nature of technological change or different degrees of mechanisation across spectra of techniques. While the measure is not valid for all possible comparisons, it must be noted that it only has validity when applied in the sense of comparisons (as given in chapter 3), that is between economies in steady tranquil growth at the same rate of profit, each having adapted to its own past experiences and future expectations.[7]

It may seem slightly odd that this measure of capital resembles the Marxian concept of the organic composition of capital (as well as

---

[7] For further applications of the real-capital ratio in comparing economies under different levels of mechanisation and bias see [85].

Keynes's use of wage units), but it is plain that Professor Robinson utilises the concept in a very different way. However, her approach to the valuation problem is similar to that found in the Classics.

Like the Classical measures, Professor Robinson's relies on external measurements in terms of labour, linked to the specific conditions ruling in the economy as a result of its past development. It differs to the extent that it attempts to expose the conditions under which it is possible to provide a measure of the quantity of capital and how that measure might be constructed. The approach thus integrates with her theory of the determination of the rate of profit, for in the post-Keynesian analysis (unlike the neoclassical) it is not possible to measure capital unless the rate of profit is determined distinctly from capital values. She thus attempts to meet and answer both the problem of the valuation of a quantity of capital and the necessity to measures changes in the overall economic system as it moves through time.

For Marx, the organic composition of capital combines not only technical production relations, but is above all an indication of the development of social relations of production. For Professor Robinson, in the light of her criticisms of the neoclassical theory of capital, the problem is to precisely measure capital as a technical factor of production. This does not imply that social relations are discounted, for they form the very bases of her models, but that they do not enter directly into the valuation problem. Professor Robinson is thus more pessimistic than the Classicists about the possibility of any actual measure that will be of practical use in actual economies that are continually undergoing dynamic change in their structural relations and are seldom, if ever, in positions of steady growth. Her pessimism is thus as much a result of her scepticism of the possibility of steady growth under a regime of *laissez-faire* capitalism as of the impossibility of producing a consistent measure of capital or output as a whole. As with the Classics, and unlike the neoclassics, the theory of distribution that she puts forward is not linked to the possibility of consistent measurement. She does show, however, that an independent theory of the determination of the profit rate is necessary to the solution of the measure of the quantity of capital.

In sum then we see that the concept that goes under the name of the measurement of capital is not a new problem, taking capital as simply part of the produced output in the system that is to be measured as it changes over time. It is a new problem as it applies to the neoclassical theory of distribution which requires a measure of the quantity of the aggregate 'factor' capital. There are two methods put forward to solve the problem of measurement over time. The Classical approach involves a measure that is external to the system and is usually taken as having labour in some form or the other as its basis.

The second is purely internal to an economic structure thought to be generally valid and never changing. Given the acceptance of supply and demand in determining prices, values and distribution, it relates to the uniqueness and stability of a vector of prices determined along an equilibrium growth path. Any change in the economy is measured in terms of deviations around this moving equilibrium vector, itself unaffected by the changes. It is also clear that this approach hides the effects of changes in distribution on the measure of output if all measurement is made in terms of the internally produced relative prices; that is it cannot analyse the problem that Ricardo first posed. In addition, the theory of distribution in this theory is directly linked up with the ability to make independent measures, particularly of capital. If market prices are accepted as the only measure of value and of distribution the problem that vexed Ricardo is not readily apparent. This is probably the main reason why the neoclassical economists have found it difficult to understand the criticisms of their approach based in the revival of the Ricardian approach to political economy.

10 An Alternative Pricing Explanation

In chapters 1 and 2 we expressed extreme scepticism about the possibility of prices becoming established in the manner outlined by the neoclassical theory of supply and demand. It was for this reason that we chose to look upon supply and demand as confirming relationships, and used the concepts of 'necessary' prices and then a mark-up of prices over costs in working out the pricing relations in chapters 4 and 5. In this chapter we try to outline an alternative explanation of the determination of prices for the post-Keynesian model and to investigate the implications of such an approach. The basis of the approach is Kalecki's theory of the degree of monopoly and, in addition, it also draws heavily on entrepreneurial expectations and normal values.

THE EQUILIBRIUM AGGREGATE PRICE LEVEL

We can describe the equilibrium price level and mark-up of prices over unit costs in the consumption sector, given the ruling technology, money-wage rate, and rate of investment with the aid of figure 10.1. On the horizontal axis we measure total employment and its allocation between the investment and consumption sectors. Given the technique of production in use there will be a direct relation between employment and output in each sector. The relationship between employment and output will be different, however, in the ranges *de* and *ef* if the technique of production in the capital and consumption sectors is different.

Along the vertical axis we measure wages and prices in money. Given the money-wage rate and the level of employment, the total wage bill for the economy is *acfd*. The investment decisions taken by the ensemble of entrepreneurs determines how this total is divided between the capital and consumption goods industries. Given some value of the ratio of investment to output, implying a value of N_i/N_c, employment in the consumption sector is *de*. The prime costs

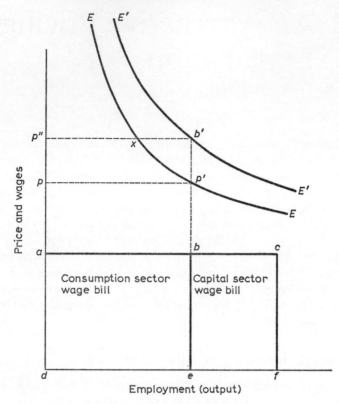

Figure. 10.1. Price Level in the consumption sector

of producing consumption output is then *abed*. The corresponding magnitudes for the capital sector are *ef* and *bcfe*.

Aggregate demand for consumption goods (when $s_w = 0$ and $s_p = 1$) is then *acfd* and is equal to total receipts on consumption good sales. Since prime costs are *abed* this leaves *bcfe* as profits earned in the consumption sector.[1]

The curve *EE* describes a rectangular hyperbola with base *ac* and constant area equal to *bcfe* (the wage bill in the capital goods sector – or total profits in the consumption sector). For the output associated with the level of employment *de* in the consumption sector, the perpendicular to *ac* at *b* will intersect *EE* at a price *p* which will

[1] This chapter draws on and repeats most of the results worked out in Part Two. The reader should be conscious of the relations involved. In most cases the symbols employed are identical with those used previously.

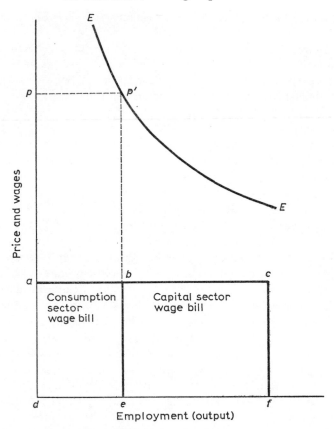

Figure 10.2. Price level with higher ratio of investment to consumption

allocate the consumption goods among all the workers. Price p yields a total profit on consumption goods of $app'b$, which is, of course, equal to $bcfe$. Looking at the same relation in terms of mark-up pricing, pa is the mark-up over costs that is compatible with the allocation of employment ef/de or the ratio of investment to consumption postulated for the diagram. A higher mark-up would cut the *EE* curve at a higher point (such as x) indicating that entrepreneurs were selling less than the output they expected to sell when they offered *de* employment. In such conditions we could not expect demand for investment to continue at the rate that justified employment of *ef* in the capital sector. The mark-up that produces price p is then the only one consistent with the entrepreneurial expectations that produced the ratio of employment ef/de between the two sectors.

In figure 10.2 we take the same system but with a higher ratio of investment to output. Here the ratio of N_i/N_c (ef/de) is higher and therefore the curve EE is higher. This situation is therefore associated with a higher mark-up (pd/ad), price, p, and total profit $app'b$.

If we had included consumption out of profits in the diagrams the EE curves would have been higher (such as $E'E'$ in figure 10.1). With a higher EE curve the ruling mark-up, the price level, and the amount of profits would have been higher (p'' and $ap''b'b$ in figure 10.1). Note that the expenditure out of profits would be just equal to $ap''b'b - app'b$, the amount that profits would be higher. In this case the mark-up that was too high in the first case (see above p. 133) now turns out to be just right and cuts $E'E'$ at b', yielding sufficient sales to justify employment de.

Likewise savings out of wages will require a lower EE curve (but the fact that workers will now earn profits and consume out of them will push the curve back up by the same amount, yielding no change[2]). All these relationships should be familiar to the reader as they are only diagrammatic restatements of the conclusions reached in chapter 4 and applied in Chapter 8.

There is thus a mark-up of price over cost (or equilibrium price or set of prices if we drop the assumption of the consumption bundle) that will be compatible with a given rate of investment and thriftiness in a given state of technology. There is also a uniform rate of profit associated with the rate of growth produced by the rate of investment, as well as a certain distribution of income between wages and profits. If both consumption and capital goods prices are calculated at this mark-up producers will be selling output produced at desired capacity utilisation and their expectations will be satisfied. If the system continues to produce these values it remains in a tranquil state on its growth path (assuming that there are no resource constraints). The problem, however, is to find out how the system might find its way to these prices and sets of expectations if we accept the fact that the operation of supply and demand will be unable to produce them over actual, historical time. We take it as given that we are working in an economy that approaches modern capitalism, with output produced by large manufacturing corporations.

[2] This relation is given in chapter 14. Some problems relating to its introduction are dealt with in chapter 11.

THE DETERMINATION OF MICRO PRICES

We now descend from the aggregate level to the individual firm (corporation) – not necessarily the representative firm in the sense of Marshall, but an approximation of what the usual behaviour of a firm might be like. We retain the distinction between capital and consumption goods on an analytical level, but need no longer identify individual firms on this basis.

The means of producing output, in the short term, are taken to be more or less fixed, as are the proportions of machines to labour which determine the technique of production in use. This means that the firm will face more or less constant costs per unit of output up to the point of full-capacity utilisation of plant. It is difficult to exactly define what we mean by full capacity, but it will suffice to say that design capacity as calculated by the engineers comes close. The concept is, of course, measured per unit of time so that shift work can always increase output (up to 24 hours) but without changes in unit prime costs.[3] After this point costs are assumed to rise at a very rapid rate. The firm's cost curves would then look like those in figure 10.3.

There remains the problem of where the firm will choose to operate in the range *OF*. Since we are not assuming strict competition there is nothing to push the firms towards full-capacity utilisation. In fact with market imperfections firms will normally operate at less than full capacity, the degree of capacity utilisation being affected by the degree of the mark-up over prime costs in relation to overall market conditions. Excess capacity may also be a matter of policy reflecting expectations about market growth. Operations at less than full capacity give the firm a margin with which to meet growing demand and swings in market preferences. When firms are battling to divide a given market it is costly to be caught without excess capacity which allows short delivery times. It also allows changes in output without a change in prices with short term shifts in demand, for repeated price changes may also be a costly process.

The firms thus have two related decisions – one with regard to price and the other on capacity utilisation. We will assume that these decisions are directly related to investment decisions, with capacity

[3] The cost curve may also fall over its relevant range, or may not exist at lower outputs. Such a case may be associated with linked processes or batch processing, or start-up costs, thus giving a minimum output well above zero with costs falling rapidly as high capital costs are spread over output.

utilisation acting as an early-warning system that new capacity is coming into use too quickly or too slowly, implying that investment decisions have been too optimistic or too pessimistic. A proper investment policy should then provide a constant average level of capacity utilisation at the chosen mark-up and resulting output price.

The relation between price and investment is linked through the amount of profits that can be earned at a given price. Given the investment decisions of the firms, which will be related to anticipated future market growth, desired changes in market share, and the potential markets to be gained through the introduction of new products, these investment decisions will require a certain amount of funds, net of available amortisation funds on equipment that is not yet ready for replacement, in order to be carried out. It would be normal to assume that firms charge the highest reasonable mark-up that the market will bear. But under such an assumption some firms will be earning more profits than they need for future expansion in their given markets and be expanding into additional markets, while others will find their gross profits insufficient to the investment that they would like to carry out and be forced to seek external finance. Since we do not wish to introduce financial markets at this point (and since evidence suggests that upwards of 80 per cent of investment is internally financed for manufacturing firms, but cf. below p. 147 and p. 169) nor introduce market diversification, we will make an assumption that allows us to ignore these problems and at the same time make a simple transformation of the aggregate relations that we have discussed above at the level of the firm.

We will assume that in order to finance their investment plans the firms attempt to set their mark-ups such that their annual accrual of gross profits is sufficient to finance their annual investments. In the aggregate version of the theory, investment generates the profits that it needs. On the level of the firm we now assume that firms attempt to set prices that will give them the profits that they need to finance investment. The point of the assumption is not whether or not firms are able to do this, but the effects that this would have on the system if they were able to do so.

When firms are successful in setting the mark-ups that yield profits that allow them to expand capacity with the expected growth of the market a stable situation is possible where investment keeps capacity growing in step with market demand. There are constant market shares, and the rate of profit will equal the growth rate of the market.

As will be quickly seen this is roughly similar to assuming that the propensity to save out of profits is equal to one. If dividends and shareholders are brought into the story there is external borrowing and the propensity to save drops below unity.[4] It is at this point that we recognize that the greatest part of profits are at the disposal of the firms, even though they may not have legal title to them, and that they are primarily used to finance investment.

To recap, we assume that the firm first makes a decision over its future investment plans. It then chooses a mark-up that will produce the required profits, and sticks to this mark-up and implied price, allowing capacity utilisation to vary around some average expected level associated with the chosen mark-up. Changes in demand are first met by changes in output and utilisation, not by changes in price or investment plans. Investment is in general planned so as to keep capacity growing in step with the expected growth in demand, and thus excess capacity is also planned at a more or less constant average level. Mark-ups and prices are, on this view, set to provide the finance required by the investment planned by the firms. These decisions are made with reference to the state of demand that experience and market research suggest to the firm as being reasonable. The actual price charged, however, is determined less by demand than by the mark-up the firm needs to generate the profits needed to finance the investment necessary to meet its future expectations of demand.

Given the assumption of competition in the broad sense, firms will thus also expect to earn profit rates equivalent to similarly situated firms in the industry, if their market share is not to be falling or unless they are using less efficient techniques of production.

Decisions about mark-ups and price are thus linked directly to firms' expectations about the future and the rate of investment that they think it will be profitable to carry out. This approach is equally valid for firms producing either consumption or capital goods and does not require any separation between the two in terms of pricing. It may, however, be true that decisions in the two types of firms will

---

[4] To make the identification complete the firms take the place of the capitalists. The existence of dividends is just like a capitalist saving propensity of less than one. However, since not all dividends are spent (in fact a very low proportion are spent) it is not strictly valid to substitute the firm's retention ratio for the savings propensity out of profits. It does, however, determine the rate of profit in combination with investment. Such an exercise is worked out in [41, chapter 12 and appendix D].

be different – capital-goods-producing firms working to a certain extent to contract, carrying smaller inventories, and thus responding to changes in expectations in a slightly different manner. Mark-ups on contract work will, however, be subject to the condition of generating an amount of profit sufficient to meet expected future investment needs.

At the same time this method would allow us to relax the assumption of equality of the rate of profit in all industries, for different markets will be growing at different rates and thus require different rates of investment, mark-ups and prices in order to preserve market shares. Thus a system in steady growth would exhibit a range of different profit rates for different individual market growth rates. A given distribution of profit rates would then be compatible with the overall savings–investment balance in the economy.

However, once we recognise that firms may find it profitable to operate in several closely related markets, or to diversify into other industries by merger with other firms, there may be no very close link between market growth rates and the profits earned by an individual corporation on its overall operations. The analysis of differing profit rates would then require the identification of particular firms with particular products in particular markets. Such an assumption, in a world of diversified corporations, would be just as unrealistic as assuming a uniform profit rate. We will therefore continue with the uniformity assumption, cognisant of the possibilities that underly it. The reader, if he wishes, may think in terms of a constellation of different profit rates, the uniform aggregate profit rate that we will use then being a representation of the distribution of these particular rates of profit.

The question that we now have to answer is whether this approach to pricing can be made compatible with the prices required for stable growth as worked out at the beginning of this chapter. Figure 10.3 shows a firm that has made a calculation of its desired capacity utilisation, OB, mark-up OS/OA, and price OS. The supply curve for the firm at levels of sales around OB is given by SS'. If the firm's calculations of market conditions are broadly correct it sells OB output at price OS and shows a profit on sales of $ASDC$ (assume an imaginary demand curve that cuts SS' around point D). If this amount of profit is sufficient to finance the firm's desired expansion through new investment the firm will not seek to change any of its decisions. The rate of profit that it is earning is sufficient to support

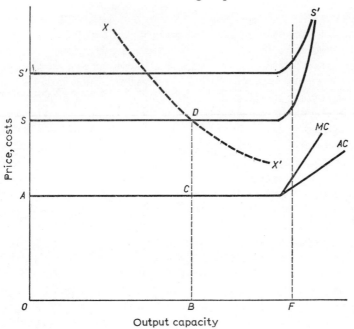

Figure 10.3. Pricing for the firm

its rate of investment, and if it is similar to that earned in other firms in industry, using similar techniques it will be preserving its market share. If this rate of profit is also similar to that earned in other industries the firm will not try to expand into other lines of production.

We must notice, however, that sales levels below or above *OB* produce different amounts of profit with the same amount of capital employed in production. Thus a level of sales persistently below *OB* yields a rate of profits and an amount of profits lower than expected. It is possible to construct a constant rate of profit curve for all levels of capacity utilisation, such as *XX'* in figure 10.3. This would show the prices that would have to be charged at different levels of capacity utilisation to yield a constant amount of profit and thus rate of profit on capital employed. There would thus be a different *SS'* curve for each desired rate of investment (and capacity expansion) and required price as given on the *XX'* curve. Thus a higher expectation of future market growth and profit requirement would yield a higher *XX'* curve, while a higher desired level of excess capacity would produce a higher SS' curve, such as $S'S'$ for example. These interrelations are important because the firm may not be able to directly control its sales, and thus the required investment, profit, price and normal capacity all interact on one another. Once a combination has been established and is supported by experience we can assume that these values become expected in the sense that they become 'normal'.

To check for equilibrium in the system we must refer to the aggregate relations as described in figures 10.1 and 10.2. We now talk about the firm pictured in figure 10.3 as an average of what all firms are doing.

If the mark-up OS/OA and price OS are the expected normal price and mark-up which will produce sales at expected average capacity OB, the firm will be able to finance its expected investment programme. The investment carried out by all the firms will then produce some overall aggregate ratio of investment to consumption. Let us say that this ratio is represented by $bcfe/abed$ in figure 10.1. This will generate an amount of aggregate demand in the consumption sector that implies mark-up pd/ad, and price p. If price p is equal to OS with sales level OB the system is in equilibrium.[5] The price and capacity level corresponding to the firms' investment plans produce sufficient demand to sell OB at price OS. That is, the investment decisions of all firms taken together produce sufficient aggregate demand on the macro level to allow each of them to sell enough product at the ruling mark-up and normal price that provides profits sufficient to finance investment. The prices that they have chosen distribute the existing consumption goods amongst demanders and generate sufficient profits to satisfy the savings–investment equality. Expectations are satisfied on the level of the firm and the macro conditions described in chapters 4 and 5 are satisfied. Sales for the single firm run in the range of OB, sometimes more, sometimes less, but the swings even out. The firms all earn the expected rate of profit on their investments

[5] Taking all firms as represented by our example there is one price p for the consumption bundle. If firms charge this price it just matches the price required for macro-equilibrium. Otherwise there will be a number of prices and a number of goods, and p is an average representative of them. To the extent that we consider capital goods producers separately we must refer, not necessarily to pd/ad and p, but to the price implied by the rate of profit p achieves for the consumption goods producers and used as a mark-up for the production and sale of capital goods (cf. chapter 5). The prices and mark-ups may be, but need not be, the same, depending on capital intensity and capacity utilisation in each sector. If we know p, however, the price in the capital goods sector is readily calculated from it and thus represents it.

and earn enough profit to continue the financing of their investment policies. Capacity keeps step with the increase in demand and the increase in sales that investment generates. Normal values become established as the system moves through time.[6] It is just as likely for prices to become established in this way for both consumption and capital goods producers as by supply and demand.

Under this scheme, however, investment decisions are elevated to primary importance, supported by expectations and the ability of market power to establish prices compatible with investment plans. Pricing decisions are then confirmed or disapproved in reference to the flow of profits or the level of capacity utilisation over time. Thus decisions in relation to a normal rate of profit, normal capacity utilisation, or normal profits all come to the same thing in relation to the firms' expectations over future investment.

TECHNICAL PROGRESS AND NEW PRODUCTS

Technical progress can be easily introduced into the analysis by recognising that gross investment in more productive techniques of production will reduce the unit costs of production. This can thus be represented by a downward shift in the cost curves of the diagrams. At given prices this increases the flow of profits and the rate of profits in excess of what the firms considered necessary before the introduction of the technique. If the costs of the new techniques do not completely take up the increase in earnings and normal investment expectations are unchanged there is then a potential for deficient aggregate demand. However, as we have seen in chapter 6, steady growth can be maintained in this situation by allowing the real wage to rise at the same rate as new techniques increase output per man. Thus with constant prices a rate of increase in the money-wage rate equal to the rise in productivity will cause the cost curves to rise by just the amount that the new technique causes them to fall, allowing the normal values to remain unchanged. This, as we have already

---

[6] It should be noticed that the diagrams given refer to a point in time. The investment being undertaken will enlarge capacity in each period. To dynamise the diagrammatic exposition one could assume that the x-axis enlarges at a constant rate (equal to the rate of investment) over time or, alternatively, that the units used to measure capacity enlarge at a constant rate, thus leaving the relations between the curves in the diagrams unchanged. In such a case the XX' curve would always show a constant rate of profit, but inscribes a larger 'nominal' area in each period to correspond to the larger capital stock.

seen, requires that technical progress leaves the relation of investment to output unchanged, i.e., that progress is neutral. If it is not,
the normal prices will be out of line with equilibrium and normal
values will no longer be satisfied or maintained. Thus changes in the
intensity of techniques of production add another dimension to the
variables under consideration in the relation between macroeconomic
and microeconomic pricing relations.

The introduction of new products is more difficult to handle, and
more important in the actual growth process. For firms the introduction of new products may be the easiest way to maintain profits
and demand in any particular industry. Over time, for any particular
product, the demand cannot continue to grow indefinitely (except in
very special cases). Thus firms may find that over time (in relation
to income elasticities) the demand for a particular product may
decline. At given prices the rate of profit earned then falls over the
life of the product, and so also does the growth of the firm if it
produces only this product. The firm then faces decline and eventual
collapse, its capital does not continue to reproduce itself. The firm
thus faces a continual fight for preservation, which is expressed in
terms of product innovation and changes in details of particular
products (as well as the dampening of competition through take-
overs and mergers). The necessity to continually stimulate demand in
a particular industry endogenously generates a certain amount of
investment in reasearch and development and in new machinery
needed to produce the new products (which need not be true of
attempts to take control of supply through mergers or take-
overs).

At the same time the firms may find it advantageous to operate
differential pricing policies at different stages of a product's economic
life, cutting prices as the life of the product progresses. This may serve
to keep up demand, but may be detrimental to profits if the cuts in
price that are necessary to maintain demand exceed potential
economies in production due to increasing returns or learning-by-
doing in production of the product. Profits may also be bolstered
by charging higher prices for newer, recently established products.
Thus the firm is actually making a composite decision over its
mark-ups on all its products in order to generate profits sufficient to
finance different rates of expansion of capacity for the production
of each of them and the introduction of new ones.

Thus while recognising this phenomenon, which is similar to the problem of differential profit rates for different firms, we abstract from it by assuming a single product with a given price in a market that continues, somehow, to grow. This makes the analysis easier, but less realistic. It does not, however, change any of our broad conclusions. It does indicate a rather large area of research still to be taken up in the establishment of the microeconomic foundations of post-Keynesian political economy.

INVESTMENT BASED PRICING AND ATTAINMENT OF STABLE GROWTH

A basic difference between the present approach to pricing through a mark-up broadly determined by investment decisions and the neoclassical theory of supply and demand, is that there is no mechanism to assure that the normal mark-up required for steady expansion will be reached, except by chance, good guess, or market manipulation (just as investment generates the profits required to carry it out, advertising of new products seems to generate, or steal from other products, the consumption expenditure that is necessary to justify their introduction).

But what happens if the firms' expectations and investment decisions are wrong; are out of line with the reality of the other investment decisions in the economy as a whole? We now move away from strict equilibrium comparisons and will talk about changes in an actual economy over time, cognisant of what this involves. We will require some very simple assumptions about the behaviour of firms. The assumption that we make is that firms' expectations of normal values, once established, are changed only slowly. In plain terms, the firms act to try to maintain their long-run investment plans when forced to make a change in their decision variables in the face of disappointed expectations. As seen above, this we can simply express as an attempt to maintain the rate of profit on capital invested, and thus price and capacity utilisation will be changed more readily than investment and profit expectations. We point out that this is *not* a 'simplifying assumption' that would leave the analysis unchanged if it were removed. If the assumption is changed the results will change. The assumption is based on the fact that it is impossible for any individual firm to either recognise the effect of its individual actions on the aggregate of all the firms' actions, or to possess easily the information that would tell it the proper investment and price policy that would satisfy their expectations. This is, of course, one of the basic tenets of Keynes's *General Theory*.

We start with the economy being in a more or less stable condition. This does not mean that all firms last forever, there may be some firms with fading markets or increasing inefficiency that are either going bankrupt or being taken over by other firms (or following product differentiation to keep up profits). On average then, expectations are being satisfied, investment is going on at a steady pace, and normal mark-ups, prices, and profit rates rule.

Now let us assume that the profit rate required and expected by the firm for its intended investment is higher than that justified by the ruling level of the *EE* curve in figure 10.1. This means that the *XX'* and *SS'* curves envisaged by the firm are too high to be compatible with equilibrium at expected capacity level *OB* and price *OS* (here $OS > p$ and $OS/OA > pd/ad$). The firm finds that it consistently sells less than *OB*. Still believing that its investment expectations are correct and that the normal profit rate is ruling in the industry its first response is to think that it has made a mistake in setting its price. Its desired position (and normal profit rate) could be achieved by charging a higher mark-up at a lower level of capacity utilisation. This implies a lower requirement of labour and may cause the introduction of new capacity to be postponed for a short period, or revised slightly downward; it remains positive at any rate.

The firm thus slides up its *XX'* curve to a new supply curve such as *S'S'* in an attempt to find a combination of price and capacity that yields the expected rate of profit required for the funding of its long-term investment plans. Depending on demand elasticities, the firm may be successful for a short period of time. But eventually the result of the reduced employment will cause a further fall in the *EE* curve. The price that would produce aggregate equilibrium in these conditions is thus still lower. The gap between the price that would give macro-stability and the price the firm sets becomes larger instead of smaller.

There are thus two effects involved. A reduction in investment orders (or a postponement) will cause *bcfe* to become smaller (figure 10.1). At the same time the reduction in employment will cause total output to fall, both in the consumption goods sector and the capital goods sector. The result might look like figure 10.4. The gap $e'-e''$ represents the decrease in employment (and thus output). The effect

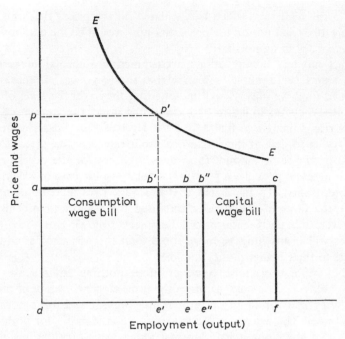

Figure 10.4. Pricing at less than full employment

on EE is a result of both shrinkage in ef and the existence of $e'-e''$ unemployment.

So we have the first round effect of overly high expectations of normal profits: rising actual prices and unemployment. At the same time we note that the price that would produce stable growth in actual conditions (if they were realised) is lower, as is the rate of profit that could be earned given the actually ruling aggregate level of investment. The money wage is constant by assumption, therefore the real wage has fallen. This is first of all due to the fact that prices have risen, and secondly to the fact that the proportion of investment to consumption has risen ($ef/de < e''f/de'$) even though total output and employment is lower.

The second effect is to a certain extent arbitrary. We could equally well have assumed that the production of capital goods is reduced in greater proportion than consumption production ($e'e/de < ee''/ef$) with the $b'e'$ and $b''e''$ lines both shifted to the right in the diagram. This may be a more realistic result, but it does nothing to halt the fall in the real wage which is calculated on the prices the firms set (figure 10.3) and not on the price that now would be the equilibrium price, i.e., p' in figure 10.4.[7]

This may lead labour unions, accustomed to a normal increase in real wages per annum, to seek higher money wages. If these are granted (and we may as well assume that they are) the level of the *ac* and *EE* curves in figure 10.4 are shifted up by the amount of the wage rise. Likewise in figure 10.3 the level of *OA* rises. The firms, still trying to defend their assumed profit rate push up prices ($S'S'$ rises) by the same amount (and possibly more for the occasion of wage increases provides a good opportunity to increase mark-ups to restore profits). To the extent that the wage rises increase demand (*EE*), the firms may find sales stabilised for a short time. This is, however, unlikely, for the price adjustments following on the rise in wages will if anything be more rapid than the households' adjustments to their higher money incomes.

The whole procedure, however, does nothing to increase the households' real income, or bring the firms closer to a rate of profit that they can no longer attain at the present rate of aggregate investment. The net result is a shaking of confidence – for both the firms and the households. Normal values and expectations now have very little meaning. With changes in expectations coming from the inability to sell output at revised normal capacity the firms revise downwards their expectations of present and future sales and thus cut employment and cut back on new investment. In Keynesian parlance the marginal efficiency of investment curve falls. At the same time the households, facing increasing uncertainty over future employment (and therefore increasing uncertainty over future income), may save more and more of their increasing money-wages, thus increasing precautionary balances – preparing for life on unemployment benefit. In Keynesian parlance this shows up as a fall in the consumption function in real terms, and an increase in liquidity preference. Thus although saving as reported on the national level may be rising in money terms, the increase in liquidity

[7] Even if the ratio of investment to consumption changes so as to bring about a higher required equilibrium price this will not affect the decrease in the real wage (though it will be less pronounced) and the eventual operation of the inflation barrier which will act to keep *OS* rising faster than p until expectations become eroded from the continually falling sales. If the fall in real wages is docilely accepted the system may come to a stable position, but at a lower volume of employment.

preference together with poor profit performance making large financial institutions less confident of the returns on financial assets, may lead to a rise in interest rates in step with rising prices. This comes about quite apart from any effect of the expectation of rising prices leading savers to demand a higher rate of interest to preserve their real rates of return.[8]

From the point of view of the firms, the negatively-sloped Marshallian demand curves that they face will be rising, but not sufficiently to offset the rise in costs due to wage increases; so that even if they are profit-maximising, marginal-cost = marginal-revenue firms, their optimum position implies higher prices and lower output.

All this combines to push demand even lower, until expectations are destroyed and investment in the new equipment falls towards zero, and real profits do the same. Trade unions now have even more incentive to bid for higher money wages for falling real-consumption output combines with rising prices to reduce real wages all the faster. We thus end up with the limiting situation of zero net investment, rising employment and rising prices. Firms find themselves with low or zero profits (England in the early 1970s was not too far from this position). These conditions can then start to generate the dismal expectations that tend to make themselves normal. No firm is willing on its own to undertake the investment necessary to start the system back on the road to full employment.

The two prime factors that we emphasise in this story are the effect of expectations of normal profits held by the firms in relation to their planned investment, and their attempt to maintain them by operating first on output and prices and, secondly, on investment. The second is a logical result of an atomistic decision-making process.

We can amplify the effect of unwarranted expectations by looking to the financial structure of the firms. We have already said that the price–capacity combination chosen by the firm will be determined by its investment policy. We now relax our strict assumption of all internal finance and look at the effects of external financing. Firms will be financing investment, and most of working capital investment (and paying off any previous borrowing), with the profits it earns.

---

[8] Thus the relation between high interest rates and inflation can be simply explained in terms of liquidity preference without reference to the effect of inflation on real rates of return, a concept that Keynes found of little use in the theory of interest.

Its ability to finance investment decisions and its ability to finance investment in excess of earned profits by borrowing will then be strongly effected by its actual flow of profits. When profits are lower than normal (expected) the investment the firm plans is in excess of what it had planned to finance internally. If it had been a previous borrower the firm will have to renew debt it had expected to retire and also arrange for new borrowing to support the investment it had expected to pay for out of gross profits. Although we have assumed that firms try to maintain long-term investment plans in the face of temporary falls in profits, it may not take much for the firm to decide to cut short its new investment. If it has maturing debt to worry about it will have a further incentive to try to increase profits by putting up prices. Rises in wages aggravate the situation by reducing still further the earnings that might have been used to retire outstanding debt – in the extreme it may require the firm to undertake short-term borrowing.

Such distress borrowing, together with the previously mentioned possibility of a rise in liquidity preference then work together to push up interest rates, making it even harder for the firms to maintain investment plans.

What investment is taking place (even if net investment falls to zero, replacement may continue) not surprisingly, will be of a type that reduces the quantity of labour per unit of output and thereby reduces current costs so as to equate them with the decline in the flow of profits. Thus 'labour-saving' equipment becomes desirable as much for the reduction in rapidly rising wages costs as for the decrease in uncertainty it gives over the size of the wage component in costs. With a lower proportion of labour to a given volume of output wage rises cut less deeply into profits.

In fact these types of equipment will usually cost more per unit of current output, but since planned output is now lower the amount spent on replacement need not be larger than amortisation on retired plant. In addition a higher ratio of capital to labour may involve a longer amortisation period due to the longer economic life of capital, so that annual total costs may be lower. Thus the decision to attempt to 'substitute' for labour may be determined not so much by the technical superiority of the new machines or the rise in wages, but more as an attempt by the firm to reduce uncertainty over its ability to produce a steady flow of profits. Thus technical choice need not be only explained by changes in the relative prices of capital and labour, but also in terms of the degree of uncertainty attached to the costs of the two.

The net result is to bring about even more unemployment, for as replacement investment in labour-saving machines lowers the amount of labour necessary to produce a given output, the amount of unemployment associated with a stationary output level with zero net investment will be growing (the relation between output and employment on the x-axis of the diagrams changes). It may also be true that in the first stages of recovery, as capacity levels are increased, employment can grow without much net capital investment but once new net investment starts employment will increase at a slower rate due to the lower labour requirements. At the same time the old expectations about prices and investment need not produce full employment, for the old levels of investment and output will yield a smaller volume of employment. The new full employment position will thus require the expectations necessary to produce a higher ratio of investment to output and there is no reason why this should be the case. It is in the analysis of such changes in techniques that chapter 7 is useful.

If the government tries to fight inflation by putting up interest rates or restricting the availability of finance to the firms it makes matters so much the worse. Higher interest rates make it harder and more expensive to borrow in order to meet short-term liquidity shortages. It also increases the proportion of interest charges for a given volume of debt. The additional debt charges provide another incentive for firms to put up prices. This induces trade unions to claim that further wage rises are necessary in order to keep their members above the subsistence level.

At the same time this may hinder recovery when it comes, for firms will be tempted to use profits to retire a debt which has been incurred on disagreeable terms, rather than immediately revising upwards their investment and employment plans. Thus early stages of recovery may show little change in investment or employment but large changes in the structure of debt.

A more appropriate government policy would be to try to increase investment and restore expectations rather than restricting the availability of credit, which only makes it more difficult for the firms to undertake new investment projects. Thus the government policy should not be to support the natural rise in interest rates that we noted above, but to try to combat it. As Keynes noted long ago, the most serious restraint to new investment is the shortage of finance obtainable on reasonable terms [36, p. 669].

Up to this point we have assumed that firms have very little hesitation about raising prices, at least in the face of wage increases that hit their competitors equally. In the case of an open economy the firms' competitors may be foreign corporations who are not subject to the same cost and demand conditions. This possibility takes away much of the ability of domestic firms to recoup wage costs in higher prices. To the extent that firms refrain from raising prices, profits are reduced and investment with them. If prices are increased above the level of foreign goods, sales are adversely affected, with a similar effect on profits and investment. To the extent that foreign goods are substituted for domestic the home country is hit by a deficit on current account. If the government reacts to the deficit by raising interest rates to defend the value of the currency, and by trying to cut back aggregate demand to reduce imports, the already weak situation of the firms is aggravated. What profits that are being earned may then be directed towards overseas investments, because profitability is higher and buying or merging with foreign firms increases the firms' control over foreign competition. The results are little better for home employment. An open economy may thus be a very serious threat to home employment. Stable growth appears as even more of a myth than in a closed system.

Thinking back to the start of our story – the whole situation arose from expectations, in particular about investment, being out of line with actual aggregate conditions. The problem is that there is nothing in the system with which to communicate to the firms what the proper equilibrium combination of price, capacity, investment and the rate of profit should be. This is, of course, as true under the pricing mechanism we have postulated as it is under that of supply and demand. As indicated in chapters 1 and 2, this was one of the main points that Keynes was making in the *General Theory*. At the same time we have been able to use our steady-state constructions to carry out an analysis of an actual situation going on over time, by looking at what would be required of the system in order to achieve stable growth and then seeing if our assumptions about the world allow it to come about. The working out of golden ages and the like thus need not be a sterile exercise in refined theory.

It is not too far fetched to think of reasons why situations such as the one we have described might come into existence. It might result from a government decision to markedly increase expenditure on armaments. Or it could result from a severe restriction of demand combined with the transfer of resources to export sectors by a government overly eager to bring about a rapid shift in the balance of payments to satisfy the international banking community. It could simply be a shift in consumption patterns due to a period of rapidly rising incomes, or as a reaction to, and attempt to control, environmental pollution. Thus it need not be the case that firms' expectations are wrong, but that what were once correct expectations become incorrect as a result of other forces in the system over which the firms have little knowledge or control.

An interesting point to note is that the same general story can be told (rising prices and unemployment) when expectations are too low. In this case the change in the proportion of investment to consumption becomes an all-important factor. Thus if prices as set by the firms are too low ($OS < p$) the real wage appears to be higher than the amount of consumption goods available to satisfy demand. Firms find themselves with too little capacity, and demands for investment are speeded up. But as firms attempt to return to normal price and capacity combinations prices start to rise and the competition for resources caused by the rise in the proportion of investment to consumption begins to push down real wages as well. Money wages then may rise more rapidly than sales and profits, for the firms are now calculating normal prices on a greater amount of capital goods than were indeed necessary, making prices and profits earned in the boom into normal or expected values. These, of course, are too high for the system to sustain in stable growth, and the decrease in employment sets in. The reader should be able to work out the details of the situation for himself.

GENERAL POINTS ON THE PRICING ALTERNATIVE

Leaving our excursion into the real world possibilities of the pricing mechanism we note primarily that if expectations are satisfied and the equilibrium prices are set by the firms they will be exactly the same prices as would have been achieved had we carried out the analysis in terms of orthodox supply and demand prices. Looking at the equilibrium position does not offer proof that it was achieved by prices calculated to produce an amount of profit sufficient to finance investment plans, or that it was arrived at by the free market forces as expressed in supply and demand, or indeed by any other possible alternative for that matter.

The difference comes in the application of the pricing mechanism. The theory with firms setting prices by some behavioural decision rule, while being compatible with equilibrium, by no means guarantees that result nor does it imply that equilibrium at steady growth will be achieved. The neoclassical theory of supply and demand, on the other hand, admits of no other result but the achievement of equilibrium. A choice cannot be made by looking at equilibrium states. What we have tried to do is look at how our postulated pricing mechanism might operate over time to achieve a final solution; it could just as well have been equilibrium. In the end it was not. As we have stated earlier, the main weakness of the supply and demand equilibrium approach is that is has not yet explained how the operation of prices in the free market might operate in disequilibrium over time to arrive at the equilibrium solution. It has shown that it exists, that there may be more than one, and that they may be stable, but not how to get there.

The reader should note that we have not rejected the function of prices as a device for the distribution and allocation of output. This aspect of prices in markets is central to the analysis, '. . . for there is solid justification for the market as a method of distributing consumer goods . . . the task of choosing what to buy is thrown onto the consumer . . .' [87, p. 71]. What we do reject is that there is any specific statement that can be made about the dynamic functions of prices, or adjustments of relative prices, to obtain full-employment equilibrium, or that the distribution of goods that is achieved by these prices (or that the prices themselves) can be in any sense called optimal. In a modern capitalist system where wages are paid in terms of money and wage goods are sold in markets at money prices, prices will indeed distribute and allocate the goods produced. They need not, however, be determined by supply and demand nor produce optimal results (whatever that may mean in the present context) nor equilibrium as a matter of course. Again we have a point that is difficult to decide on simple logic, both explanations of prices can equally well produce the equilibrium positions, in theory, under the proper assumptions. The end results of the two approaches when used in analysis are, however, rather different.

We note in closing this chapter that the equilibrium growth constructions that we have formulated in earlier chapters only become potent tools of analysis when we match them up against postulates about real world behaviour.

In the preceeding chapter the effect of a uniform ratio of capital to labour [cf. p. 114] on the relation between labour values and prices, and the value of capital and the profit rate was discussed [see also 14]. In any actual economy we would expect to find differences in techniques of production for different products represented by different capital-labour ratios. We would also expect normal capacity utilisation to be different for different firms and industries. It is for these reasons that we have pointed out (pp. 71, 140) that mark-ups of prices over costs will not generally be uniform in the economy (or in our two sectors) for this would require a uniform level of capacity utilisation and capital-labour ratio for all firms in the economy. Thus although we have assumed in Chapters 4 and 5 that production relations in the two sectors are uniform to simplify the numerical presentation, the general relation between real wages and investment and capitalists' consumption outlined there will hold whatever the differences in production relations in the two sectors. Likewise, the graphical analysis of this chapter is further complicated if we separate firms by sector with differences in technique or capacity utilisation (cf. n. 5 above). It is for this reason that we have used a firm representing the economy as a whole, emphasising its relation to the aggregate of the system with differences in capacity utilisation and techniques a possibility for particular firms.

11 Money Variables, Real Variables and Financial Assets

We have already posited a close relation, in terms of methodological approach, between Classical political economy and post-Keynesian theory. This we said was in terms of emphasis on the distribution of income among broad social classes through the approach of real physical costs of production (most especially labour) and the concept of a surplus of output over real input costs in a world where output is produced and reproducible in an historical context. The role of relative prices in distributing a given quantity of already produced (and thus scarce, but not in the classical sense of not being reproducible) output was not an integral part of this scheme.

The Classical economists did, however, accept the teaching of Say's Law in the broad sense (as we have described it in chapter 2 above) as well as the Quantity theory of Money. It is on these two points that the post-Keynesian theory differs in a crucial way from the Classical modes of thought.

MONETARY AND REAL ECONOMY

The post-Keynesian approach to monetary matters is rooted in Keynes's short-period theory of effective demand and Keynes's view of the relations of a monetary system, which taken together invalidate both Say's Law and the Quantity theory of Money. The most crucial point is Keynes's view of a monetary economy as differentiated from a real-barter exchange economy. It is from this distinction that his theory of output and employment logically followed.[1]

It is this view of a monetary economy that is maintained in the post-Keynesian theory, although it does not give money itself a primary role in the analysis, for monetary relations are closely tied

[1] Joan Robinson [72] comments on this relation that Keynes 'failed to notice that he had incidentally evolved a new theory of the long-period analysis of output'.

to disequilibrium, and as a first approximation it has focussed on the basic structural relations of the system as they might develop undisturbed by persistent disequilibrium.

For Keynes, money was important because the future was uncertain and unpredictable. Money provided the most certain link between the present and the uncertain future because it was the most liquid and least risky of all assets available as stores of value over time. It was for this reason that, in a monetary economy, people were willing to hold money for transactions purposes rather than physical goods, and that all contracts, debts and exchanges were denominated in terms of money.[2]

Further no meaning could be attached to an equilibrium value of money. The value of money, being primarily determined by the effect of the level of money wages at any particular moment of time, was viewed as more or less an historical accident, thus forbidding the identification of an equilibrium value of money or an equilibrium price level. Thus while Keynes did not assume or require wages and prices to be inflexible, the maintenance of the monetary economy required that money wages be more or less stable to keep the value of money from changing so rapidly as to deny it pride of place as the most certain link between present and uncertain future values. Perfectly flexible wages and prices, while theoretically admissible, were inconsistent with the existence of a monetary economy.

Changes in the money price level were thus linked to changes in the level of money wages. Money wage changes, which could be affected by labour through the wage bargain, were related to the real wages that were determined along with employment by the real relations in the system and the level of investment.[3]

Thus one of the crucial features of a monetary system is that wages are not paid in real terms, not in a proportion of the product produced by labour, but in money, the real value of which is determined by the overall operations of the economy and not by any single market. Neither was the wage bargain made in real terms, but

[2] It is not intended, or possible here, to give a full analysis of Keynes's monetary theory in relation to the *General Theory* as a whole. A good compact statement is given in Keynes in [34] and [37]. Paul Davidson [6] has recently analysed the relation of Keynes's monetary theory to models of long-period growth.

[3] Although the main goal of the *Treatise on Money* was the determination of a stable level of prices. The relation between the level of money wages and prices is clearly stated by R. F. Kahn in 'Lord Keynes and Contemporary Economic Problems, I', in [25].

was, and only could be made, for money wages. It is in the determination of the real consumption value of the money wage that the physical relations of production and investment play the major role.

The payment of labour in money creates a sharp distinction between the consumption value of the wage (the real wage), the value in terms of commodities produced by the payment of the wage (cost in terms of own product of labour to the employer) and the nominal money value of the wage. Thus, unless the wage bargain can effect the physical relations in the system and investment decisions, the wage bargain cannot determine the real wage. The rejection of this possibility in a monetary economy is the source of Keynes's assumption that the wage bargain is made for the money wage, and could not, even if labour desired, be made in terms of the real wage.

At the same time, in a monetary economy, unlike a real-barter exchange system, potential production need not always be equal to the sale of goods, nor will investment always be of an amount sufficient to exhaust potential savings at any given level of employment. Through the introduction of the consumption function one can conceive of the level of effective demand that would be forthcoming at any level of employment. This amount of consumption demand, given techniques of production, will require a certain amount of the total employment. The difference between this amount of employment and that initially posed, will not be needed to produce consumption goods, but incomes from some type of employment for this labour was assumed in the derivation of consumption demand. Keynes's point is that entrepreneurs of their own accord, in the face of an uncertain future, will not automatically command the investment goods necessary to provide employment and incomes for the remaining labour. Thus the point of effective demand that would have resulted from the employment of these labourers is not realised, leading to less, rather than more, optimistic expectations about the ability to sell future output. When incomes need not be fully spent, or unspent incomes need not be offset by investment there is no inherent reason for the system to produce full employment. In a real barter-exchange economy these conditions are always fulfilled; in a monetary economy they are not.

The role of money in a monetary economy then exerts influence primarily by providing finance for investment irrespective of the amount of personal saving obtaining in the economy (or, in the case of a fringe of unsatisfied borrowers, limits the amount of investment that can be carried out irrespective of saving). The obverse is that the level of the interest rate may also exert an effect in as much as it colours entrepreneurial expectations. It also exerts a real force, but a secondary one in relation to expectations, in terms of the amount of profit on a given investment that must go to interest charges, or in terms of the effect of the proportion of debt to assets (or interest charges to profits) on the ability to obtain finance for investment.

Thus although Keynes was careful to specify what he called the 'essential properties of money' [35, p. 222 ff.], he was more concerned with these properties as a means of defining a monetary economy and the deployment of real physical resources within such an economy in difference with a real barter-exchange economy, than he was in outlining what the specific physical characteristics of money should be. The emphasis is on the utilisation of physical resources within the context of a monetary system *rather* than the real forces that were said to be hidden behind a 'veil of money'.

In this context the problem of achieving full-employment of labour was twofold. It required that first the physical resources should be available for investment, and second, that the capitalists should be willing and able to make use of the resources by undertaking investment.[4] While it is true that in a monetary economy both these relations are related to monetary factors, it is not necessarily true that simple operations on monetary factors will bring about the two conditions required. Putting it another way, although money is the most certain link between the present and an uncertain future, and has this link because the future is uncertain, changes in monetary variables need not have a direct effect on expectations about an uncertain future, i.e., the decision to invest (utilise physical resources for investment).[1]

It is precisely this division of emphasis that is adopted in the monetary assumptions of the post-Keynesian extension of Keynes's theory. The system is a monetary system, but the emphasis remains

[4] R. F. Kahn emphasises this physical resource base of Keynes's revolutionary approach: 'It was the physical use of resources which mattered.' 'Even today attempts are still made to escape from the harsh physical realities which Keynes emphasised back into the old-fashioned world of mumbo-jumbo in which the economy yields to a few waves of the magic wand of credit.' [25, pp. 109–10.]

[5] As Kahn points out, it is not suitable to think 'of a schedule of liquidity preference as though it could be represented by a well-defined curve or by a functional relationship expressed in mathematical terms or subject to econometric processes'. [25, p. 90.]

on the utilisation and allocation of the physical resources of the system. The monetary relations are crucial in the theory to (1) insure the provision of physical resources for investment, and (2) provide finance to the entrepreneurs so that investment need not be limited by individual saving decisions.

MONETARY AND REAL RELATIONS IN POST-KEYNESIAN THEORY

We can highlight these relations by looking at their function in the theory that we have surveyed in Part Two. In showing the possibilities of different possible rates of growth for economies with given money-wage rates and thriftiness, it was the real wage that was affected by the higher rates of capital accumulation. A higher rate of accumulation requires a greater amount of resources available for investment and thus implies a lower real wage represented by a lower proportion of real resources available to satisfy the consumption desires of labour. The possibility of the divergence of the real from the money rate of wages as found in a monetary economy is crucial to this exposition of the theory of distribution.

If labour were paid, for example, in real goods there could be no difference between real and money incomes. Only the physical surplus that remained after the deduction of wage goods would be available for investment. In such a case any investment in excess of this residual would be limited by the willingness of the wage-earners to forego some of their wage goods, leaving the resources that would have produced them available for the production of investment goods. In such conditions the real-wage bargain and the real savings decisions in the system would determine the resources available for investment. When investment always equals this amount such a representation resembles a neoclassical system where investment is determined by individual decisions to save.

When wages are paid in money the real value of the wage is determined by the investment decision of entrepreneurs, which need no longer be limited by the wage bargain nor the real savings desired by the individuals in the system. In the Keynesian system it is the investment decision that takes prominence, it is not limited by individual desires to save, and broadly determines the real wage of labour.

But when all this has been said and done, it remains broadly true that the standard of living depends on the physical realities of the situation and not on the behaviour of money wages. By the physical realities I mean the quantity of consumer goods which it is physically possible and worth while to produce, and the total amount of employment, including all the employment on things other than consumer goods – things such as defence and investment.[6]

In the more direct applications of the post-Keynesian theory[7] the relation between real and money wages is even more important for if wages were fixed in real terms, investment would be fixed as a technical maximum and thus the growth rate would have a single equilibrium value, which may or may not be the full employment rate.[8] Thus any attempt to increase the rate of investment would be handicapped by the lack of real resources to carry it out, any change from the ruling rate of investment determined by savings preferences being logically impossible. This brings up the second, and related, aspect of the role of finance.

The ability to create monetary claims in advance of (or without reference to) actual output is the feature of the monetary economy that allows those who can obtain finance (investors) to command physical resources in excess of their real earnings or wealth position. The ability of the capitalists to command finance for the appropriation of resources to investment purposes gives them ultimate control over the proportions in which the system's available resources are divided between investment and consumption. The difference between the money wage and what it will buy in terms of consumption goods then acts simply to confirm this division of resources that has already taken place on a different level.

As above, if investment were limited to finance out of profits (and/ or voluntary savings) there would be only one feasible combination of investment to consumption. The availability of finance in excess

---

[6] R. F. Kahn [25, p. 106], the passage continues, 'These two quantities – the quantities of consumer goods and total employment – have to be fitted to one another, due allowance being made for saving. The fit is secured by the real wage being established at the necessary level. The process is the pressure of demand on the supply of consumer goods. This determines the extent to which prices are held up above money wages – the ratio of one to the other, rather than the absolute level of either – and it also determines the level of profits, which in so far as devoted to consumption reduce the amount of consumer goods available to support the real wage.'

[7] E.g Kaldor, see chapter 13, below, for references.

[8] Thus making the result much similar to that which produces the knife-edge in Harrod's theory.

of earnings (and without reference to savings) allows investment to be a truly independent and autonomous variable in the system, affected more by entrepreneurial expectations (animal spirits) than anything else in the system. It supports the Keynesian proposition that only production creates income, that investment is necessary for production, and thus that investment determines income, employment and saving.

While it is true that finance is also available to consumers to finance consumption expenditure in excess of income, this does not provide a defence against the power of the capitalists to appropriate resources, for such expenditure takes place after the distribution of resources has been determined and only acts to put pressure on the prices of the existing available quantity of consumer goods. It may be true, however, that consumers who have recourse to credit may be able to improve their consumption positions relative to other consumers without access to credit. As will be seen below, there is a possibility for definite relative improvement by households with greater earning capacity or greater wealth positions.

The two aspects of the effect of monetary relations on the physical relations in the system are neatly linked in long-period analysis by Joan Robinson's concept of the 'inflation barrier' where the effect of the proportion of investment to consumption on the real wage of labour brings the labour force into action to try to redress the situation by means of demands for higher money wages. Because labour can only have an indirect effect on the process of production and investment decisions through the money-wage bargain the balance cannot be redressed and must result in spiralling inflation which eventually breaks confidence and produces a slump, with consequent rising unemployment. The inflation barrier thus represents the interaction between the real relations and their monetary consequences. It also underlines the crux of the problem of inflation in the struggle over income distribution.

MONETARY ECONOMY AND THE LONG-PERIOD

In working out the basic structural relations of the capitalist system in a long-period framework the post-Keynesian theory has stressed the physical relations necessary to the derivation of growth at full employment. It should not need emphasising that this exercise is a first step in the understanding of these relations and why or why not the system does not usually tend to conform to them. The disequilibrating effects of the existence of uncertainty are overcome by the assumption of tranquillity, which also must reduce the direct role of money in the analysis. This does not imply, as some have suggested, that the post-Keynesian approach to political economy is non-monetary. It is based in the relations of a monetary economy; it could not function, and would have no sense, without them. To gain a better understanding of the underlying physical structure of the system it is, so to speak, anaesthetised into tranquillity, but the roles of uncertainty, expectations, disappointment, money, etc., are still there to come into force when the assumption of tranquillity is relaxed.[9]

It is perhaps true to say that the explicit introduction of monetary institutions has been side stepped[11] in an attempt to clarify the physical relations of the monetary economy growing through historical time. This tendency, if it can be said to exist at all, and the reason why it can no longer exist, can be explained by reference to some technical coincidences in the simplest explanations of the post-Keynesian model.

THE DISTINCTION BETWEEN WAGES AND PROFITS, AND WORKERS AND CAPITALISTS

Following the Classical tradition, the post-Keynesian theory drew the lines of the problem of distribution around broad social classes as represented by wages and profits income. In the simplest version of the post-Keynesian model all profits are saved and all wages are consumed ($s_w = 0$, $s_p = 1$). Under these assumptions social and income classes are unambiguously identical, capitalists receive profits, workers receive wages. Further the entire system can be theoretically conceived in real quantities, in physical terms.

When wages are completely spent on consumption and money-wages are uniform, the real wage of labour is simply the consumption output divided by the number of workers. The share of labour is then the consumption output in the system. Both can readily be conceived of as physical amounts; reference to money wages or prices is

[9] As, for example, the exercise of the previous chapter. It should be emphasised that tranquillity does not imply either perfect foresight or perfect knowledge.

[10] Although Joan Robinson [85] devotes over fifty pages to problems of money and finance and Kahn [24] deals directly with the required rate of interest in the long-period context.

not needed. Talking about the money wage divided by the level of consumption goods prices or the simple quantity of consumption goods divided by the number of labourers is the same thing.

Likewise profits can be directly viewed as the net production of capital goods in the system for the corresponding period – a quantity of machines, without reference to prices. The sum of profit can be looked at as the total net output minus consumption output. The share of money profits in income or the share of machines in total output comes to the same thing. As a proportion of the system's output the physical quantity of capital has just as much meaning as the money sum that is exchanged for it.

Thus the share of labour in output is identically equal to the mass of consumption goods produced, and the share of profit is the net accumulation of machines. The distribution of income can be viewed just as easily in physical as in money terms. This physical representation has the further quality of directly corresponding to the proportion of investment to consumption goods as determined by the decisions of capitalists to command resources for capital goods production.

The rate of profit and the rate of growth have similar physical counterparts (in the absence of technical progress other than Harrod neutral), for the rate of profit is a quantity of machines as profit in relation to the existing machines in service, and the rate of growth of output is the ratio of physical output, capital and consumption, to similar quantities in preceding periods, i.e., the system can be treated as if it were moving along a von Neuman ray, for it has the same assumptions.

The possibility of explaining the system in this fashion, and the ease of emphasising the effect of the physical relations on distribution has *mistakenly* led many to believe that there was no place in the system for money, money relations or monetary institutions. As emphasised above, the system being treated is always a monetary system, in the sense of Keynes. Indeed the whole analysis would make no sense if it were not. However, it is only under the simple assumptions about savings propensities that the description of the relations of the system can be made as easily in physical terms as in monetary terms. That is, it is only in this simple case that the correspondence between physical and monetary quantities is unique.

When the analysis is opened up to include the possibility of savings out of wage income, the simple correspondence between physical and monetary quantities is lost. Much confusion is created if the consequences of this disinction are not clearly appreciated.

As Pasinetti emphasised, when there is saving out of wages, the simple correspondence between functional income categories (workers and capitalists) no longer holds [66]. If there is saving out of wages there must be some way for these savings to be employed or disposed of to useful purpose. This immediately suggests that some sort of financial intermediaries or financial assets are a necessary requirement if wage savings are not to be limited to being hidden under a mattress.

If wage savings are used to finance investment (as Pasinetti assumed) then workers become entitled to income represented by the profits on these investments. When workers receive both wages and profit as income the identity between the functional income categories (wages and profits) and social categories (workers and capitalists) no longer holds.

Despite the introduction of the assumption of saving out of wages Pasinetti was able to show that this change had no effect on the determination on the rate of profit or the distribution of functional income between *wages and profits* (but that it did effect the distribution between workers and capitalists). The rate of profit could still be explained by the simple formula $\pi = g/s_c$ with s_c representing capitalists' propensity to save (to match s_w the workers' propensity to save out of wages and profits on invested savings), replacing s_p, the propensity to save out of the functional income category profits in the original formula.

It is at this point that the non-identity between wages and profits and workers and capitalists causes a serious conflict between social appearance and physical relations. First, s_c enters the determination of the rate of profit in a masked form. In actuality it represents *the propensity to save out of total profits* as a functional income category, i.e., the two are equal (but not identical), $s_c = s_p$. It is only the fact that, under Pasinetti's assumptions, the propensity to save of the capitalists is equal to the propensity to save out of total profits that allows s_c to enter the determination of the rate of profit. Thus the original formula holds as the more general form.[11] Thus the post-

---

[11] Cf. chapter 14 below. The formula is worked out under more detailed assumptions, with the same results in [41, chapter 12]. R. F. Kahn touches on the same point when he notes that the results depend very crucially on the way income is defined [24].

Keynesian formula for the determination of the rate of profit (as Pasinetti pointed out) holds strictly only for functional income categories, and to explain the distribution of income between wages and profits. The introduction of $s_w > 0$ will have an effect on the distribution between workers and capitalists, but not in physical terms.

Thus, secondly, the correspondence between physical quantities and the distribution of income between wages and profits cannot be directly translated into the relations between workers and capitalists when there is saving out of wages, and social relations depart from functional income categories. In this case the real income of workers must be calculated by deflating money receipts by the prices of consumption goods. But this index need not correspond to real physical consumption. Thus, for example, if there is saving out of wages the workers receive income in excess of wages in terms of profits on their invested savings. The workers' money receipts divided by the level of consumption goods' prices thus indicates a higher real income, despite the fact that, in equilibrium, the purchase of physical consumption goods by workers is unchanged. In return for this nominally higher real income the workers receive some kind of paper assets for their savings – claims over future consumption which the class of workers as a whole can never realise; the higher real income does not mean higher real consumption.

The concept of real wages thus ceases to have a simple and direct physical meaning in terms of social classes, so also with real income. Real consumption still corresponds to the output of consumption goods in real terms, but there is no direct correspondence to this amount in social income terms, or in terms of income (wage + profits) divided by prices.

At the same time the physical description of profit is no longer possible. In the social sense profits as well cease to have a simple direct meaning, for some of them are now paid out as income to workers and thus are available for workers' consumption, being replaced by savings out of wages.[12]

Two levels of the theory thus become evident, with the functional income categories underlying, but no longer directly corresponding

[12] We should perhaps again emphasise that profits as a conceptual economic category will always exist, although they may be difficult to pin down in practice or company reports. This has caused some to suggest that cash flow is a more suitable and definable subject for the analysis of company finance decisions. This would then roughly correspond to gross profits in our terminology.

to, the visible social categories. The theory of distribution that would result from the visible level would be directly associated with personal income distribution. In such a case the major question becomes the distribution of claims over profits and the relations between corporations and households (producers and consumers), or extending the explanation to as many individual groups as one desires or views as meaningful.[13]

The major question at issue in this second approach is thus radically different, as are the structural and institutional relations necessary to analyse it. Pasinetti was able to make the simple assumption that workers pass their savings to the capitalists who invest them, i.e., an arrangement similar to common share ownership. The analysis, even at this simple level, thus suggests that it is absolutely necessary to introduce financial assets and institutions into the analysis. To answer the question of the distribution of the claims to profits this becomes of primary importance.

At the same time, however, it remains true that $\pi = g/s_p$ determines the overall rate of profit and that only the propensity to save out of total profits is important in the distribution of income between wages and profits. This simple relation will always underly the visible categories, and we can thus use it as a benchmark which allows the elaboration of distribution to whatever social categories we might find interesting.

For example we might want to look at the distribution of income in relation to income size. If we assume that the propensity to save is an increasing function of income then higher incomes will have a higher proportion of savings and thus claim a higher proportion of the profits income than lower groups. Thus a higher rate of investment that requires a lower amount of real consumption will come about through a lower real consumption by the low income groups (just as in the simple theory it was at the expense of real wages) for they have a smaller income reserve to meet the higher prices and they get back a smaller proportion of the higher profits than individuals with high incomes. Thus saving is made equal to the higher level of investment by lower real consumption and saving by lower income groups and higher saving by high income groups due to their greater ability to save. The manner of operation of this type of analysis is the same as that between wages and profits, which serves

---

[13] Pasinetti originally suggested this possibility [66], although it has not been taken up to date.

as a base for the analysis which now deals with markedly different categories.[14]

The recognition of the difference between functional and social categories, and physical and nominal quantities thus signals the enrichment of the theory in a number of ways. First of all financial assets must explicitly be introduced. With the introduction of financial assets, as the last example indicated, we also must be ready to take into account the two types of income from these assets: direct incomes and capital gains incomes.[15] Secondly the introduction of assets other than money will effect the behaviour patterns for both households and firms that will be analysed in the model. In addition it will allow us to make statements about general problems of monetary and financial policy. We will try to indicate, in very general terms, some of the possible effects on spending units (households) and firms.

WORKERS AND FINANCIAL ASSETS

Following our analysis above, the introduction of a range of different financial assets allows savings to be held in a wide variety of forms in addition to money or direct investment. Taking an overall ruling rate of profit for the economy we can rank returns to different types of financial assets in a descending order using the ruling rate of profit as a maximum: shares, preferred shares, bonds, bills, money. Assuming for the moment that the money supply is always sufficient to satisfy the demands by firms for investment funds so that there is no financing constraint, the answer to some of our questions about the distribution of profits will be answered by looking at differences in returns for different assets. The distribution of claims to profits is answered primarily by the type of assets that are held by any class, groups or individuals in the economy.

The proportion of profit that can be claimed by any class or group could then be explained by differential risk or liquidity preferences. But this is at best a liberal rationalisation, for it rests on the assumptions that (1) all individuals have equal incomes to place in assets, which implies, (2) that there is equal opportunity for all to enter

---

[14] The relation between high and low incomes is suggested in [41, chapter 12].

[15] This was taken up by Kaldor in his 'neo-Pasinetti theorem', developed in the appendix to [29]. A more elaborate approach is found in R. F. Kahn's 'Notes on the Rate of Interest and the Growth of Firms' [25]. See also [58, 59] for a treatment of the problems from a slightly different standpoint.

financial markets with equal information. Unless these assumptions are satisfied we cannot say that certain individuals or groups receive a higher proportion of total profits as income due to the higher returns earned on the assets they hold because of the difference in risk or liquidity preferences. A point of major importance in this type of investigation of the distribution of profits claims is the ownership of different asset types in relation to income level or income class, as well as the management of cash balances by different income and wealth groups.

When the composition of cash balances and different financial assets is different for different income groups these groups will be affected differently by changes in interest rates, share prices, investment, and government monetary policy. It is one of the great deficiencies of the analysis of the effects of monetary policy that it seldom looks at how monetary policy may effect income distribution, usually assuming that all individuals are affected equally and the distribution of income not at all.

The real value of claims on future output in terms of gains on and holdings of financial assets will be affected by changes in monetary policy and will thus bring about different reactions on individual consumption and savings decisions. If we want to argue that changes in monetary policy will affect all spending units equally we must assume that all such units have the same consumption and asset positions, as well as equal opportunity to invest in assets of all ranges of return; but such an assumption makes the analysis of money and financial assets nugatory in the analysis of the effects of monetary policy. If we are interested in explaining distribution by social categories as well as by functional income categories the inclusion of these differences is crucial.

Let us make some simple assumptions. Access to financial markets and information are associated with the level of income. Thus savings from low incomes will be held primarily in cash or fixed interest earning assets such as deposit accounts or national savings schemes. Middle incomes have sufficient income to allow investments in government securities and investment trusts. High income earners place their savings in common or preferred shares, the returns from the former varying with the profitability of the corporations and the general state of confidence in the market.

Now we can start with a simple comparison of differences in the rate of accumulation as between two economies made up of households with different income levels and thus different holding of financial placements. The quantity of money in each case is appropriate to allow the entrepreneurs the finance they desire. The system with the higher rate of accumulation will require more profits and thus have higher prices for its relatively lower output of consumption goods. For the high-income groups in the high-accumulation economy the higher profits come back to them in terms of higher dividends and capital gains in greater proportion than the rate of interest is higher than in the low-accumulation economy. The low-income groups on fixed interest returns in the high-accumulation economy have a lower purchasing power of total income than their counterparts in the low-accumulation economy. Income claims are thus the same, or are lower in a lower proportion for high incomes than for low incomes as between the two economies. Just as in the functional income analysis, where the real wage would have been lower, now the real value of income claims for low income groups is lower. Instead of saying that investment is at the expense of wage consumption we can now say that it is at the expense of low incomes. Thus it is probable that macroeconomic stabilisation and full employment policies, as well as monetary policy, may have direct effects on the distribution of income, and these effects are the same whether we talk of wage incomes or the low paid.

If we look at the relations in an economy moving over time and add the effects of expectations in a system where prices do not necessarily fall with deficient demand we find the same general relation. Low incomes may be harder hit by rising prices, and in an effort to provide for an uncertain future try to increase their savings in liquid assets. The consumption in the present and the claims on future consumption of the low income groups then will decrease to a greater extent than for high incomes. Such a situation would be in direct contradiction to the postulated Pigou or (asset) wealth effect.

In the orthodox analysis a change in the general level of prices affects the value of wealth held in financial and other assets. Rising prices should then reduce the value of wealth held in assets. But when some asset holders get back all of the rise in prices in terms of dividends and capital gains while others are limited to fixed returns on their wealth it is the high income and wealth groups that can retain their consumption and wealth positions – in fact they may well increase their claims on future output at the expense of low incomes. Thus the rich become richer as the poor become poorer, the wealth effect may work in the opposite direction once we look at the distribution of assets by types of return as held by different income groups.

The failure of prices to fall with deficient demand forbids the Pigou effect from working in the opposite direction, but even if prices did fall, disappointed expectations would forbid the required increase in demand, thus making the explanation of full employment via the Pigou effect suspect in a world of unequal incomes and asset ownership.[16]

ASSET STRUCTURES AND PRODUCTIVE ENTERPRISE

Now let us turn to the other side of the financial asset relationship, to the firms which issue assets to gain finance. Like the household, the firm has a balance sheet – one side has assets (machines, buildings, etc.) the other liabilities (financial assets to the rest of the community). At one time or other the two were roughly equal. Investment was funded by retained profits, share issues, bonds, long-term bank borrowing or short-term paper. The proportion of these assets and the proportion of external debt to assets will not be determined randomly. The liabilities are all similar in the sense that they place an obligation on the firm's flow of profit. The time structure of these assets will differ from the time structure of the physical assets they brought into existence. It is in relation to earnings and the time structure of assets that the structure of liabilities may at any particular time appear so inappropriate as to attain an aura of randomness.

Firms, given expectations (including those about expected rises in wages), attempt to gear their investment to the conditions prevailing in the financial markets. These conditions, of course, are to an extent of their own making for they control the primary emission of assets and the level of income (through their combined investment decisions) along with the banks and the government. Their expectations to a certain extent spill over into the expectations of the purchasers of their liabilities, through changes in the level of income resulting from investment and funding decisions.

If the corporation is funding part of its investment externally it will assume that the flow of profit will roughly balance the necessary

[16] It should be recalled that it was the role of the Pigou effect (or wealth effect) to show that the operation of relative prices, when perfectly flexible, would eventually lead the system to full employment.

redemption of liabilities, interest and dividend payments, and investment planned with internal finance. However, unforeseen changes in any number of variables, e.g. demand, interest rates, liquidity preference, government policy, can rudely upset the rough balance. Just as the economy carries the skeleton of its past investment decisions in the existing stock of capital, it also has these relics in its portfolios – they may be no easier nor less costly to dispose of.[17]

Thus once we admit the existence of financial assets into the model the conditions of steady growth become much more difficult to achieve (and to analyse) than in the simple case where wages are fully spent and profits are identical to the investment that caused them. Not only must the broad relation between total savings and total investment be satisfied, but there must also be a rough correspondence between the financing decisions of firms (given market conditions) and the liquidity preference (and income distribution) of the public, given their expectations and expectations of the share market. To this must be added the decisions and market interventions of the banking system.

Thus the technical and structural effects of the firms' liability positions, along with their expectations will have a direct effect on their real decisions and the appropriation and use of the real resources in the system. As indicated in the preceding chapter, these effects may make monetary policy not only ineffective, but damaging to the ability of the system to maintain full employment.

One of the biggest problems of the traditional explanation of investment decisions is that it emphasises interest rates (which reflect governments' or households' expectations of asset prices) in the determination of the relative prices of capital and consumption goods output and thus the decision to invest, completely ignoring the possibility of the firms having expectations and concerns over a very different set of variables and that their control over them is only impinged by their ability to satisfy these expectations in relation to the extent that government monetary policy eases or aggravates the ability of firms to form the liability structures they desire for their investment programmes. Like the effect of policy on the household, it is too often assumed that the kinds of liabilities a firm is forced to acquire has no affect on its decisions, or that all firms are affected equally by monetary control.

[17] Much of this type of analysis is to be credited to the work of H. P. Minsky [56, 57].

To bring the effects on households and firms together, we indicated that the total level of consumer demand would be affected by the distribution of asset ownership and expectations. Also the liability structures of firms and their expectations will strongly effect their ability to carry out investment and employment decisions. Monetary policy may then affect both sides through the link between households and firms of financial assets and their distribution. Whether monetary policy that would be beneficial to the firms will also be for the households, is a question that cannot be answered *a priori.*

Movement along a path of steady growth in conditions of tranquillity is a much simpler proposition to prove than to achieve in practice. Thus while there is no reason or necessity to restrict the analysis to the simple cases outlined in Part Two above, these preliminary relations must be worked out before more complicated analysis, especially in terms of money and financial assets, can be attempted. As R. F. Kahn puts it, 'I desire to learn to walk before I try to run' [24]. Many of those who try to run before they can walk have deprecated the usefulness of walking. What has been presented above is just a rough outline of some possible areas of analysis that could be approached with a concrete knowledge of the simple model.

12 An Open Economy

Many of the standard results of the neoclassical theory of international trade also come into question when exposed to the possibilities of capital heterogeneity and production through historical time. Since this criticism is well documented (cf. [54, 55, 102, 103, 105]), as are the extensions of Keynes's short-period theory to trade (e.g. [76, part III]) these aspects will not be taken up here. The reader is, however, directed to Steedman [102] and Steedman and Metcalfe [103] for a reappraisal of Ricardo's theory in relation to later neoclassical interpretations of Ricardo's approach.

In the present chapter we will be more interested in the application of the post-Keynesian approach to an open economy. We cannot pretend to supply a full reworking of international trade theory, but will content ourselves with general indications towards such a development. We are particularly interested in how international exchange in goods will effect the results we have obtained above for a closed system.

In an economy which is open to trade many of the results obtained for the closed system will naturally be modified. The general method of analysis, however, remains substantially the same. We begin by noting several general areas in which the analysis will be modified.

GENERAL EFFECTS OF INTERNATIONAL EXCHANGE

First, exchange with other economic systems removes the limits on available resources; trade may increase or decrease the available resources or change their composition.

Second, as mentioned in chapter 10, competition from foreign producers may limit the ability of domestic producers to set the prices they desire and require to finance their planned investment, thus forcing a greater reliance on external finance or a reduction in investment plans. At the same time foreign markets provide the possibility of using profits in excess of domestic expansion needs for investment abroad.

Further the possibility of spreading production and sales over several national boundaries (as for example multi-national corporations) reduces the uncertainty over costs and competition for sales both at home and abroad. A multi-national firm grouping can thus effectively limit the uncertainty over its sales and prices by becoming both the domestic producer and the foreign competitor at the same time. With diverse national markets the firm will be less susceptible to changes in national market demand, national wage costs, and individual government's economic policy. Thus sales and production will take place in diversely placed, but commonly directed, national units.

Larger size of productive units may also bring higher productivity due to large-scale processes, but it should be noted that international expansion and large size go hand in hand, for the reductions in unit costs associated with large size require stable, growing markets. To ensure this stable production, firms will be less willing to submit themselves to the vagaries of market growth, wage costs or government economic policy in any one country.

Third, international exchange in consumption goods may effect the 'inflation barrier'. The strict relation between investment, profit and real wages may be broken when workers are free to spend their incomes on imported goods. Thus the real wage implied by a given ratio of investment to consumption can be increased by the import and purchase of less expensive foreign goods. At the same time (unless imports of consumption goods are just matched by exports) the price level and profit rate implied by a given rate of investment may be lower when imported goods are consumed. The 'inflation barrier' may thus come into effect at a higher ratio of investment to consumption than without imports of consumption goods.

Such a situation, however, would imply a rising deficit on current account which must be balanced by earnings from investment abroad, by exports of capital goods, gold payments or devaluation. Thus we may find that the 'inflation barrier' is replaced by a 'balance of payments barrier' which produces broadly similar results. If, for example, the government uses demand restriction, a programme to favour exports, or devaluation (or all three together) to adjust a payments deficit the effect will be to reduce real purchasing power, reduce available domestic consumption goods, or make imports more expensive, all three acting to reduce the real consumption value (or the rate of increase) of wage incomes. If this encourages unions to press for higher money-wages, the resulting wage-price spiral of the 'inflation barrier' analysis comes into action. Just as the unions' reactions to the inflation barrier in the analysis of the closed system prevents the system from retaining its stable full employment growth position, the action of the 'balance of payments barrier' may make it more difficult to sell exports, preventing the return of a stable payments balance necessary to allow full employment. The depressing effects on output and employment of both cases are well known. In addition devaluation will have effects on the terms of trade which affects the physical resource position of the country, with a higher quantity of produced output now required to attain a given amount of foreign product.

Thus, in analysing trade, we will find it useful to distinguish among imports and exports of both capital and consumption goods output, for the consumption of imports and exports will have a direct effect on the physical resources available to a country, the compostion of its final available and non-available output, as well as the distribution of income.

Fourth, the open economy allows direct analysis of policy questions, especially in terms of interest rates to control the level of international capital flows, and the effect of exchange rates on the terms of trade. It is also obvious that only in rare cases will there be compatibility between the economic goals (and utilised policy measures) of individual nations and the multi-national corporations that might be located within them. Of course this is one of the reasons for the existence of such corporations.

Fifth, we also recognise that some of the significance of certain variables used in the analysis will be different. For example, the level of real wages in any one country has very little meaning in another economy, and we have no meaningful method for comparing them. The real wage embodied in an imported good is of very little significance to the price of imports in relation to home produce. The level of money-wages, which directly effects money prices, is what will be important; so in terms of international competitiveness the most important factors will be the relative money-wage levels and relative productivity. The level of real wages will effect the competitiveness of internationally traded products only to the extent that it acts on the level of money-wages and prices, tempered by differences in productivity.

These relations will, of course, be effected by the exchange rate which translates foreign prices into home prices, but we can draw no general rule about the effect of exchange rates for they need not be directly related to differences in real or money-wages, nor to productivity differences among countries. To the extent that exchange rates are fixed, their periodic changes will be linked most closely to changes in money-wages relatively to other countries, and the degree of confidence multi-national firms place on the stability of the exchanges.

ANALYTICAL DIFFERENCES

The standard analyses of international exchange take imports and exports in terms of homogeneous national product, and look only at the effect of trade on the level of aggregate demand through the relations of saving to investment, exports acting to increase demand relatively to home production and vice versa for imports. Policy questions are also treated in this framework.

By looking directly at the composition of exports and imports in terms of our two sectors (consumption goods and capital goods) we can directly analyse the effect of trade and balance of payments policy on distribution and profitability. It would be a mistake, in this context, to consider all exports as equivalent to investment and all imports as equivalent to saving, although this is often done. The import and export of capital goods may do nothing to change the relation of available to non-available output, although this will be true of consumption goods.

In addition we are faced with some problems between analysis and reality in employing the approach of dynamic comparison. For a system to be in steady growth it will be necessary for its trade to always be in balance; or, in the case of overall imbalance, an ever-increasing deficit or surplus on trade account, or an ever rising or falling exchange rate in the case of easily changed or flexible rates of exchange, will be necessary. None of these possibilities are particularly becoming or realistic. At the same time it would be a mistake to start right out with the analysis of change over time. We thus start by looking at the conditions that would be necessary for a country that engages in trade to produce the same characteristics as a closed system. We can then use this as a benchmark for looking at the effects of imports and exports of capital and consumption goods taken first separately and then in combination.

COMPLETE TRADE BALANCE AND COMPARATIVE COSTS

A country that has what we will call a complete trade balance will have balanced trade in both consumption goods and capital goods. Thus import of capital goods are just balanced by exports of same, and exports of consumption goods just equal consumption imports. Overall trade is thus in balance ($X_i = M_i$, $X_c = M_c$) and the trading country has the same proportions of investment to consumption goods as a non-trading country under the same production conditions. It is only under these restrictive conditions that the trading and non-trading country will be identical. As we shall see, they will not be identical under other combinations of imports and exports that yield balance of payments equilibrium. We again point out that we are forced to take the analysis at the start from the position of equilibrium of the trade balance, for without this assumption forces would be set up to correct a surplus or deficit and involve us in change over time in one economy before we are ready to analyse it.

There is one possible case where the trade and no-trade economy may not be identical, so we shall deal with that first. If there are differences in productivity or natural resource endowments between the trading countries, the doctrine of comparative costs may explain a benefit for the trading country. Normal arguments about trade flows follow the theory of comparative costs. Thus, for a given expenditure of labour on a given good, if it can be exchanged for another with higher domestic labour requirements, the total of goods that can be procured with a given labour force will be higher if production and trade are concentrated in goods with comparative advantage. Thus, under the comparative cost principle, the real wage could be higher for a given ratio of consumption to investment when trade and specialisation takes place in consumption goods with comparative advantage. Likewise the accumulation of capital goods could also be higher for trade and specialisation in comparative advantage capital goods. The total of goods available for a given expenditure of labour and ratio of investment to output may thus increase with comparative advantage trade. Thus as long as overall trade remains in balance for both sectors the trading country could have a higher real wage and rate of growth of capital than the non-trade country when both have the same resources and the same ratio of investment to output. This is the only case in which there can be a difference between the trade and no-trade countries in conditions of complete trade balance for the trading country, and we thus leave it to one side along with the problems of technical choice that comparative cost exchange in capital goods may involve.

INDIVIDUAL EFFECTS

We now look at the effects of imports and exports of capital and consumption goods, each taken separately, without worrying about the trade balance or the repercussions that these exchanges may cause for the trading partners, or on the ability to find export markets. For each category of imports and exports we look at the difference such trade will have in relation to the non-trading position of the country, assuming that the ratio of investment to consumption, level of money wages, etc., remains unchanged. We thus, for example, do not discuss exports of capital goods that result from an increase in the production of capital goods, but export of the given capital goods produced; likewise for consumption goods.

Export of capital goods

If capital goods only are exported the internal accumulation of capital will be lower. The ratio of investment to consumption is unchanged, the internal accumulation of capital is lower, but balanced by the trading surplus. The direct effect will be on the level of employment, for if the trade causes the internal accumulation of capital to be less than the rate of growth of employable labour the level of employment will fall. On the other hand, if the rate of capital accumulation had been above the rate of growth of labour, exports will have the beneficial effect of making investment more profitable and thus high enough to produce full employment. The export of capital thus primarily effects the level of employment and the profitability of capital goods production. With an unchanged ratio of capital to consumption production the mass of consumption goods available for wage consumption is unchanged, and thus the real wage is unaffected. The changes in the profitability of capital goods production may set up forces that act to increase the ratio of investment to consumption which would affect the real wage and thus also react on the choice of technique.

Import of capital goods

Imports of capital goods increase the productive capacity of the economy and increase the demand for labour to man capital. As in the case of exports, the major effect will be on employment and the profitability of capital goods production. To the extent that labour was unemployed in the absence of capital imports such imports represent borrowing in the present to increase present and future production. If the rate of growth of output that the import of capital allows is greater than the interest on the finance that must be used to cover the deficit it may be in the long-run interest of a country to carry out such a policy despite the deficit on the balance of payments that it causes, provided that it can persuade the rest of the world to allow it to do so.

The potential effects on the choice of technique will also be similar to that of the case of exports of capital. Taking the two cases together we must also recognise that when trading countries are on different positions on the ruling spectrum of techniques (or on different spectra) trade provides the possibility of the employment of different techniques without an actual change in the ratio of investment to output. This is, of course, just a slightly different way of looking at the doctrine of comparative costs.

Export of consumption goods

The export of consumption goods reduces the available domestic supply of a given output of consumption goods and thus will promote higher market clearing prices and profits on home production. The real consumption of labour is thus reduced. To the extent that this increases expectations it may give a boost to accumulation or make domestic markets more desirable: the former detrimental; the latter favourable to real wages.

The export of consumption goods itself does nothing to free resources for higher investment, as the same quantity of resources must still be devoted to their production even though they are not consumed internally. The surplus on trade account can, however, be used to command more foreign resources. Thus the higher share of profit and lower share of wages associated with a given ratio of investment to consumption with exports of consumption goods is in a sense illusory from the point of view of command over internal resource utilisation, but allows total resources for investment to increase to the extent that the surplus is used to command foreign capital. Such a position may be beneficial to exports as a whole to the extent that firms require profitable home markets before they are willing to enter export markets.

Imports of consumption goods

The existence of competitive imports of consumption goods will act to increase the available consumption goods in the system and thus decrease the revenue received for the sale of a given quantity of domestic goods. The price of consumption being lower due to foreign competition, the real wage of labour will be higher. Thus an economy that allows a free flow of competitive imports may find its level of prices and profits lower. To the extent this blunts the spirit to invest the growth rate will be depressed, with detrimental effects on employment.

The real problem is, of course, that such a situation creates a deficit on the balance of payments that must eventually be paid – thus a charge is placed on capital accumulation or future consumption to make good the deficit. This is true whether the debt is paid off in terms of consumption or capital exports or financial assets, or if the exchange rate is adjusted. Thus the import of consumption goods can change the distribution of resources between consumption and investment for as long as the country can find reserves to support the deficit. This case is then just the opposite of the export of consumption goods, except for the reaction to a deficit being in the long-run more detrimental to employment than for a surplus. It is, however, more favourable to the level of the real wage.

The sort of reasoning implied here resembles the neoclassical theory of time preference, for the time distribution of consumption is altered. Perhaps it would make more sense to guage time preference in relation to balance of payments figures than interest rates, as consumers may have more control over imports in the short run than over the rate of investment which is the major determinant of the rate of profit and the rate of interest. In the sense that the interest rate is tied to balance of payments policy, the use of consumption imports as a measure of time preference may be even more desirable. Unfortunately the regulation of international trade would never allow a full expression of such preferences, for both governments and international agencies assure that deficits are not allowed to become too great – balance of payments policies being in the hands of the capitalists and the government, not the consumers.

Imports and exports

Of course imports and exports do not always balance. It is usually the case that countries find themselves in a position where they must actively search for sufficient exports to balance the imports that are occurring. There are a number of ways by which this balance can be maintained, but for present purposes we will be interested in only two, which act most directly on the position of real wages and capital accumulation. As a contrast to the position of 'complete trade balance' that we outlined above we now look at situations where trade is in balance ($X_c + X_i = M_c + M_i$) but exports of consumption goods may be greater or less than imports of consumption goods and likewise for capital goods. We will then compare these positions of trade balance with those of a no-trade (or complete trade balance) economy.

We start by identifying the following variables.

$I = I' + X_i$, where I' is capital used domestically and X_i, capital exports.
$I'' = I' + M_i$, or the internal capital available for production.
$C = C' + X_c = C' - M_c$, or the internal production of consumption goods.
$C' = C - X_c$ or $C + M_c$, or available consumption goods.

In terms of the relation of investment to consumption and thus the real wage and profit relations we are primarily interested in I, the total domestic production of capital, and C', the available consumption goods in the system. We thus have two possible positions of equilibrium trade balance

$$(1)\ \ X_i > M_i = X_c < M_c,\ \ I > I'' = C < C',\ \ I/C > I/C'$$
$$(2)\ \ X_i < M_i = X_c > M_c,\ \ I < I'' = C > C',\ \ I/C < I/C'$$

In more simple terms case (1) could be reduced to $M_c = X_i$ and (2) to $M_i = X_c$.

It can be seen that these positions of trade balance have different effects on profits and the real wage. In position (1) the effective ratio of investment to consumption goods is lower, I/C representing the resources committed to investment and consumption and I/C' showing the relation between investment and available consumption goods due to trade. In this case the real wage is increased at the expense of capital accumulation for I'' is less than I. With the same overall rate of growth of GNP the rate of profit is lower and the real wage is higher. The second case is just the opposite. In general we could say that in case (1) the country is trading capital accumulation for consumption and in the second the country is foregoing consumption for higher capital accumulation. It is unlikely that in either case stable growth could be maintained at the same technique of production for in (1) capital will become scarce and in (2) will be in surplus relative to the available labour force. There will be some level of mechanisation which would allow each system to maintain a stable growth path, but (a) this position will be different from that for the no trade economy, and (b) will be different from the trading economy with 'complete' trade balance. We thus see that in the analysis of growth it is not sufficient to look simply at the balance of overall imports and exports, for the combination and composition of imports and exports will have a direct effect on the growth path, the real wage and the profit rate. In an open economy there is no way to draw a direct relation between the ratio of investment to output and the distribution of income or between the growth rate and the profit rate.

The usefulness of such a formulation depends on the social relations that one puts into it. If imports are free to vary and the system is assumed to stay in equilibrium, then exports of capital goods must adjust to preserve trade equilibrium. In such a case the wage-earners will always be in a position to react to a rate of investment that they feel implies a real wage that is too low. If both imports of capital and consumption goods are free to vary then exports of both may have to adjust and the net result will depend on the final composition of trade. The most realistic result is that neither category will adjust quickly enough and that government policy intervenes to cut down the imports of consumption goods by restricting demand and the 'balance of payments barrier' comes into effect. This raises the prices of exports and makes it even harder to restore payments balance. To the extent that there is foreign competition, the rise in prices implied by case (2) may bring about a lower real wage, but this is dampened by the effect of the reduced rise in prices due to the fear of foreign competition.

The simple relation $\pi = g/s_p$ that we used in the analysis of a closed system thus becomes more complicated when trade in goods is taken into account. Taking account of the relations that we have discussed the formula would take the following form

$$\pi = \frac{g' + (X_i + X_c)/K - m_w(W/K) - (M_i/K)}{s_p}$$

where $g' = I'/K$ and m_w is the propensity to purchase imports out of wages given $s_w = 0$. When there is complete trade balance the formula collapses to the simpler form; if not it must be taken in the more complicated version. Under the assumption that total investment inclusive of exports of capital is constant, and postulating a relation between imports of capital and profits such that $mP = M_i$ we would have

$$\pi = \frac{g + X_c/K - m_w(W/K)}{s_p + m}$$

which highlights the relations that we have been considering, i.e., the effect of imports and exports of consumption goods on profits and real wages when exports and imports of capital goods adjust to preserve the trade balance. Thus the formula tells us that the consumption of imports has a detrimental effect, and the export of consumption goods a positive effect, on the rate of profit, no account being taken of the effects on internal accumulation and employment. We should note, however, that the formula cannot be used with the same facility as the simple formula in the case of the closed (or complete trade balance) system.

In general, it is obvious that the capitalists in the system may not have the same direct control over exports and imports that they have over the ratio of investment to consumption. Thus the most important change brought about by the introduction of trade is that stable growth is even more difficult to achieve, for workers can always offset the distributional consequences of any particular rate of accumulation by the purchase of imports, and the capitalists may have to settle for a lower rate of profit for a given rate of investment due to the existence of foreign competition. The payments deficit that such situations can create usually brings enough pressure from the capitalists to convince the government to abandon support of growth with full employment in favour of support of the value of the currency.

One of Keynes's most important contributions to economic policy was to try to set up institutions that would safeguard against the possibility of such reactions taking place. Provision of international credits and adjustable exchange rates were to allow freedom to adjust to deficits that would not prejudice full employment. Unfortunately this is another part of the Keynesian revolution that did not succeed, for neither devaluation, international debts, nor weak currencies are in the interest of capitalists' profits.

For stable growth to occur balance is necessary between both trade in goods and capital flows. The general approach that we have presented here links exports to the profitability of the home country (exports of capital goods or investment abroad) and imports to the prevailing level of the real wage (and thus primarily to consumption goods). A higher ratio of investment to consumption taken internally then promotes both capital exports (and investment abroad) and imports of consumption goods (through the real wage). This extends the struggle over the distribution of income to the composition of trade as well as the overall ratio of internal investment to consumption. In this sense both inflation and a trade deficit are involved in the struggle over the distribution of income and cannot be separated in the analysis of an open economy.

The relations that we have tried to work out are of the simplest kind. We have not included the possibility of saving out of wages, explicit policy relations and the flow of capital that results from the existence of international corporations. Nor have we specifically examined the effects of exchange rates and the terms of trade, or the use of profits. Such additions would signal application to the problems of developing countries. The simple model, however, is open to be adapted to these modifications.

Even on the simple level, the introduction of trade in goods makes stable growth in a capitalist system more of a myth, for it provides the possibility of both inside and outside forces to upset it. The imports of consumption goods become an active variable in the determination of the real wage, while the level of money-wages and prices along with the level of real income directly effect the level of consumption imports. These imports are the easiest to explain, and the hardest to curtail. Any attempt to do so may bring the 'balance of payments' version of the 'inflation barrier' into action, making it almost impossible to bring about the correction of the trading position without a deep slump. Thus we find that not only is full employment growth not a natural result of the system, but that balanced trade is an even less likely result when combined with full employment. We also see that the problem of the trade balance may be directly related to the problems of the distribution of income and thus to inflation. The post-Keynesian relations and tools are thus not limited to the analysis of a closed system and gain even greater relevance when applied to an open economy.

Part Four

13 Alternative Post-Keynesian Analyses – I

As implied in the first chapter, it is an oversimplification to say that a homogeneous school of thought exists in the post-Keynesian approach to economics and economic dynamics. The basic similarities of the post-Keynesians' approach are rooted in the fact that they all take Keynes's work as the starting point. However, there are major differences in emphasis, as among the major contributors to the post-Keynesian reconstruction of Political Economy. In this, and the following chapter, we attempt to briefly highlight the most important of these differences.

KALDOR AND STYLISED FACTS

The first explanation of distribution and growth by Nicholas Kaldor [26] appeared at about the same time as the publication of Joan Robinson's major work on the same subject [85]. In this chapter we will compare the approaches of the two authors. Since we will not be able to present the evolution of Kaldor's views in detail, the student is referred to his major works [27, 28, 30, 31].

The first difference to be noted is that Kaldor explicitly builds abstract models. But while they are abstract they are meant to correspond to what Kaldor calls the 'stylised facts' of the real world (more or less constant wage share in national income, generally stable growth, low or zero saving out of wages, steady growth of output per head and capital stock, etc.). The models are thus meant to reflect reality and to be used to analyse it in both a theoretical and a practical policy sense. In this sense Kaldor does not have any particular qualms about analysing changes over time in a particular economy, an exercise that Joan Robinson treats with the utmost caution.

For Kaldor stability is a natural property of long-period analysis, for Professor Robinson it is a myth. The same difference is apparent in the treatment of full employment. In Joan Robinson's models a number of quasi-golden-age situations are possible at less than full employment of the labour force. In Kaldor's approach, if the system is in a position of long-run steady growth, full employment is a necessary outcome. Although Kaldor has been accused of achieving this result by assumption, he does, in fact, provide a logical analysis of its necessity which rests primarily on the assumption that available labour is the basic constraint to full-capacity utilisation of capital and growth [28, 30].

PRICES AND DISTRIBUTION

The Kaldor approach also differs markedly in its analysis of pricing, price response, and the operation of the distribution mechanism. This is largely because Kaldor chooses to analyse movements through time in a single economy. He generally follows the method of price determination that involves the addition of the normal rate of profit to wage costs of production in order to arrive at selling price fixed by the firm.[1] An increase in the rate of investment in the system then causes excess demand for consumption goods which drives up prices. As prices are assumed to adjust more quickly to changes in investment and aggregate demand, and money-wages slowly or not at all, the real wage falls as profits rise in response to a higher rate of investment. Actual changes in consumption goods prices bring about the reduction in consumption out of wage incomes as market-clearing is established. The rise in prices equally increases profits to accommodate the equality between savings and investment. This equality is assured by the assumption that the propensity to save out of wages is less than that out of profits (Kaldor in general assumes that $s_w < s_p < 1$) which allows the system to achieve stable equilibrium growth at any rate of investment that produces a rate of profit high enough to encourage entrepreneurs to continue at that rate.

The major difference is that Kaldor assumes that this is a process that actually occurs over time. This requires the assumption that consumption goods' prices are flexible (at a minimum in an upward direction) or that there are rapid changes in entrepreneurs' expected gross profit margins (at least in the consumption goods sector); either of which respond quickly to the pressures of demand. On the other hand money wages must be assumed to respond very slowly or not at all (or in lesser proportion than prices).

[1] This is also the basis of some of the analysis presented in chapter 10, above.

If prices are not easily changed due to market imperfections, or are changed only with discretion, or if labour is quick to respond to a rise in prices by demanding higher money wages, the process will not operate as simply as Kaldor implies. Although the distribution mechanism is sound, it does not allow for large price fluctuations and thus instability; for if prices are not easily changed the profit share may not rise, thus damping investment, or if prices are flexible the result is inflation due to wage claims, markedly increasing uncertainty about real future consumption and investment projects. It is for this latter problem that Professor Robinson introduces the concept of the 'inflation barrier'. The former cannot occur because she would find it difficult to make a definite prediction about change occurring over time. These problems in the adjustment process of Kaldor's model do not do much to support his claim of 'stylised' stability of the actual economy.

In his later models, e.g. [31], Kaldor introduces a slightly different pricing convention in terms of a 'corporate pay-off period'. Corporations are assumed to determine a fixed period of time (estimated at say 3–4 years) in which they want to recover the cost of an investment project. Prices are then set, given expectations of demand high enough to generate profits over the pay-off period equal to the cost of the investment project. All revenue earned after the period is thus pure profit.

This type of pricing policy corresponds to entrepreneurial reactions in the face of rapidly changing technology. If technology is changing rapidly, present investments may be quickly superseded by machines of higher productivity per man and higher profitability. Thus the concept of pay-off period pricing reflects the entrepreneur's attempt to at least cover the costs of investments before they are made technologically inefficient by new, more productive techniques. This reflects Kaldor's concern about the importance of technical change on a realistic description of the process of growth, and the behaviour of capitalists in that process.

This institutional change in the method of price determination in Kaldor's theory does not affect the ruling rate of profit achieved by the system as much as it effects the role played by the profit rate in his models. Since Kaldor is dealing with changes over time in a model that is more or less to reflect reality, the rate of profit being earned on existing investment is of very little consequence to new investment decisions which relate to new types of productive equipment. Thus investment decisions are taken in regard to the rate of profit expected on new investments in terms of the expected pay-off period and the expected life of the equipment, in relation to others in the industry and closely related industries.

From this basis Kaldor rejects the valuation of the existing stock of capital as unrealistic and unnecessary. He thus works solely with the *expected* rate of profit (as symbolised in the pay-off period) on the value of new gross investment calculated at existing demand prices. While this approach has great practical appeal by short-circuiting the capital valuation problem, it represents the most marked difference between the methodological approaches of Kaldor and Mrs Robinson.

It is one of the prime goals of Professor Robinson's analysis to derive a theoretical groundwork for the determination of the rate of profit and the distribution of income between wages and profits. Kaldor, attempting to set up a model descriptive of behaviour rejects the necessity of deriving concepts such as the rate of profit and the value of capital on the grounds that entrepreneurs (a) cannot know what they are, and (b) do not use them in practice.[2] They are thus unnecessary to Kaldor's analysis and he replaces them with his unique concept of the 'technical progress function', which is the crux of his particular approach.

TECHNICAL PROGRESS AND ITS FUNCTION

In relation to technical progress Kaldor first of all explicitly rejects any possibility of analysing the choice of techniques in terms of capital intensity. He considers such analysis basically neoclassical and chides Professor Robinson for making such a detailed analysis of the problem. It is, of course, easy to see that this position results directly from denying the necessity of the valuation of capital or the determination of the rate of profit, for choice of technique considerations, as we have seen in chapter 7, rely on explicit knowledge of the rate of profit to be used in calculating the capital costs of different techniques.

Instead Kaldor posits a simple decision rule for capitalists investing in new techniques. They are assumed to always choose the

[2] This, of course, does not resolve Professor Robinson's concern with deriving a theoretical explanation of the determination of the rate of profits and distribution of income.

technique that gives the greatest increase in output per head at the lowest cost of capital per man, without bothering to decide if the new technique is more capital or labour intensive than existing techniques. While this observation is undoubtedly realistic it causes some problems for the underlying theoretical model. In order to preserve the stability of the growth path in Kaldor's model it is necessary for the continuous introduction of new techniques to produce (on balance) a constant capital–labour or capital–output ratio. In other words technical progress must be broadly neutral over time. Thus, although the concepts of bias in technical progress are rejected, Kaldor does not hesitate to employ the integrally related concept of neutrality in the technical change that does take place. The technical position is thus not much different from an analysis that takes account of bias, but the methodological application of the principle is the distinguishing feature.

It is in this regard that the technical progress function becomes the *deus ex machina* of the Kaldor model. The technical progress function ranges all existing techniques of production in terms of the rate of increase in productivity they produce associated with the rate of change in investment per man that they require. Assuming that there is some technique for which a higher investment per man results in a smaller increase in productivity than for previous techniques implies that there is some point on the function at which the rate of increase in investment required for the technique just equals the rate that it increases productivity per man. At this point investment per man just equals output per man in terms of rates of increase. If the system is always at this point on the function the capital–output ratio will be constant (in the terms of chapter 6 the ratio of investment to output is constant) and thus relative shares of wages and profits in income, and the rate of profit will be constant. Thus when there is diminishing returns in terms of productivity to increases in the rate of investment there must also exist a point of constant returns, which for all practical purposes represents neutral technical progress over time.

Thus if one can show that the economy will always be at this point of constant returns on the technical progress function it follows that the system will exhibit steady growth with constant shares of wages and profits in output. In such conditions the pay-off period will be uniquely determined, as will the length of time that each plant of given technique is held in production before being replaced by a plant of the newest available technique. Since the rate of profit will also be constant if the rest of the variables in the system are constant, Kaldor can reject the necessity of actually finding out what the rate of profit actually is for it adapts to the other variables in the system.

This is all quite sensible, if one can derive an explanation of how the economy reaches and maintains the desired position of neutrality on the technical progress function. Unfortunately Kaldor does not provide a convincing analytical explanation of this result which is crucial for the rest of his propositions in his analysis (cf. [41, pp. 137–40, 203–7]). It does, however, match Kaldor's view of the 'stylised facts' of post-war capitalism and the technical progress function itself has been shown to be a useful macro-economic policy tool (cf. [3, 4]). The only problem is to explain how and why the free enterprise capitalist system can (should), through its internal logic, produce neutral technical progress as a necessity.

SUMMARY

Professor Robinson places the determination of the rate of profit and distribution at the base of her theoretical analysis, taking into account practical social considerations of capitalism. From this base she attempts to work towards an explanation of the growth process in realistic terms. It is only when all the prior theoretical problems have been worked out that the analysis is carried to the explanation of actual changes in actual economies, and then only with the greatest care.

Kaldor rejects both the methodology of her approach and the necessity of determining these concepts, introducing the concept of the technical progress function as the base of his stylised model, which is used to analyse changes in a single system over time. He thus attempts to go directly to a realistic description of the process of economic change over time. This presents a certain gap between the formal model aspects of Kaldor's approach and the worldly wisdom with which it is applied. In reality Kaldor's theoretical model attains and retains steady growth more by assumption than by logical analysis, suffering from an inadequate explanation of how the economy reaches and maintains the position of neutral progress.

While Joan Robinson is highly sceptical about stability and only derives positions of steady growth to better understand why they are not attained, Kaldor's belief in 'stylised' stability leads him to underplay the destabilising forces in his model. His method also denies the explicit determination of the profit rate[3] and thus limits the usefulness of his model for a theoretical analysis of distribution and growth. This, we must realise, is not of much consequence to Kaldor's approach, for both its aims and methodology are distinctly different from those of Professor Robinson. Kaldor addresses himself primarily to a realistic description of the process of growth and to the insights that this gives for realistic policy recommendations. This, of necessity, implies gaps between the strict theoretical base and the use to which the base is put. This would only have grave consequences if the world were an economic model created by economists.

In summary then we find basic differences between the two approaches under the headings of: (a) methodology, (b) the pricing mechanism, (c) the determination of the profit rate, (d) the analysis of technical progress, (e) the valuation of capital, and (f) the stability of the growth process. This comparison is not meant to depreciate the significance of Kaldor's analysis, but simply to highlight the varied nature of approach and analysis that has stemmed from the underlying Keynesian mechanism and is included under the name of post-Keynesian.

[3] Although in [26] and [28] Professor Kaldor held a position very close to that of Professor Robinson.

14 Alternative Post-Keynesian Analyses – II

In marked contrast to the approach of Kaldor are the long-run equilibrium models of Luigi Pasinetti. Although occasionally drawing directly on Kaldor's work, Pasinetti's approach is primarily technical and logical. His models are worked out to find what conditions and assumptions are the 'necessary relations to achieve full employment' in conditions of long-period equilibrium growth. Pasinetti takes very seriously the methodological approach (and limitations) implied by the long-run analysis of equilibrium growth at full employment. He has on one occasion explained this approach as follows:

> To those readers who still find it difficult to follow the logic of the long-run equilibrium growth models I would suggest a device. We have normally been used to think in terms of a free market economy and then to extend the results to the case of a centrally planned economy. Here, it turns out to be much more helpful to reverse the procedure and to think first in terms of a centrally planned economy. For, in this case, the relationship (an equilibrium relationship) between the long-run rate of profit and the natural rate of growth emerges immediately. The corresponding relationship for a free market economy will then appear much easier to grasp. [67, p. 77].

SAVINGS OUT OF WAGES AND THE POST-KEYNESIAN MODEL

One of Pasinetti's most striking contributions to the extension of post-Keynesian theory was rectification of a logical slip in one of Kaldor's early models [26]. The problem, as we have seen above (chapters 4 and 11) involves the introduction of savings out of wages in the determination of the rate of profit and distribution. Under the simple assumptions of $s_p < 1$ and $s_w = 0$, the rate of profit is determined by the simple equation, $\pi = g/s_p$. However, when $s_w > 0$ there are two separate effects introduced in the system; one in terms of effective demand, the other in terms of the ownership conditions of the stock of capital (or the legal claims to the profits on capital).

Aggregate demand for consumption goods is lower, for any given level of output, when savings from wages are positive and not equal to zero. On the other hand, if wage earners are saving they will be accumulating wealth, making bank deposits, buying bonds, or whatever. It is rather unrealistic to assume that savings out of wages simply disappear in a hole in the ground or under the mattress. Kaldor had overlooked both these aspects of the problem and Pasinetti set about to make the necessary changes to bring them explicitly under analysis.

However, to great surprise,[1] Pasinetti was able to show that even when savings out of wages were taken into account the rate of profit and the distribution of income between the functional categories of wages and profits, was still explained by the simple formula, $\pi = g/s_p$. The result is quite straightforward when the method of analysis, and its attendant problems, are taken into account. First the problems, then the method.

THE PROBLEMS

When savings from wages are explicitly incorporated in the analysis, some conventions must be introduced for the placement of those savings. Pasinetti took the simplest assumption, that the wage-earners simply passed their savings to the capitalists to invest, and in return received the ruling rate of profit on these invested savings. This is simple enough as an assumption, but it creates an additional division in the analysis, of which Pasinetti was well aware and which he stressed [66, pp. 270–1].

In the revised model functional income categories – wages and profits – are maintained. But at the same time social categories – workers and capitalists – also arise, for the capitalists can no longer claim either ownership (although they have control) of the capital stock financed by savings out of wages, or the profits accruing to the capital financed by savings out of wages. Thus, in terms of income flows, wages and profits and the incomes of workers and capitalists are no longer identical. Wages and profits and the income of workers and capitalists mean different things. Although Pasinetti worked

---

[1] At least to some economists, see [99].

out the relations for both sets of income divisions, he only claimed that the simple equation held for the distribution of income between the functional income categories of wages and profits, i.e. that savings out of wages by workers would not effect the distribution of income between wages and profits. Likewise, savings out of wages did not effect the rate of profit.

Since the rate of profit and the distribution of wages and profits could be shown to be independent of wage savings, nearly any assumption about savings out of wages could be introduced into the analysis without changing Kaldor's initial conclusions.[2] This result had the effect of reducing the severity of what appeared to some to be extremely unrealistic assumptions about savings propensities in the post-Keynesian approach, i.e., $s_w = 0$, $s_p = 1$. Very evidently the introduction of savings out of wages does affect the distribution of income between *workers* and *capitalists*. Some additional problems caused by this double division have been taken up in chapter 11.

THE METHOD

Pasinetti's conclusion is most easily demonstrated by making a simple comparison of two systems in long-period, full-employment equilibrium at a given growth rate. There is no question about whether they will achieve this state of their own accord, they are there. The problem is to find the relations necessary for them to be in this happy condition.

One economy is the simple post-Keynesian case with $s_w = 0$. In the second $s_w > 0$ and $s_c - s_w > 0$. In the second we write s_c in place of s_p to indicate the propensity to save by capitalists out of their profits, and s_w indicates the propensity to save out of wages plus any profits earned as a result of the investment of these savings. The question is to find if there is any difference between the distribution of income between *wages* and *profits*, and in the rate of profits earned, in the two systems under the condition that both achieve stable equilibrium growth with full employment.[3]

[2] The initial issue has become exceedingly confused by a failure to distinctly separate functional income and social classes, as appears to be the case in [99], where it was shown under certain conditions s_c would not enter the formula $- s_p$ however (no matter which social class makes the savings out of profits) still determines the rate of profit along with investment.

[3] Stability requirements also turn out to be the same as Kaldor's.

As we saw in chapters 4 and 5, prices, profit rates, distribution and the rate of profit will be related to the aggregate supply-and-demand conditions generated in the consumption goods market as a result of the equilibrium relation of savings and investment given the ratio of investment to output. Thus if we can show that savings (consumption) and investment are the same in the two systems we can say that the assumption of savings out of wages has no effect on the rate of profit or the wages–profits distribution, for then the prices in both systems will be the same and with given employment and money-wage rates the real wage must be the same.

In the first system total saving is

$$S = s_w W + s_p P = s_p P \tag{14.1}$$

since $s_w = 0$. In the second system profits (P) are claimed not only by the capitalists, but also by the workers, for the workers finance part of total capital accumulation with their savings from wages and the savings out of the profits they receive on those savings. Thus total profits P must be divided into profits received by the capitalists, P_C, and profits accruing to the workers, P_W. Since the capitalists pay the workers the ruling rate of profit on their savings that are invested by the capitalists, total profits will be divided between capitalists and workers in proportion to the finance (savings) they provide for capital accumulation. Thus, in steady equilibrium over time the relation

$$P_W/S_W = P_C/S_C \tag{14.2}$$

will determine the division of profits. Total savings by the workers are then $S_W = s_w(W + P_W)$ with $S_C = s_c P_C$ for the capitalists. Total savings in the system are then, in the second system

$$S = s_w(W + P_W) + s_c P_C \tag{14.3}$$

Thus we must compare total savings (assumed equal to investment in equilibrium) for the two sytems (14.1 and 14.3). If they are different the rate of profit and distribution in the two systems will not be the same, but if they are the same then both systems have the same total saving, investment, consumption, prices, capital accumulation, distribution and profit rate.

We first of all note that savings out of wages are higher in the second system by the difference between 0 and $s_w W$. What about the savings from total profits? In the first economy saving from total profits was $s_p P = s_c(P_W + P_C)$.

It is clear that savings from the P_C portion of total profits has not changed. Savings out of the P_W portion of total profits, however, is lower in the second system for $s_w < s_c$. Thus savings from total profits are lower in the second system by $(s_c - s_w)P_W$. In the second system overall, savings are higher by $s_w W$ and lower by $(s_c - s_w)P_W$. If the two offset one another total savings will be unchanged in the second system as compared with the first.

We said above that if the system were to be in long-period equilibrium over time with a constant rate of profit and constant rate of growth, profits for each group would be proportional to their savings, i.e., (14.2) must be satisfied. In fact, it turns out that the relation (14.2) is simply another way of expressing $s_w W = (s_c - s_w)P_W$, the condition required in the preceding paragraph.[4] Thus the two systems, if they are in steady equilibrium growth and satisfy condition (14.2) will both have the same total savings. With the same total savings they will also have the same rate of profit and distribution of income between wages and profits. Thus the simple formula $\pi = g/s_c$ determines the rate of profit and the existence of savings out of wages has no effect on either the equilibrium profit rate or the distribution of income between wages and profits.

That s_c rather than s_p enters the simple formula without changing the results can be simply shown. Condition (14.2) also implies that $P_W/S_W = P_C/S_C = (P_W + P_C)/(S_W + S_C) = P/S$. Thus $P_C/S_C = P/S$, and $s_c P_C = S_C$. By substitution $P_C/s_c P_C = P/S$, from which $S = s_c P$ follows directly, and S and P are total savings and profits made by workers and capitalists together. Thus s_c is of the same value as a propensity as the conceptual propensity to save out of total profits, s_p, irrespective of who receives them as income. Although the two propensities are equal in magnitude, they are not identical, s_c referring to the savings propensity out of capitalists profits, P_C, and s_p to the proportion saved out of all profits by the workers and capitalists together. The savings propensity of a particular group then only enters the formula when it carries the same value as the savings propensity out of profits as a functional income category. This emphasises the contention that the determination of the rate of profit and the distribution of income between wages and profits is not effected by the existence of saving out of wages. What is important is the propensity to save out of total profits as a functional

---

[4] This can be simply seen by substituting $S_W = s_w(W + P_W)$ and $S_C = s_c P_C$ into $P_W/S_W = P_C/S_C$ and rearranging terms.

income category; whether it is written s_p or s_c (to take account of social classes) makes no difference.

Again, we must stress that the result pertains only to the wage–profit distribution and the rate of profit. The distribution between *workers* and *capitalists* will be affected by the magnitude of the propensity to save out of wages if the system is to be in equilibrium growth with full employment. Differences in s_w, by affecting S_w will bring, via (14.2), differences in P_W. Thus a higher s_w implies a higher ratio of P_W/P_C which obviously effects the distribution of income between workers' income $(W + P_W)$ and the capitalists' income (P_C). In this sense it is the difference in the distribution of profits, P, between P_W and P_C that allows the stable growth path at different values of s_w, while at the same time these differences do not effect the rate of profit or the shares of profits and wages in functional income. The method here still depends on the comparison of two systems with the assumption that both are in equilibrium, long-run growth with full employment maintained over time. The assumption that workers receive the ruling rate of profit on their invested savings is not crucial to the result.[5]

Further, the analysis does not imply anything about changes over time, only the results of comparing two equilibrium growth figurations with the relations necessary to achieve full employment. It does not imply that if s_w *changes* the change will have no effect on the performance of the system – it will (probably cause a slump), but such analysis is outside the analytical method that Pasinetti employs.

Thus Pasinetti, while working from a model of Kaldor, is closer in his methodological approach to the method of analysis used by Joan Robinson. Practical conclusions that can be drawn from his analysis are only in terms of long-period planning (e.g., in a socialist economy where deficient aggregate demand need not be a major concern). At the same time, however, the model does bring out some striking revelations about social relations and power relations under a regime of *laissez-faire* capitalism.

---

[5] It could, for example, be assumed that the capitalists keep for themselves part of the workers' profits, thus giving the capitalists a rate of return higher than the ruling rate of profit (and the workers a lower one). This would give a higher proportion of S and I for a given growth rate $(s_c > s_w)$ and thus acts like a higher propensity to save by capitalists. Cf. [59]. Pasinetti's results are further generalised in [29].

OTHER WORKS

The model of Pasinetti's that we have discussed, due to the confusion it engendered in the neoclassical camp, is out of proportion in importance to his other contributions to post-Keynesian analysis. One of his most important, if least well known, works is the introduction of technical progress, product differentiation, differential profit rates, and individual prices into a long-run econometric model of a dynamic economy. This model is a monumental enlargement of his early model, removing many of the simplifying assumptions [67].

In addition Pasinetti has been closely related to the revival of interest in Ricardo [65] and has provided one of the first applications of Sraffa's work to a critique of neoclassical economic theory [68]. In this respect he has been concerned to search the underlying deficiencies in both the Walrasian and Fisherian branches of neoclassical explanations of the determination of the profit rate [69].

15 Where do We go From Here?

In concluding our brief exposition of the post-Keynesian revival of problems of Political Economy we review some of the main points, assess future possibilities, and draw a comparison between future possibilities of post-Keynesian and neoclassical approaches to economic analysis.

WHERE WE'VE BEEN

The post-Keynesian method of thought and economic analysis which we have developed primarily from the contributions of Joan Robinson, is aligned closely with that of the Classical economists and Marx. In addition it incorporates the Keynesian theory of effective demand. From both the Classical economists and from Keynes comes the emphasis on real variables and real costs in the analysis of the logical relations necessary to produce a steady growth path. This comes through clearly in the emphasis on conditions of production and supply.

From Keynes directly comes the analysis of aggregate demand in a monetary economy. Although the explicit effects of purely financial and monetary matters are often minimised, emphasising real physical relations, the analysis is in no sense carried out in a non-monetary or barter system. The system considered is conditioned to uncertainty through the assumption of tranquillity, but money continues as a store of value between the present and the future and money is the sole basis of the system's circulation and distribution relations. The analysis is always carried out with wages paid in terms of money with money profits being earned. Although a 'money commodity' is seldom explicitly introduced, the analysis always refers to a 'money economy'.

The analysis of growth and distribution is grounded in the determination of the economy-wide rate of profit on capital by the combined forces of investment and conditions of thriftiness. This relation is symbolised by the formula $\pi = g/s_p$. The determination of the rate of profit in this manner leads directly to a theory of distribution that relates the share of investment in output with the share of profit in income necessary to preserve the equilibrium $S = I$ relationship. In such a system profits will be such as to provide the saving required to balance the investment undertaken by capitalists when the ability to save out of profits is greater than that from wages.

In much of the analysis where $s_w = 0$ and $s_p = 1$, the system can be analysed in physical terms; real wages correspond to the physical amount of consumption goods and profit to a certain amount of physical equipment. Functional income categories and social categories come to the same thing. When these savings assumptions are not maintained these simple identities no longer hold, but this does not vitiate the analysis. As was seen in chapter 14, Pasinetti was able to show that the determination of the profit rate still holds when there is positive savings out of wages. In Chapter 11 we saw that not only was the simple wage–profit relation undisturbed by the difference between social and functional income classes, but that it provided a ready means for enlarging the analysis to include financial assets as well as the analysis of a large number of different distribution problems besides wages and profits as functional income classes.

The concepts of steady growth and especially the 'golden age' are set up to explore the logical requirements for a system to achieve stable growth. These constructions can then be used to analyse what Joan Robinson calls the 'rules of the game' and conflicts in the economy that cause divergence or convergence from (to) stability. They are in no sense used to depict the path of any actual economy or to create the belief that such positions will be the natural state of affairs in any economic system. If there is any such implied belief it is that free-enterprise capitalistic economies will tend to be unstable.

The use of comparisons of steady growth paths in the face of technical progress requires the definition of neutral technical progress which leaves the relations between investment and consumption unchanged. From this norm, capital saving and capital using bias can be analysed. However, in chapter 13, we saw that Kaldor rejects the usefulness and necessity of such an exercise.

This leads directly into the discussion of the choice of techniques of production to be used at a point of time, highlighting the importance of the rate of profit in calculating the costs of potential techniques. This analysis also produced what Professor Robinson called a 'perverse' case which is now recognised as the general problem of capital reversal. It is this result along with that of double switching that provides the logical disproof of the neoclassical postulate of the inverse relation between the rate of profit and capital intensity.

The problem of technical choice also raises the problem of the measurement of capital which also forms a part of the critique of the neoclassical analysis of capital and technical change via the aggregate production function. In chapter 9 the problem of measurement was shown to be a more general problem, relating to all produced output and well-known in economics at least since Ricardo's time. The measure of capital adopted was shown to be a long-period generalisation of Keynes's method of measurement in the *General Theory*.

The basic model can be extended to provide for varying assumptions about savings by different classes, but this in no way effects the determination of the rate of profit by investment and savings out of the income categories wages and profits. It is again necessary to note that this determination is carried out in terms of functional income categories, wages and profits, which need not (and probably will not) correspond in a direct fashion with specific classes of income receivers. The confusion of functional income classes with social classes has caused much misunderstanding of the theory. In chapter 11 we have shown how this provides a possibility for making the theory richer and more realistic, but it by no means undermines the simple relations based on functional classes which will always exist, even if only conceptually.

Imperfect competition can also be directly introduced into the analysis, either on the macro level [91] or as in chapter 10 at the firm level. This was related to an attempt to suggest a possible method of price determination for the model other than simple supply and demand. The microanalysis of the macro theory remains one of the least refined areas of post-Keynesian theory.[1]

The general method of thought of the post-Keynesian approach, as we humourously tried to suggest with the rabbits and elephants analogy of chapter 1, is distinctly different from that of the orthodox neoclassical approach. In the Classical tradition of Political Economy

---

[1] An initial attempt at integration of post-Keynesian macro theory with non-neoclassical micro theory is [48]. A more integrated approach is found in [12].

it looks at a system that is growing and changing over time, with conflict between classes and nations. In this context the analysis of the distribution of scarce resources at a point in time, though not nugatory, is of secondary importance.

To put logical rigour into the analysis of such problems the post-Keynesian theory tends to favour the method of comparison rather than dynamic change as the starting point. This alerts one to the dangers of drawing conclusions about dynamic change from comparisons of static positions of equilibrium as the neoclassical analysis is wont to do, without specifying just exactly how the system moves from one position of equilibrium to another. In addition the post-Keynesian method highlights the pitfalls involved in analysing a system that changes through time with its own unique past history and future expectations affecting its performance.

The method of dynamic comparison used is readily admitted to be unrealistic, but it provides a start in showing the conditions necessary for steady growth and why it need not naturally occur. This then opens the way to the analysis of disequilibrium growth and all the attending difficulties. How this type of exercise might be approached was taken up in chapter 10. The analysis of an open economy and the effects of trade on growth have been sketched out in Chapter 12. It is in these areas that the extension of the theory to the analysis of disequilibrium can yield the most fruitful results.

Chapters 13 and 14 indicated that the post-Keynesian approach is not identical in its approach or application to specific areas or problems. We have tried to show, however, that the general base of the theory is unified and coherent in that it stems from the work of Keynes and is potentially able to analyse all the problems that classical political economy found of interest. In this sense it qualifies as a true alternative to the existing neoclassical orthodoxy. It remains true that it will not answer all the questions posed by neoclassical theory. If it did it would not be an alternative. At the same time it provides a method of approach and a point of view widely different from the neoclassical, offering questions that the neoclassical approach cannot treat. It is in this sense that it becomes a true alternative.

Much of the post-Keynesian analysis has suffered from being a negative rather than a positive approach, that is it has spent as much effort trying to solve neoclassical puzzles as it has trying to work out its own methods. As an example, when Joan Robinson set out to find a theory to determine the rate of profit she found that the existing theory was logically inconsistent. She then set about to find one of her own. This theory has subsequently been attacked as being unsuitable to further analysis of disequilibrium. This is of course true, the theory was never meant for that, but it does solve the existing gap in the theory and spells out the conditions necessary for the rigorous determination of a rate of profit. It seems better to start out from a theory that is logically consistent than one that is not. It is in this sense that the positive contributions of the post-Keynesian theory have just begun to be explored. For this task there is little question that the Keynesian short-period analysis will, in conjunction with the long-period results of the generalisation of the general theory, provides the groundwork for the Keynesian revolution that never was.

Further the post-Keynesian approach has clarified criticisms of the neoclassical theory that were hazily put in Keynes work. The two most important that we have singled out are the effect of historical time on equilibrium analysis, and the role of relative prices as an adjustment mechanism in a non-static world. With the post-Keynesian analysis in hand it is possible to directly question the efficacy of relative price adjustments, for the neoclassical theory has never shown their operation over historical time. It has been shown that a market clearing vector of prices can exist and under what conditions it will be stable at a point in time, but there is as yet no proof that it will be established or by what method, in a world that moves through history.

THE STRAW MAN AND SELF CRITICISM

Throughout this book we have tried to present the post-Keynesian theory as a positive approach to economic analysis, showing along the way some similarities with what the classical economists called Political Economy. We have not paid too much attention to, or attempted to present fully, the post-Keynesian critique of neoclassical theory. It is now more or less accepted that this critique is logically sound and that it applies directly to the sort of neoclassical theory based on the aggregate production function or Fisher's concept of the aggregate rate of return [69]. This critique has left untouched to a certain extent, the fully general equilibrium approach which requires neither the aggregate production function nor the Fisherian concept of the aggregate rate of return, and is based on the extensions of the Walrasian theory by Debreu, Arrow and Hahn [7, 1].

It has become fashionable for the more erudite of the strict general equilibrium theorists to claim that the post-Keynesian critique of neoclassical theory has been aimed at a straw man, that the critique logically does not touch the full general equilibrium approach, and that this approach was never meant to be realistic or positively useful in the first place. The continued refinement of the general equilibrium approach has been carried out just to show the extent of the unrealistic assumptions necessary to make it applicable, and thus in what actual conditions it will not be applicable. Thus no good general equilibrium theorist ever tried to describe reality, or claim that the theory should be used to explain it. The whole theory is set up, so to speak, to show why it has no value. Its positive contribution is then to show us what we cannot say, i.e., that the answers derived from the models are the wrong answers, so at least we know that out of all possible answers which ones not to choose. If this were all there was to neoclassical theory it would be a harmless, though expensive, intellectual game.

Unfortunately not all neoclassical theorists are so erudite or so honest. The theory as it is written in the textbooks, taught in the lecture hall, and explained to royal commissions is taken by those who use it as a description of the real world. The theory is used to explain the operation of markets, to make policy recommendations; its results are taken as what is and should be, not as a statement of what doesn't exist.

Even more importantly there are those who think that all that is necessary to make the theory realistic is further refinement. Thus, for example, the theory can be made more realistic by explaining racial discrimination in terms of the high disutility associated with working with a black man. If this is increased realism then the theory can be refined to explain anything and everything – it ceases to be a theory for it can never be falsified.

Further there are few econometricians, who, after testing a facet of neoclassical theory, are willing to say that his results show which results out of all possible results are the wrong ones because the theory he has used is based on assumptions that do not hold in the world that he has used to produce his data.

There is a world of difference between saying that even though a theory is patently unrealistic, it can have a positive benefit because of what it removes from a set of possible solutions and the method and practice of the theory in the actual world. It would be refreshing if all proponents of neoclassical theory and its refined state of general equilibrium where as honest as this, in fact they are not.

Much of the post-Keynesian theory is taken in this same sense of honesty. The 'golden age', for example, is set up as an unrealistic state of affairs to show why it will not normally exist. The post-Keynesian theory starts from the basis of Keynes and the world of the present. The neoclassical theory is a refinement of nineteenth-century conditions which took 200 years to show us that we are no longer in the nineteenth century.[2] At the very least the post-Keynesian theory offers us a possibility of understanding present conditions, and a rational reason for attempting to use it as a basis for further research rather than the approach of general equilibrium. There is certainly no reason to reject it simply because we have no idea of the fruits it will bear because it has not yet reached the state of refinement of general equilibrium analysis. Thus the case I am putting to you favouring the post-Keynesian theory as a full alternative to the neoclassical approach is less on the grounds of the logical faults of that approach than on the basis of the ability to take current Keynes's short-period theory have found applications in all fields of economics so should the extension of this theory into the areas of dynamic change.

WHERE DO WE GO FROM HERE?

This leaves us a final question: where do we go from here? First of all, as we have tried to suggest, the results achieved in the long-period analysis of growth are not unique to it. Just as the bases of Keynes's short-period theory have found applications in all fields of economics so should the extension of this theory into the areas of dynamic change.

In terms of strengthening the theory, the largest gap remains on the micro level. As with Keynes, the micro bases of the theory are not always explicitly spelled out, or are assumed to be those of standard micro theory. In combination with microeconomic theory and the rejection of the neoclassical price mechanism, it is necessary to find out just exactly how prices are formed and how they function

2 It has been suggested that the neoclassical theory is not even a realistic description of nineteenth-century conditions. Cf. [88, 39].

in a corporate capitalistic system. This leads directly to a rethinking of the concepts of markets and purchase and sale relations.

In the preceding chapters we have tried to suggest some of the possible areas of analysis and lines of approach to be followed. These are mere indications of what can be done. The role of the government has only been hinted at. The entire field of government and public finance is open to be taken up (cf. [9, 10, 11, 104, 53]). The theory of planning for economic development can also be treated on a post-Keynesian basis [51]. The explanation of economic history is another waiting field. In this respect we should note a major difference between the Classical economists and the post-Keynesians: that in terms of population growth. In the post-Keynesian theory investment is 'treated as an independent variable governed by technical progress and population growth' [66] both of which are also taken to be independent of the workings of the system. This was not true of the Classical economists, at least in respect to the growth of population, which was determined by the growth and distribution process. Leon [46] looks on exogenous technical progress as one of the most unrealistic parts of the post-Keynesian models. Both problems bear further investigation.

There need be no limit to the basic analyses that can be worked out on the lines that we have presented above. The only reason that the theory may appear to some to be only a critique and not a fully-fledged alternative is that the way is still open for positive contributions to be made. The neoclassical theory was not born full-grown to replace the Classical, there is no reason why the post-Keynesian must be so to be taken as a serious alternative.

Finally, we must note the need for a wholesale rethinking of the concept of dynamics. It should now be obvious that the difference between statics and dynamics is quite different from the difference between equilibrium and disequilibrium. In fact, equilibrium encompasses both statics and dynamics and as a result greatly hinders the application of the models to the actual process of growth in historical time with uncertainty a natural phenomenon. What is worse, the concept of equilibrium itself is reactionary in the sense that it voids the analysis of any other position by the mere fact that it is the reference position we use to judge change. In this sense real economic change is incompatible with equilibrium analysis. How far analysis can progress in this direction is difficult to say. Now that the basic relations of steady growth paths have been worked out with precision, attempting such analysis should be much easier. It is clear, however, that it is time to slough off our impermeable skins of steady-state equilibrium analysis by bringing together into a unified whole the Keynesian short- and long-period analysis. Once this is done, economics can again become political economy and cease treating human relations as though they were interchanges between atomic particles.

References

1. K. J. Arrow and F. H. Hahn, *General Competitive Analysis* (Edinburgh: Oliver and Boyd, 1971).
2. Krishna Bharadwaj, 'Value through Exogenous Distribution', in *Capital and Growth*, ed. Harcourt and Laing (Harmondsworth: Penguin, 1971).
3. A. Cigno, 'The Technical Progress Function and the Aggregate Production Function Revisited', mimeo, Univ. of Birmingham, 1972.
4. A. Cigno, 'Technical Progress with Imperfect Diffusion of Innovations', mimeo, Univ. of Birmingham, 1972.
5. P. Davidson, 'Money, Portfolio Balance, Capital Accumulation, and Economic Growth', *Econometrica*, xxxvi (April 1968).
6. P. Davidson, *Money and the Real World* (London: Macmillan, 1972).
7. G. Debreu, *Theory of Value* (New York: Wiley, 1959).
8. Dorfman, Samuelson and Solow, *Linear Programming and Economic Analysis* (New York: McGraw-Hill, 1958).
9. J. L. Eatwell, 'On the Proposed Reform of the Corporation Tax', *Bulletin of the Oxford Institute of Statistics* (Nov 1971).
10. J. L. Eatwell, 'A New Approach to the Problem of Public Goods', unpublished paper (Cambridge, May 1971).
11. J. L. Eatwell, 'State Intervention and Income Distribution: Some Theoretical Considerations', unpublished paper (Cambridge, July 1971).
12. A. S. Eichner, *The Mega-Corp and Oligopoly* (unpublished, New York 1970).
13. G. R. Feiwel, *The Intellectual Capital of Michael Kalecki* (Knoxville: University of Tennessee Press, forthcoming 1974).
14. P. Garegnani, 'Heterogeneous Capital, the Production Function and the Theory of Distribution', *Review of Economic Studies*, xxxvii (July 1970).
15. G. C. Harcourt, 'A Critique of Mr Kaldor's Model of Income Distribution and Economic Growth', *Australian Economic Papers*, ii (June 1963).
16. G. C. Harcourt, 'A Two-Sector Model of the Distribution of Income and the Level of Employment in the Short Run', *Economic Record*, xli (March 1965).
17. G. C. Harcourt, *Some Cambridge controversies in the theory of capital* (Cambridge U.P., 1972).
18. R. F. Harrod, 'The Expansion of Credit in an Advancing Economy', *Economica*, i (Nov 1934).
19. R. F. Harrod, 'A Rejoinder to Mr D. H. Robertson', *Economica*, i (Mar 1934).
20. R. F. Harrod, *Economic Dynamics* (London: Macmillan, 1973).
21. J. R. Hicks, 'Mr Keynes and the "Classics": A Suggested Interpretation', *Econometrica*, v (1937).
22. J. R. Hicks, *Value and Capital* (Oxford U.P., 1939).
23. R. F. Kahn, 'The Elasticity of Substitution and the Relative Share of a Factor', *Review of Economic Studies*, i (Oct 1933).
24. R. F. Kahn, 'Exercises in the Analysis of Growth', *Oxford Economic Papers*, xi (June 1959).

25. R. F. Kahn, *Selected Essays in Employment and Growth* (Cambridge U.P., 1972).
26. N. Kaldor, 'Alternative Theories of Distribution', *Review of Economic Studies*, XXIII (1956).
27. N. Kaldor, 'A Model of Economic Growth', *Economic Journal*, LXVII (Dec 1957).
28. N. Kaldor, 'Economic Growth and the Problem of Inflation', *Economica*, XXVI (Aug, Nov 1959).
29. N. Kaldor, 'Marginal Productivity and the Macro-Economic Theories of Distribution', *Review of Economic Studies*, XXXIII (Oct 1966).
30. N. Kaldor, 'Capital Accumulation and Economic Growth', in *The Theory of Capital*, ed. Lutz and Hague (London: Macmillan, 1961).
31. N. Kaldor and J. A. Mirrlees, '*A New Model of Economic Growth*', *Review of Economic Studies*, XXIX (June 1962).
32. N. Kaldor, 'The Irrelevance of Equilibrium Economics', *Economic Journal*, LXXXII (Dec 1972).
33. J. M. Keynes, *A Treatise on Money* (London: Macmillan, 1930).
34. J. M. Keynes, 'On the Theory of a Monetary Economy', reprinted in *Nebraska Journal of Economics and Business*, II (Autumn 1963).
35. J. M. Keynes, *The General Theory of Employment, Interest and Money* (London: Macmillan, 1936).
36. J. M. Keynes, 'The "Ex-Ante" Theory of the Rate of Interest', *Economic Journal*, XLVII (Dec 1937).
37. J. M. Keynes, 'The General Theory of Employment', *Quarterly Journal of Economics*, LI (Feb 1937).
38. J. M. Keynes, *The Collected Writings of John Maynard Keynes*, ed. D. Moggridge (London: Macmillan, 1973).
39. J. Knapp, 'Economics or Political Economy?', *Lloyds Bank Review*, No. 107 (Jan 1973).
40. J. Kornai, *Anti-Equilibrium* (North Holland: Amsterdam, 1971).
41. J. A. Kregel, *Rate of Profit, Distribution and Growth: Two Views* (London: Macmillan, 1971).
42. J. A. Kregel, *The Theory of Economic Growth* (London: Macmillan, 1972).
43. T. Kuhn, *The Structure of Scientific Revolutions* (Chicago U.P., 1963).
44. A. Leijonhufvud, *Keynesian Economics and the Economics of Keynes* (Oxford U.P., 1968).
45. R. Lekachman (ed.), *Keynes' General Theory: Reports of Three Decades* (New York: St Martin's Press, 1964).
46. P. Leon, *Structural Change and Growth in Capitalism* (Baltimore: Johns Hopkins Press, 1968).
47. C. B. MacPherson, *The Political Theory of Possessive Individualism* (Oxford U.P., 1962).
48. R. Marris, *The Economic Theory of 'Managerial' Capitalism* (London: Macmillan, 1964).
49. K. Marx, *Economic and Philosophical Manuscripts of 1844* (Moscow: Foreign Languages Publishing House, 1961).
50. K. Marx, *Theories of Surplus Value*, Part III (Moscow: Progress Publishers, 1972).
51. G. Mathur, *Planning for Steady Growth* (Oxford: Blackwell, 1965).
52. J. E. Meade, *A Neo-Classical Theory of Economic Growth*, 2nd ed. (Oxford U.P., 1961).
53. J. S. Metcalfe and I. Steedman, 'Some Effects of Taxation in a Linear Model of Production', *Manchester School* (Sep 1971).

54. J. S. Metcalfe and I. Steedman, 'Reswitching and Primary Input Use', *Economic Journal*, LXXXII (June 1972).
55. J. S. Metcalfe and I. Steedman, 'Heterogeneous Capital and the Heckscher-Ohlin-Samuelson Theory of Trade', in *Essays in Modern Economics*, ed. Parkin and Nobay (London: Allen and Unwin, 1972).
56. H. P. Minsky, 'Keynesian Theory and the Current Crisis in Economic Policy', talk given in Bonn, Germany, 16 Sep 1971.
57. H. P. Minsky, 'An Evaluation of Recent Monetary Policy', paper to Midwest Economic Association, St Louis, 21 April 1972.
58. B. J. Moore, 'The Pasinetti Paradox Revisited', *Review of Economic Studies* (forthcoming).
59. B. J. Moore, 'Old Results in a New Framework', *Review of Economic Studies* (forthcoming).
60. E. J. Nell, 'Two Books on the Theory of Income Distribution: A Review Article', *Journal of Economic Literature*, X (June 1972).
61. E. J. Nell, 'The Revival of Political Economy', in *Ideology in Social Science*, ed. R. Blackburn (London: Fontana, 1972).
62. D. M. Nuti, 'The Degree of Monopoly in the Kaldor-Mirrlees Growth Model', *Review of Economic Studies*, XXXVI (Apr 1969).
63. D. M. Nuti, 'Vulgar Economy in the Theory of Income Distribution', reprinted in [100].
64. D. M. Nuti, 'Amortisation and Replacement in the Neo-Keynesian Theory of Income Distribution', *Oxford Economic Papers* (forthcoming 1973).
65. L. L. Pasinetti, 'A Mathematical Formulation of the Ricardian System', *Review of Economic Studies*, XXVII (Feb 1960).
66. L. L. Pasinetti, 'Rate of Profit and Income Distribution in Relation to the Rate of Economic Growth', *Review of Economic Studies*, XXIX (Oct 1962).
67. L. L. Pasinetti, 'A New Theoretical Approach to the Problem of Economic Growth', in *Semaine d'Etude sur le Rôle de l'analyse économetrique dans la formulation de plans de développement* (Rome: Vatican, 1965).
68. L. L. Pasinetti, 'Changes in the Rate of Profit and Switches of Technique', *Quarterly Journal of Economics*, LXXX (Nov 1966).
69. L. L. Pasinetti, 'Switches of Technique and the "Rate of Return" in Capital Theory', *Economic Journal*, LXXIX (Sep 1969).
70. A. C. Pigou, *Employment and Equilibrium* (London: Macmillan, 1941).
71. D. Ricardo, *The Works and Correspondence of David Ricardo*, ed. P. Sraffa (Cambridge U.P., 1951–72).
72. Joan Robinson, 'The Theory of Money and the Analysis of Output', *Review of Economic Studies*, I (Oct 1933).
73. Joan Robinson, 'Euler's Theorem and the Problem of Distribution', reprinted in [79].
74. Joan Robinson, 'A Fallacy of Laissez-faire', *Economic Journal*, XLV (Sep 1935).
75. Joan Robinson, 'Indeterminacy', reprinted in [76].
76. Joan Robinson, *Essays in the Theory of Employment* (London: Macmillan, 1937).
77. Joan Robinson, 'Rising Supply Price', reprinted in [79].
78. Joan Robinson, *An Essay on Marxian Economics* (London: Macmillan, 1942, 1966).
79. Joan Robinson, *Collected Economic Papers* Vol. I (Oxford: Blackwell, 1951).
80. Joan Robinson, *The Rate of Interest and Other Essays* (London: Macmillan, 1952).
81. Joan Robinson, *On Re-Reading Marx*, reprinted in [95].

References

82. Joan Robinson, 'The Production Function and the Theory of Capital', reprinted in [84].
83. Joan Robinson, *Exercises in Economic Analysis* (London: Macmillan, 1960).
84. Joan Robinson, *Collected Economic Papers* Vol. II (Oxford: Blackwell 1960).
85. Joan Robinson, *The Accumulation of Capital* (London: Macmillan, 1956, 1969).
86. Joan Robinson, *Essays in the Theory of Economic Growth* (London: Macmillan, 1962).
87. Joan Robinson, *Collected Economic Papers* Vol. III (Oxford: Blackwell, 1965).
88. Joan Robinson, *The New Mercantilism* (Cambridge U.P., 1966).
89. Joan Robinson, *The Economics of Imperfect Competition* (London: Macmillan, 1933, 1969).
90. Joan Robinson, *Freedom and Necessity* (London: Allen and Unwin, 1970).
91. Joan Robinson, 'Harrod After Twenty-One Years', reprinted in [95].
92. Joan Robinson, *Economic Heresies* (London: Macmillan, 1971).
93. Joan Robinson, 'The Second Crisis in Economic Theory', reprinted in [95].
94. Joan Robinson, 'What Has Become of the Keynesian Revolution?', Presidential Address, British Association, Section F, Leicester, 1972.
95. Joan Robinson, *Collected Economic Papers* Vol IV (Oxford: Blackwell, 1973).
96. P. A. Samuelson, *Economics* (New York: McGraw-Hill, latest edition).
97. P. A. Samuelson, 'Parable and Realism in Capital Theory: The Surrogate Production Function', *Review of Economic Studies*, XXIX (June 1962).
98. P. A. Samuelson, 'Understanding the Marxian Notion of Exploitation: A Summary of the So-Called Transformation Problem between Marxian Values and Competitive Prices', *Journal of Economic Literature*, IX (June 1971).
99. P. A. Samuelson and F. Modigliani, 'The Pasinetti Paradox in Neoclassical and More General Models', *Review of Economic Studies*, XXXIII (Oct 1966).
100. J. G. Schwartz and E. K. Hunt (eds.), *A Critique of Economic Theory* (Harmondsworth: Penguin, 1972).
101. R. M. Solow, 'A Contribution to the Theory of Economic Growth', *Quarterly Journal of Economics*, LXX (Feb 1956).
102. I. Steedman, 'On Foreign Trade', unpublished paper (Manchester 1971).
103. I. Steedman and J. S. Metcalfe, 'On Trade Between Countries with the Same Ricardian Technology', unpublished paper (Manchester, 1971).
104. I. Steedman, 'The State and the Outcome of the Pasinetti Process', *Economic Journal*, LXXXII (Dec 1972).
105. I. Steedman and J. S. Metcalfe, 'Reswitching, Primary Inputs and the Heckscher-Ohlin-Samuelson Theory of Trade', unpublished paper (Manchester 1972).
106. P. Sraffa, 'The Laws of Returns Under Competitive Conditions', *Economic Journal*, XXXVI (Dec 1926).
107. P. Sraffa, *The Production of Commodities By Means of Commodities* (Cambridge U.P., 1960).
108. T. W. Swan, 'Economic Growth and Capital Accumulation', *Economic Record*, XXXII (Nov 1956).
109. Symposium: The Future of U.S. Wage-Price Policy, *Review of Economics and Statistics*, LIV (Aug 1972).

Index